EVOKING CHANGE

For Dr. Rose who cares for my body, mind & soul.

Anna J. Christie

EVOKING CHANGE

CHANGE

Make a Difference in Your Life and in the World

Anna S. Christie

iUniverse, Inc.
New York Lincoln Shanghai

EVOKING CHANGE
Make a Difference in Your Life and in the World

Copyright © 2007 by Anna S. Christie

All rights reserved. No part of this book may be used or reproduced by any means, graphic, electronic, or mechanical, including photocopying, recording, taping or by any information storage retrieval system without the written permission of the publisher except in the case of brief quotations embodied in critical articles and reviews.

iUniverse books may be ordered through booksellers or by contacting:

iUniverse
2021 Pine Lake Road, Suite 100
Lincoln, NE 68512
www.iuniverse.com
1-800-Authors (1-800-288-4677)

Because of the dynamic nature of the Internet, any Web addresses or links contained in this book may have changed since publication and may no longer be valid.

The views expressed in this work are solely those of the author and do not necessarily reflect the views of the publisher, and the publisher hereby disclaims any responsibility for them.

ISBN: 978-0-595-44455-7 (pbk)
ISBN: 978-0-595-69248-4 (cloth)
ISBN: 978-0-595-88782-8 (ebk)

Printed in the United States of America

978-0-595-44455-7
0-595-44455-5

Drawings were created exclusively for this book by Alexandria Bois

Figure 13 courtesy of the Alzheimer's Disease Education and Referral Center, a service of the National Institute on Aging. Used with permission.

All other graphics were created exclusively for this book by Jessica Marshall

Quotations from the Christian Bible are the author's own translation from the original languages

The information contained in this book is not intended to serve as a replacement for professional medical or psychological advice. Any use of the information in this book is at the reader's discretion. The author specifically disclaims any and all liability arising directly or indirectly from the use or application of any information contained in this book. A health care professional should be consulted regarding your specific situation.

Except where indicated, names and identifying characteristics of people in this book have been changed, and some stories have been amalgamated, to protect the privacy of the individuals.

For Peter, who saved my life

I define love thus: the will to extend one's self for the purpose of nurturing one's own or another's spiritual growth.

—M. Scott Peck

Contents

Acknowledgements xiii

Introduction xv

Part One   The Nature of Change 1
    Chapter 1:   *Labour Pains* 3
    Chapter 2:   *The Five Bourns* 13
    Chapter 3:   *Evoking Change* 21
    Chapter 4:   *The Leadership Trinity* 27

Part Two   The Bourn of Self 35
    Self-Definition 37
    Chapter 5:   *Self* 39
    Chapter 6:   *Not Self* 51
    Emotional Intelligence 61
    Chapter 7:   *The Healing of Self* 63
    Chapter 8:   *Leviathan* 77
    Chapter 9:   *Leviathan: Nature or Nurture?* 91
    Chapter 10: *The Brain Made Easy* 99
    Chapter 11: *Attunement and Attachment* 115
    Chapter 12: *The Nature of Emotion* 125
    Chapter 13: *Emotional Awareness: Fear and Anger* 129
    Chapter 14: *Emotional Awareness: Shame* 143
    Chapter 15: *Emotional Awareness: Sorrow and Joy* 151
    Chapter 16: *Emotional Awareness: Nurture* 161
    Chapter 17: *Lesser-Known Emotions* 169
    Chapter 18: *Growing into Leadership* 177

Meaningfully Connected 181

    Chapter 19: Bourn Leaders *183*

    Chapter 20: Listening *191*

    Chapter 21: Giving and Receiving Feedback *203*

Part Three   **The Bourn of Relationships** 211

    Chapter 22: Thinking Systems *213*

    Chapter 23: Systemic Anxiety *227*

    Chapter 24: Triangles *241*

    Chapter 25: Emotional Process I *249*

    Chapter 26: Emotional Process II *259*

    Chapter 27: Curious Change *273*

    Chapter 28: Extraordinary Leadership *279*

Part Four   **Distant Bourns: Societal context, nature and the supernal** 283

    Chapter 29: Changing the World *285*

Afterword 295

Suggested Readings: Leadership and Personal Growth 297

Bibliography 299

Index 305

Acknowledgements

I would like to express my appreciation, first, to my amazing husband, Charlie Bois, who has both changed and evoked change in me over the 27 years of our life together. This book could not have been written without your support, wisdom and enthusiasm. It means so much that you believe in me. I will love you forever. My daughter, Alexandria Bois, spent countless hours hashing out theory with me and being my best critic. She also created the artwork for this book. Alex, I thrive as much on your perspicacity as on your daily hugs. To my daughter, Katrina Bois, thank you for reading my manuscript and simply saying, "I really liked it a lot." You are the most well-read young adult that I know, and your integrity is unquestionable. To my son, Adrian, for designing my website and for loving me enough to keep asking my advice, thank you.

To my most respected friends and colleagues who read the manuscript and who gave me feedback about my theory, this book is as much yours as it is mine. Without your brilliant, thoughtful critique, it would not have come together into this integrative masterwork:

- Loranne Brown, sessional writing instructor, Trinity Western University; author of the highly acclaimed *The Handless Maiden* (Doubleday Canada, 1998). Special thanks to Loranne for editing the original manuscript
- Ryk Brown, philosopher and theologian, my hero, my friend.
- Clinical psychologist, registered play therapist and neuroscientist, Dr. Geoffrey Carr, PhD. Dr. Carr has been on faculty as a professor at both the University of British Columbia and Simon Fraser University. Thank you for pointing out my errors and enlivening the text with your commentary.
- The Rev. almost-Dr. Jeff Crittenden, my most well-read colleague. Thanks for your comments and encouragement.
- Syndicated columnist, author, entertainer and three-time winner of The Stephen Leacock Award for Humour, Gordon Kirkland. Thanks for believing in me as a writer from the very beginning.

- Bruce Sanguin, United Church minister, therapist and author of *Darwin, Divinity and the Dance of the Cosmos* (Copperhouse, 2007). It's great to have a friend who's another theolog cum scientist. I enjoy our chinwags about God and quantum theory and psychotherapy. You're my inspiration.
- Social worker and psychotherapist Peter Silin, author of *Nursing Homes: The Family's Journey* (Johns Hopkins, 2000). Thank you for your critique and support.
- Murray Speer, I am as much your student minister as you have been mine. Thank you, Murray, for some of the most insightful criticism I received.

A special thank you to Dr. Joan Wyatt, who took a chance on letting me teach her M. Div. students at Vancouver School of Theology. Also to Rev. David Anderson who spread my reputation as a "leadership guru" far and wide, long before I deserved it.

To my teacher and favourite Bowenian, Randy Frost, director of *Living Systems*, Vancouver, BC, I learned so much from you.

I am very appreciative of Barb and Will Watkins of River Run Cottages for providing me with the beautiful and tranquil setting for the solitude I needed to complete this work.

I am indebted to the following theorists for the inspiration behind my theory of leadership: Stephen Covey, Scott Peck, Edwin Friedman, John Gottman, Leslie Greenberg, Murray Bowen and Fred Craddock. Although I don't quote Dr. Craddock in this book, it was he who first taught me to integrate the words I proclaim with the life I live and within all my relationships.

Thank you to the 100+ participants in my leadership classes who have allowed themselves to be guinea pigs of this theory. You are all unique and amazing.

Finally, to the congregation of Gilmore Park United Church, who are such mature leaders themselves that my job is effortless. You are a blessing to me every day, but more importantly, you are, and will become, an agent of change in the world. I Love you all.

Introduction

Life's Lesson

I was the graduate who had it all—all the skills, knowledge and gifts necessary to become a great leader and change the world. I was bright and ambitious, a never-ending source of energy, enthusiasm and optimism. As an upbeat, joyful charismatic visionary with a shelf of trophies in public speaking, I could easily draw a crowd. You would think this combination was destined for greatness, but I did not become a great leader. Instead, I failed miserably.

Inside the body and soul of this gifted young woman dwelled brokenness and fear in overflowing quantities. It spilled over into everything I did and every relationship I entered into. By the time I was in my mid-thirties, I was involved in a career and a trio of community groups all enmeshed in conflict. To top it off, I wasn't speaking to my entire family of origin, I didn't give my husband the time of day, and I had three children I barely knew. In 1996, when I was out of work and suffering from burnout, I was diagnosed with cancer. This triggered the age-old anxiety disorder that I had been dealing with—and hiding—for over 30 years. Did I mention that I was an ordained minister, yet I had no idea where God was? There was but one certainty in my life: *things needed to change.*

It's not like my entire being came crashing down at once; it was a slow and steady degeneration, and I didn't realize until some time later that the common denominator in all these failures was *me*. Gee, I thought it was the state of the church, my dysfunctional family and/or the going-to-hell-in-a-handbasket world. It was not so much that I blamed everyone and everything for my problems but more that I thought I could have evoked some meaningful change in my situation if I had simply learned more information or had more skill.

In my great quest for the acquisition of this skill, I attended numerous continuing education classes on preaching, teaching, theology, counselling, small group theory and the Enneagram. I devoured literature on church growth, enlivening worship, the latest Bible study curriculum, congregational organization and every program under the sun. I did marriage enrichment weekends and parenting courses, and spent more "quality time" with the family. I became exceedingly skilled in "communication," "conflict resolution" and "training leaders." I even studied in depth Stephen Covey's *The 7 Habits of Highly Effective People: Powerful Lessons in Personal Change*, which describes a great theory and is a great book, but despite my knowledge of it, I was far from highly effective.

I saw a therapist for two years who sat like a dummy bridge hand and nodded agreement that my mother was to blame for almost everything. I underwent psychoanalysis, hypnosis, original grief work, primal scream therapy, cognitive-behavioural therapy, embraced my inner child and studied my family system. I enrolled in an M.B.A. program. I began working on a PhD in psychology. Then I got cancer. With similar enthusiasm, I attacked it on all fronts: surgery, radiation, chemotherapy, healing touch, prayer, herbal remedies and a vegan diet. Out of this entire quest for more information, the only thing that seemed to be of any lasting value was whatever I did that contributed to not dying of cancer. Who knows what it was, out of all that! Instead of dying young, I was left alive, by the grace of God, or some fluke of the universe, to figure out how on earth I could make sense of it all.

Sometimes life leads you to an Alcoholics Anonymous "Step One" whether you've ever been an addict or not. Step One is known as "bottoming out." I came to believe I was powerless over [all this crap] and my life had become unmanageable. It's a humbling experience for anyone, perhaps more so for the one voted most likely to succeed.

Since I had some time on my hands while recovering from illness, I set out to learn how to do leadership properly. If I could no longer blame God or the world, then poor leadership must be at the root of my failure in my career, in my family and within my own life. After all, when I went to theological college in the 1980s, the word "leadership" was frowned upon. It was hierarchical, patriarchal and indicated an abuse of power. We were encouraged instead to use words like "collegial" and "community." Assuming more knowledge about techniques was what I needed, I set out to research and absorb as much data as possible on the topic of leadership.

Theory, Controversy and Discovery

Some of what I studied was very good: I value it to this day. Tops among the good stuff was Stephen Covey's emphasis on "the inside-out approach."[1] It turned on a light bulb for me. If I wanted to change anything or anybody, I had to start by getting my *personal* "act together." I came to realize that my failure in ministry was linked to the quality of my relationships at home and everywhere else.

---

[1] Stephen Covey, *The 7 Habits of Highly Effective People*, 15–44.

Unfortunately, much of what is written about leadership is technique or tricks of the trade: manage people in 60 seconds; learn communication, delegation, negotiation; draw on teamwork, empowerment and methods to inspire, enthuse or challenge. "Experts" talk about leadership *style* as if being a good leader depends on choosing a way of being as one would choose accessories.

In the midst of the worst years of my existence, my friend Ian gave me a book that marked the beginning of real change in my life. It was Edwin Friedman's *Generation to Generation: Family Process in Church and Synagogue*. The late Edwin Friedman was both a rabbi and a family therapist. As a therapist, he was a student of Murray Bowen, the founder of "Family Systems Theory," based on the theory of (natural) living systems.

Bowen was a psychiatrist who became dissatisfied with the lack of scientific precision in a psychoanalytic approach. He began work in the 1950s studying families in a residential/institutional setting, in particular, families with schizophrenic children. Bowen discovered that there was an *emotional process* in these families that was common to them all and that if the process were changed, the schizophrenic's functioning improved, even if some other family members or relationships appeared to worsen.

One of Bowen's most important conclusions was that the family is an emotional system, and as such, it is interconnected and functions as a whole. Bowen theory therefore joins the concepts of systems thinking and emotional process. Since the focus is no longer on the symptom bearer (in the original study, the schizophrenic child), but on the emotional process within the family, then it is more fruitful to modify the process than to try to "fix" the individual with the problem. Of course, Bowen came to believe that once these patterns could be seen in schizophrenia, it was possible to see them in other families without problems (or with less serious problems) as well.[2]

Edwin Friedman studied with Bowen at the Georgetown University Family Center, now known as the Bowen Center. Since Friedman was a practicing rabbi as well as a family therapist, he brilliantly applied the insights of Bowen theory (systems thinking and emotional process) to human institutions such as the church or synagogue.

---

[2] General information on Bowen is derived from Daniel Papero, PhD, LCSW, at his Vancouver conference "The Therapist's Own Family," October 17–19, 2003. Dr. Papero is a long-time colleague of Bowen, faculty member at the Georgetown University Family Center at Dr. Bowen's invitation, and the author of *Bowen Family Systems Theory*.

In his latter years, Friedman gave seminars and consulted to leaders in all sorts of organizations—community groups, medical facilities, education systems and the world of commerce. If you have the incentive and enthusiasm to investigate these themes more intensely, then by all means examine Friedman's writings and the videos of his seminars. They are an invaluable legacy to the study of leadership. It is also tremendously worthwhile for students of leadership to examine Bowen theory at its source. Once I got started with this theory, I couldn't learn enough about it. Although Friedman's theory is brilliant, like Bowen's, both are lacking the integration of recent research into human emotion.

If I could have recommended any of Friedman's writings as textbooks to the lay people in my two-year-long leadership program, I probably would not have begun writing this book. Unfortunately, Friedman is pretty technical, and the reading is "heavier" than most folks are willing to take on. So I set out to write this book as a discussion of living systems theory for lay people. I thought that if lay people can even become aware of the emotional process at work in their organizations and families, then these systems would begin to stabilize and function better.

I quickly became paralyzed in what began to be a simple writing of Bowen theory, largely because I do not even agree with some of Bowen's most central concepts: his fundamental (unproven) theory of the scale of differentiation of self, for example, and in particular, his idea that one cannot substantially move up the scale.

My main problem with Bowen is related to my own personal story of the overwhelmingly successful treatment of severe symptoms of post-traumatic stress disorder. I gained success in treatment through "traditional" psychotherapy, which focuses on emotion and attachment with a particular emphasis on the relationship between therapist and client. Bowen and his most prominent disciples (Kerr, Papero) are adamantly opposed to the two most widely agreed-upon principles of psychotherapy: a) that healing is contingent upon a good client-therapist relationship and b) that therapy should focus on the emotional experience of the client. I do believe that the Bowenians are wrong about this. Unfortunately, most theorists who focus on emotion and attachment theory discount all of Bowen, throwing out a perfectly good baby with the bathwater.

A few years ago, I was privileged to attend a conference with the leading Bowenian, Michael Kerr, and the most prominent academic researcher in couples' therapy (who has an emotion-focused perspective), Dr. John Gottman. Listening to the debate between these two led me to explore aspects of both Bowen and emotion-focused theories further. My formal training in counselling was first in a person-centred (Rogerian) approach, and later in Bowen theory; my greatest interest at this point in my career is in emotional awareness, attachment theory and the use of emotion in healing. If this conference were any indication, then the two "sides" do not understand each other. This book attempts to integrate aspects of both as they relate to our common journey as human beings toward changing ourselves or evoking change in the world. People who are willing to change themselves for the sake of evoking change in their closest relationships or in the world are called *leaders*. True leadership, therefore, does not necessarily come by virtue of office.

A Critical Time

There is a crisis in leadership in our present day. It was no wonder that Daniel Goleman's book, *Emotional Intelligence: Why It's More Important Than IQ*, was so popular when it was released in 1995. People naturally knew there was something more to good leadership than appointing the person with the most IQ points, skill or expertise to lead them. Hiring or appointing leaders for their intellectual ability alone may have appeared to work at one time, but it hasn't worked at all since about the 1960s, if it ever really did.

Equally popular today to the topic of leadership is that of conflict management. Although conflict is normal and natural, poorly handled conflict is killing us. It is killing our marriages, our businesses, our institutions and governments, and the way we raise our children. In my own work in the church for over 20 years, as well as in observing people's behaviour in small groups and community organizations, I have seen the degree and amount of destructive conflict escalate. Conflict points to a crisis in leadership and until we figure out what good leadership is, conflict will continue to infiltrate every human institution and slowly destroy us.

There are lots of techniques being marketed today for "resolving" or "managing" conflict, but they are just that—techniques. They do not address the real problem, which is a crisis in leadership. They are temporary bandages at best, covering up wounds but not curing the infection. Ronald Heifetz in his thought-provoking book *Leadership without Easy Answers* refers to conflict management skills as "technical solutions" and urges leaders to move their organizations toward identifying and working on "adaptive challenges" that force both the group and its leader to grow. [3]

---

[3] Ronald Heifetz, *Leadership without Easy Answers*, Chapter 6.

Author, speaker and business consultant, Stephen Covey, in his first book, *The 7 Habits of Highly Effective People,* implies that conflict management techniques are an example of using "the law of the school," when what is needed is "the law of the farm." Covey's "laws" remind us that when we are in school, we can cram for the exam the night before and still pass the course, but this approach cannot be used on the farm. It's no good to plough, plant, water and fertilize the night before you expect a harvest. It just can't happen. Leadership, says Covey, is based on natural laws like the "law of the farm" and must therefore not begin with techniques but with the inward transformation of the leader.[4]

The answer to the crisis of leadership and ensuing conflict is not a quick fix. Change requires patience. True leadership that evokes lasting change is a journey—a lifelong process that begins and ends with personal or *spiritual* growth.[5] Edwin Friedman emphasized repeatedly in his seminars that the answer to the problems in our organizations is not for the leader to acquire more knowledge or expertise. It is for the leader to improve his or her functioning.[6]

Many, if not most, people are not even *aware* of their own functioning and have no idea what is going on inside their heads—or hearts, as the case may be. Increasing your awareness of self as well as the awareness of the emotional process going on in the system is critical. The degree to which you are unaware of your own emotions and emotional process directly relates to the degree of conflict (or sometimes chaos) in the systems you hope to change.

A business executive may be the most intelligent, visionary, organized and creative person in the company. This leader's résumé may appear to "have it all": education, experience, knowledge, skill—even "interpersonal skills." The leader of the local art gallery, church board or service club may be the most dedicated, faithful, hard-working volunteer in the group (and usually is). Leaders of families may be loyal partners and parents, good providers, nurturing mothers, caring husbands. Couples may go to marriage enrichment classes, weekly dates, spice up their sex life and never fight. But if these leaders have no awareness whatsoever of their own pain and accompanying emotional triggers, or of the emotional process going on in the room, the only change they will experience is a descent into troubled waters. It is a trouble that is common to us all.

---

[4] Stephen Covey, *The 7 Habits of Highly Effective People,* 22.

[5] Growing personally is a spiritual journey. By "spiritual" I do not mean religious. The term "spirit" encompasses all that we are: the sum total of intellectual, emotional, psychological, creative, sacred and meaning-filled. If you feel more comfortable with it, you may substitute the term "personal growth" whenever "spiritual growth" is mentioned.

[6] Edwin Friedman, *Reinventing Leadership* (video).

Part One

The Nature of Change

Chapter 1:

Labour Pains

Emotional pain is a disconnection from the source of human joy.
—*Elliot Essman*

We live in a time known as "postmodern." Just when you thought you were getting used to the idea of all things "modern," now even the word "modern" means something right out of the 1960s—old, washed up, passé. Our world has changed more in the last 50 years than it has through all the previous years of human history combined. Not only has the world changed quickly and dramatically, but also the rate at which it changes seems to be ever increasing. Even the nature of change itself has changed. But in this reality of incredible, fast-paced, ever-changing change, one thing has remained constant: the world and its people are in pain, and in need of healing.

It should be fair to assume that you are reading this book because, even in some small way, you are unsatisfied with your life and wish for something to change. Or perhaps you are unsatisfied with the state of the world or the way it seems to be heading. Perhaps your dissatisfaction is confined to governments, the media, businesses, or your own workplace or community group. And it's probably fair to say that despite your original reason for reading this book, you would love to see some change in your family members.

You also want your life to matter. You may be young, one foot on the dock of life's foundation, another in the boat of adventure, ready to sail. You want to chart the right course. Or perhaps you are middle-aged and have begun asking the big questions:

> ➢ What am I doing on this earth?
> ➢ How can I be of importance in the lives of others?
> ➢ What is the purpose of my work?

- Will I see the world change in my own lifetime?
- Does my life make a difference?
- When I am gone, will it matter that I was here?

You may have reached the end of life and are wondering if there is still any hope, any chance that you can do something before you die that will leave a legacy. Or you could be any age at all and simply wish that things would change so that your life would be more:

- Simple
- Meaningful
- Hassle free
- Caring
- Loving
- Fun

The problem with wanting anything to change is not in the desire but in the methods that many attempt to employ to evoke the change. People tend to hold rigidly to their ideas and values, expecting everything to change but themselves. They repeat the same behaviours time and time again, clinging blindly to the fanciful notion that one day something will work. It is akin to stumbling in the dark, eternally groping for a light switch that just isn't there. Speaking of light switches, it was Benjamin Franklin who said the definition of insanity is to do the same thing over and over and expect different results. It would seem logical that what we need is a new method. I am proposing something altogether different.

The Problem

Every method or technique that focuses on change will ultimately fall short if you continue to hold a world view that professes you can somehow change (yourself or others) without acknowledging, experiencing and enduring *pain*. I really hope you've paid for the book already. Honestly, don't run away screaming or throw it on the dresser with a declarative "pfffffffft!" The truth is that the world is in pain and you are in pain, whether you realize it or not. You do not need another means or technique for ignoring the pain or covering it up, but rather a means of healing it so that your life (and the lives of those you love, and of generations to come) grows to become something better.

You may be so used to your pain that you have buried it. Or you may be so aware of it that it hurts or tortures you daily. Whether or not you are aware of your condition, you feel it and you live in response to it every day—and it can be hell.

Many seek to overcome their pain by finding simple, shallow solutions—fulfillment in the temporary or the worldly. You think if only you could get that job, or money, or possessions, or that special relationship—or if only you could get one of those things *back*—then you would not be in pain. You may believe that if you could only fix another's problems or control his behaviour, then you would not be in pain. Whatever it is you seek, it is a substitute for spiritual growth, which, although a painful experience itself, is the only route to ultimate healing.

Many experience hopelessness in striving for ultimate relief from their pain in their own limited ways. The journey to healing requires such tremendous effort that you would rather remain in pain than exert the energy to heal it. This may lead to despair, manifested in the rampant depression that plagues human beings all over the planet. In despair, you may realize that you cannot heal the pain on your own, so you seek inwardly to smother it by taking it out on yourself. You may do this with alcohol, drugs, sex, food, perfectionism, overwork or other ways. In despair, you may become satisfied that life offers only fleeting, temporary moments of happiness, which you seek through food, entertainment, shopping or even relationships. In despair, you may search endlessly for that "special person" who will love you, thus soothing your pain. When your relationships prove to be only temporary solutions (since the other's needs are as great as or greater than your own), you might turn this unrealistic expectation onto your children.

In despair, you might realize that you cannot heal your pain yourself, so you seek outwardly to destroy the pain by projecting it onto other people. You may do this by trying to control others with your anger or through "helping" others to the point that they cannot even help themselves. You project your pain onto your partner, your children, your friends, co-workers or subordinates. This projection of pain infects every human institution and system, for whenever we gather together with others, we gather as a people in pain. People who project pain are usually unaware of it. Because they are also unaware of the emotional process involved when others are projecting their pain, there is a profusion of human conflict and a crisis in leadership.

And so the problem remains. You are in pain and wish you had the power to evoke real change. This causes a great ache inside you, and you assume that the way to heal it is to run away from it and avoid it. This, of course, only makes it worse. For the only solution to your pain is to grow. Without this necessary growth, you do not have a hope of changing yourself, let alone your marriage, your children or the human systems you exist in or attempt to lead.

The Solution

The good news is that you do not have to fear your pain, dread it, or try to avoid it. Most importantly, it serves no purpose for you to be unaware of it. It is a good thing to become aware of your pain, its sources and the way you act out of it. You can feel your pain and not die, go crazy or become worse. Awareness of your pain is the first step in healing and therefore the first step in evoking change in your own life.

The goal of this book is to raise awareness of the human ability to *grow*. If you grow, you will grow out of your pain, rather than grin and bear it, cover it up or project it onto others. If you are *aware* of your pain and the emotional systems functioning within your own brain as well as the human systems that you and others exist in, then you will heal. Healing yourself is the avenue that leads to change in others and in the world.

Giving Up on the Quick Fix

What is the purpose of awareness of your pain, or of your journey toward spiritual growth, if not to bring you and the groups or systems you exist in or lead a change that endures? The frustration you will inevitably experience is that you may be willing to endure pain in order to grow, but you will want to see results quickly. The process of change is exceptionally slow. It is possible to experience some changes in yourself almost immediately; seeing change in others will take more time, and you may not see the effect of your efforts to change larger systems or the world in your own lifetime.

When I was a young minister, my ambition was to save the entire national church from its bad theology, declining membership and cumbersome bureaucracy. It never occurred to me until 20 years later to change to a different denomination (that has good theology, declining membership and a cumbersome bureaucracy). Besides saving the church, I also aspired to save the world. There was no option of changing worlds, unfortunately. Unaware of my pain, I forgot to save myself first. I forgot that the work of evolution—for us to begin as single-cell organisms and become this magnificent and complex human life form—took about four billion years. Why would the whole church, let alone the world, change in the span of my 40-some years of ministry? More importantly, were my lofty goals not more about trying to *be* God rather than to serve God?

Surely, change will come; evolution cannot possibly be over. Psychiatrist and renowned author Scott Peck wrote in *The Road Less Traveled* that the current stage of evolution is a spiritual one.[7] Although I agree with him, who really knows? Perhaps even our physical brains, and thus our emotional systems, are evolving as well, and this will one day better enable our spiritual evolution, an evolution that could also take billions of years.

The evolutionary perspective reminds us that we are but a speck in a vast universe of time and space that has existed and will go on to exist for eternity. Perhaps when humans evolve spiritually in the next four billion years or so, we will grow into divine beings and the universe will become *shalom*.[8]

Once we become fully aware that we won't even be alive when the changes that we want in this world come about, it helps us to see differently our role in the systems within which we function. I have a Buddhist colleague named Sabanno to whom I sometimes relate my silly problems in case his Buddhist perspective is more profound some day than my Christian one. Sabanno always says the same thing to me: "Anna, meditate on the impermanence of these things."

It is a Buddhist spiritual practice to meditate on impermanence. Why don't you give it a try right now? It may increase your awareness of the universal condition and lift the sails for your voyage of spiritual growth.

1. Begin by finding a comfortable position.
2. Breathe deeply and relax your body as much as possible.
3. Become aware first of your breathing and how impermanent it is. As soon as you feel satisfied with an in breath, you must let it out. Similarly, the satisfaction of the out breath lasts only a moment.
4. Become aware of your body—your aches and pains, perhaps. Then meditate on the fact that your body is impermanent; one day it will simply be gone from this earth.
5. Meditate now on the floor and the building you are sitting in. Think about how one day it, too, will be gone from this earth.

---

[7] Scott Peck, *The Road Less Traveled*, 263.

[8] The Jewish concept of "shalom," often used as a greeting or simply translated "peace," is actually a state of being that encompasses peace, healing, wholeness and abundant blessing. "Shalom" may refer to the inner state of individuals; however, Jews and Christians also use it to refer to an anticipated state of being for the whole earth. Shalom may be the state of existence that Jesus referred to as "the kingdom of God."

6. Think about the city, town or countryside you are sitting in. One day it will no longer exist.
7. Meditate on the problem you are experiencing, whether it is a problem with work, human relationships or health. Realize that one day it will no longer exist, just as you will no longer exist.

Awareness of your impermanence, the fact that your life is merely a speck in the universe, helps you put your problems and pain into perspective. It helps you not take yourself too seriously. For you are not in control of the universe, and your life does not really make much of a difference nor does the work you do make much of a difference in the grand scheme of things over billions of years.

Imposing the Will

People spend a lot of time *trying* to make a difference and trying to change or control what they cannot change or control. Most of the time these efforts are directed toward others, but many people also attempt to control situations and even world events.

Leadership expert and family therapist Edwin Friedman referred to this human need to control others as the "*imposing of the will.*" As he sat and listened to couples talk about their problems, he would always notice one of them allude to, or outright declare, the imposing of his or her will upon the other.[9] If only she didn't nag so much; if only he were home more; if only my co-workers would do it my way; if only the banks didn't raise interest rates; if only I could impose *my* will on everyone else. We all waste a lot of time imposing our will or wishing we could, as though it were possible to essentially control the thoughts and actions of others or the universe itself when we are not even aware of the pain that is controlling *us*. Our lives are a flash, a fraction of a trillisecond. The future is long—very long—and we are not a part of it.

Our need to control others and situations, and thus impose our will, is born out of our anxiety. Our anxiety is the fear of our pain. It is fed by the idea that we are not impermanent but somehow can control our own lives, the lives of others and the state of the universe. Subconsciously we believe that if we could do that, we would no longer be in pain. The more anxious we are, the more we need to impose our will on others so that we do not feel our pain and are less anxious. This futile exercise reveals our insignificance and impermanence. We are but a molecule of a speck of flour in the dough of *shalom*. If you are willing to become

---

[9] Edwin Friedman, *Emotional Process and Process Theology*, (video).

aware of your pain and endure it in order to grow, then perhaps you will have a chance to become a molecule of yeast, an agent for change that, while seemingly small, is vitally important. Whether your life is the flour of the universe or the yeast of *shalom*—either way—you will die and not ever know.

Grief and Loss

You might well ask: Why do you think that everyone on this earth is in pain? Surely, there are people who are happy, joyful, upbeat and optimistic. Aren't people only in pain if something painful happens to them, such as loss of a loved one, trauma, abusive parents or some such thing? Is the "default setting" of everyone on the planet *pain*?

I am no stranger to joy. People who meet me often describe me as happy, positive, exuberant, even funny. I am not *against* joy, assuming all of life should be about experiencing and resolving painful feelings. I sing, dance, drink exquisite wines, scream with delight down waterslides and dress up in funny costumes on Halloween. My favourite pastime is to get together with family and experience the kind of laughter that doesn't stop until you dissolve in tears and someone pees her pants. Although I am obviously a religious person, the highest holy day of my year is April Fools' Day. Okay, I'm kidding about that—it's Easter—but the point is, please don't misunderstand all this talk about pain. Healing pain is not a stifler of joy but ultimately a vehicle for it.

For over 20 years, I have worked as a grief and crisis counsellor, and in that time, I have probably counselled a thousand people who have experienced grief and loss. At first, I worked only with people who had lost loved ones through death. Then my work gradually branched out to those who had lost their jobs, their pets, their relationships, their independence or their good health. I found that the same grief response is triggered in all these situations. No matter what the loss, people go through the same predictable seven-stage pattern of shock/fear, denial, anger, bargaining, guilt, sadness and finally acceptance.[10]

My role as not just a counsellor but the people's pastor brought me into contact with families at every stage of their lives (marriage, births, illness, promotion, bankruptcy, retirement, death). I began to notice that the same grief response could present itself in all circumstances of life, to varying degrees. I also noticed one other critical thing: *the grief that people experienced, with a few obvious exceptions such as the loss of a child, never seemed to fit the loss*. By this, I mean that there was always more grief present than the loss seemed to call for.

---

[10] Elisabeth Kubler-Ross first identified five stages of grief in her book *On Death and Dying*.

For instance, the loss of a job might be met with some sadness, anger and fear in one person and complete devastation in another. For sure, I have never met anyone who could deal with such a loss by feeling no pain at all. Some might *say*, "It doesn't bother me," but the look on their faces tells me otherwise. Pain is seen in the eyes, not heard from the lips of those who are either unaware of it or refuse to speak of it.

The disciplines of psychiatry and psychology revolve around the central belief that people are in emotional pain. Most major theories of psychology include the understanding that the very mentally ill are merely people with magnified conditions of the basic human condition. Put the other way around, the plain, everyday worries, frustrations or sadness of the average person are merely a microcosm of what can be observed in larger "quantity" in the mentally ill. Our pain is universal; our experience of it is varied.

Most people have shut down their pain and refuse to look at it, consider it or address it. The average human fears thinking about this pain, assuming that feeling it will be so overwhelming that it will be intolerable. Many fear becoming "mired" in the pain, spiralling downward into more pain and thenceforward living a life that is filled with excruciating pain and nothing else. Although it seems to be a human instinct to feel this way, the exact opposite is true and real lasting joy can be found nowhere else but at the bottom of the pit of your pain.

Taking Leadership

You want something to change, and you are willing to become an agent of that change. This makes you a leader. The word "leader" may excite you greatly, or it may frighten you beyond belief. If it excites you because you think it holds some reward or recognition, you may be sorely disappointed. If it frightens you, fear not! By leadership, I do not mean that you have to hold an office, stand up in front of people, come up with ideas or, God forbid, *impose your will* upon anyone. I will say more about the definition of leadership in chapter 3, but for now, it will suffice to say that anyone who cares enough about change to be willing to grow and to endure pain in order to do so is by definition a leader in this world. Every family, organization, institution, community or group needs leadership. The more leaders there are in each of these organizations, the better. It is a myth that there can be too many leaders.

As someone who cares about making a difference, you are willing to take leadership if only by enduring pain in order for that to happen. But the pain has to be *worth it*. There has to be a way out—a better, more hopeful way, and an expectation that the change will be *permanent*. I promise you that there is. There is a way to make a difference in your own life, in the lives of others around you and in the world. In order to do that, you must begin with a clear understanding of the sure and certain path that change always takes. Most people err by trying to evoke change in ways and in areas over which they have no power. Allow me to introduce you to a new way of looking at the universe.

Chapter 2:
The Five Bourns

It is a flaw in happiness to see beyond our bourn.
—John Keats

The world is changing. Some say it is getting better; others disagree, and most don't really know. I suppose it depends on your perspective. What would you like to see changed? Here's my list, for what it's worth. Feel free to add in some of the ways you wish you could make a difference.

Things I'd like to see changed include:

- World peace
- An end to injustice, poverty and oppression
- Better care of the earth, including plants, animals and the ecosystem
- A cure for every disease that kills us before our time
- More love, respect and care for one another
- Harmony and a communal spirit
- True friendship
- Better parenting of all our children
- Less fighting or distance among family members
- More happiness and enjoyment of life
- Someone, other than myself, cleaning the toilets
- _____
- _____
- _____

I hope I've left enough room for the things you care about. Be sure to write in the book; someone may find your copy a hundred years from now and take up where you left off. It was an English professor of mine who advised me of the wisdom of writing in one's book. He announced to the class on the first day, "A virgin book is a virgin mind."

Now that you've decided what you want changed, let's take a look at how change comes about. Hopefully, you will already understand that your longing for change is rooted in your pain. Pain is not useless in the universe; if nothing else, your pain has the power to instil in you the desire for something better.

In order to be healed of your pain, you must take leadership in your own life. The world needs wise, integrated leaders. Leadership is not as difficult as it sounds, but it is by no means simple. Most people go about it the wrong way. They approach the challenge like Stephen Leacock's Lord Ronald who "flung himself from the room, flung himself upon his horse and rode madly off in all directions."[11]

Change happens in a very systemic and predictable way. It doesn't matter if the change is within you, in a relationship system or in the whole world: the theory is the same. Yeast can only change the dough it is sitting in, not the dough on the table beside it or the dough next door. The smell of fresh-baked bread is only pleasant to those within the house and has no effect on those in the next town or the people in Africa. Each agent of change is a small entity that is surrounded and enveloped by an entity larger than itself.

I don't like the word "entity" much. It seems rather hollow and dead. I thought about "realm," but I'm picky about words, and that one comes from the root of "regal" and denotes empires and rulers and such. "Reality" was a fleeting thought, but it seems that "reality" is up for grabs these days. Thanks to the little bit of knowledge I have of quantum physics, I now doubt whether anything is "real." Perhaps some of the ancient philosophers were right all along—reality is only what we perceive it to be. There is a word that better describes the concept I'm trying to convey, but it is an old word that isn't used much anymore, so I hope you will indulge me and bring it back into use for the time being. It is the word "bourn." I like this word primarily because of its close association with geography. John Keats, in his poem *To Autumn*, writes, "And full-grown lambs loud bleat from hilly bourn."

bourn–noun, archaic.

---

[11] Stephen Leacock, *Nonsense Novels IV—Gertrude the Governess: or, Simple Seventeen.*

1. realm; domain
2. destination
3. bound, limit, edge

[Origin: 1515–25; earlier *borne* < MF, OF, orig. a Picard form of *bodne*; see bound, boundary] [12]

I propose that within our understanding of the universe, there are five bourns, as shown in Figure 1, below.

The Five Bourns

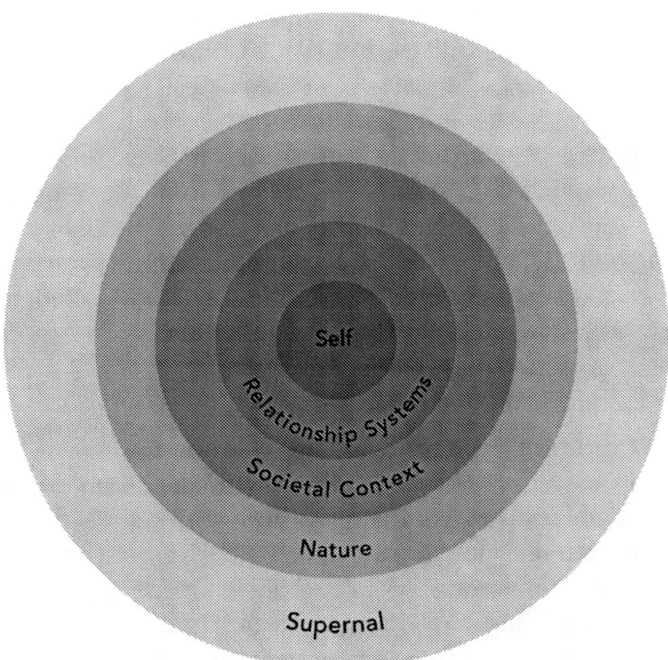

Each of these bourns has a specific relationship with the others. *Change can only happen in the movement of one bourn to another, and with respect to the*

---

[12] The definition is an amalgamation from several dictionaries and word books. The word origin is taken from www.dictionary.com, referenced on February 15, 2007.

relationships the bourns share with one another. The five bourns in order of smallest to largest are:

> Self
> Relationship Systems
> Societal Context
> Nature
> The Supernal

The Bourn of Self

As far as you need be concerned, all change begins (and ultimately ends) at the centre in the bourn of self. It is impossible to evoke change in a family, community group, in business or even in the world unless you take leadership in your own life beginning with the healing of your own pain.

In order to lead others, we must first lead ourselves. In my travels as a teacher and seminar speaker, I encounter leaders from every walk of life who struggle with some problem or other in their organization. Some folks who come to me for therapy struggle with their marriages or family life. Almost all of these inquirers have one thing in common: they perceive the problem to be in others or beyond themselves. I am amazed at the amount of human energy expended on this planet in efforts to change others, and the lack of willingness to lift a finger in an attempt to change self in relation to others.

The Bourn of Relationship Systems

The bourn of relationship systems is different for every person on the planet. It includes the circle of other human beings who are nearest to you. Your closest relationship system is always your family—both your nuclear family and your family of origin. You may not have a good relationship with your family. Many people blame their families for this. It is only a change in you, in relation to your family, that will bring about change in your family.

Others who make up your relationship systems are friends, co-workers, those you interact with in religious or community groups or those you lead or govern by virtue of your job or office. Your relationship system may be small—it is for most of us. Nevertheless, you are able to take leadership at the local diner where you work, among the soccer moms or on the finance team at the synagogue. If you are the pope or the prime minister, your relationship systems are large and involve makers of law or makers of doctrine. Even so, the pope and the prime minister will have minimal positive effect on the world if they cannot take leadership in their own lives and within *all* their closest relationship systems (their families and small groups of confidants). Whoever you are, you have great power to evoke change in the groups of which you are a part. Change in those closest to you, however, comes only *after* you can change yourself. If your goal is to change others, but not yourself, you will most certainly fail.

The Bourn of Societal Context

Societal context is the world we have created as a human species. It is culture and societies, governments and world orders. It is also any collection of ideas, beliefs, values and norms. It includes science, philosophy, law and religion. Not all people on the planet share the same societal context, but we all exist within several at the same time. We may not even share the same context with our next-door neighbour. We have a different cultural heritage, a different religion, a different set of beliefs. Nevertheless, both we and our neighbours are living *subject to* a societal context.

The Bourn of Nature

"Nature" is an imperfect word for this bourn, but I cannot think of a better one. The bourn of nature includes the whole universe of which we are a part. It is the earth in all its glory, the planets and the "laws" that govern them. It includes all creatures great and small from the tiniest and simplest viral particle to the immensely complex human being. Nature is also the *substance* of the universe—once thought to be matter or things material. This has now come into question. The bourn of nature also includes forms of energy or waves of some yet-unknown substance or reality that make up all that exists in the universe.

From within the bourn of societal context, we humans *decide* what this bourn of nature essentially is. We come up with "laws of nature" or "laws of physics." We decide what reality is and isn't, what makes sense and what doesn't, whether the world is round or flat, what a black hole is and whether or not "miracles" are possible. It is important to remember that even the laws of nature or of physics change as we discover more about them. They aren't *givens*. We as humans (in a societal context) create and re-create them with the passage of time.

The Bourn of the Supernal

"Supernal" is another one of those words that doesn't get used much. I went looking for a word that would be inclusive of almost everyone's belief systems.

Supernal is an adjective, and I admit that I'm taking some liberty by using it more or less as a noun. I found it when I looked up "supernatural," which I concluded had too much baggage. The word, literally, means this:

Supernal—*adj*
1. lofty
2. of more than earthly or human excellence
3. powerful
4. heavenly, divine, celestial

[Origin: 12th c; fr L. *supernus* "situated above"][13]

The supernal refers to whatever force or power in the universe you believe is greater than human power and greater than nature. Perhaps you are an atheist, in which case your belief system might involve the conviction that nature itself is the greatest power there is. If this is so, the theory of the bourns will still work—but you will have to include both nature and the supernal together as one bourn. Your beliefs may be non-theist, as in the Buddhist tradition, Confucianism, other existentialist philosophies and even some postmodern Christian understandings. In this case, the supernal may represent "the ground of all being," the Buddha (as a concept), "Enlightenment," "the Way" or the "More." The supernal does not have to represent a *being*; however, the theory as I describe it best fits with such a being. The theory also acknowledges that there is some sort of *force* in the universe that is both powerful and ultimately to be desired or *good*. If your religion is "Starwarsianity," you will be right at home.

The majority of people in North America believe in a deity or, simply, "God." This is true even though they may not describe themselves as religious people. The trend nowadays is to be "spiritual but not religious." If you do believe in God, then you may substitute the term "God" for "supernal" anywhere that it occurs. Your idea of God does not need to encompass a being who is omnipotent, omniscient, omnipresent or omni-anything.

Goodness and Love

Whatever the supernal is, it is about goodness and love. "Good" is a term we understand and generally agree on. "Love" is more complex. I do not define the word "love" for the purposes of this book, in the sloppy, meaningless way

---

[13] This definition is an amalgamation from several dictionaries and word books.

it normally gets thrown around in movies and songs, that warm fuzziness that applies equally to chocolate, your precious offspring, or your cat. I am talking about capital L *Love*.

The best definition of Love ever written is Scott Peck's in his best-selling book about spiritual growth, *The Road Less Traveled*. Peck wrote:

> I define love thus: The will to extend one's self for the purpose of nurturing one's own or another's spiritual growth.[14]

He goes on to describe Love as an action rather than a feeling. Although Love involves compassion and kindness, at its heart, it is neither, and may, from time to time, be interpreted as unkindness or a lack of compassion. Love is manifested in your willingness to *tolerate pain* in order to grow or so that another might grow.

Love is a positive force in the universe, working only for the good. It beckons everything to grow, to become better, more Loving. The supernal will go to great lengths to bid a person to grow. Because the supernal is the force of Love itself, it is willing to endure pain for our spiritual growth. The supernal will change itself for our sake.

The supernal is not infinite in size but is of a particular size, with infinite ability to grow. The supernal's size is the accumulation of the amount of Love that the whole universe, including humanity, has grown into. Whenever we grow spiritually, we add to the ultimate size of the supernal (the supernal "grows"). You will note that the diagram shows the supernal bourn with dotted lines, indicating a capacity to grow in size (quantitatively).

Growth

As we grow or evolve, we become more like the essence of the supernal itself. Theoretically, we could grow until we become completely "one" with the supernal. The religious greats (Buddha, Moses, Jesus, Mohammed) are said to have had a special connection with the supernal. Many of them are described as God-like or even God. It is certainly an accepted belief of religious people throughout history that reaching heights of divinity, enlightenment or ultimate reality *is* possible for a human being. It is a bourn that few will reach but everyone can strive for. It is in the striving that spiritual growth occurs. If we reach the bourn of the supernal, even in part, we have more power to influence the universe and its peoples *for the good* than we can ever imagine.

---

[14] M. Scott Peck, *The Road Less Traveled*, 81.

Chapter 3:
Evoking Change

*Be not angry that you cannot make others as you wish them to be,
since you cannot make yourself as you wish to be.*
—Thomas á Kempis

The power to change yourself, the people around you or the world, as well as the *way* that change happens, lies in the relationship of the bourns to one another. The arrows in Figure 2 show the means of influence each bourn has in connection to the others.

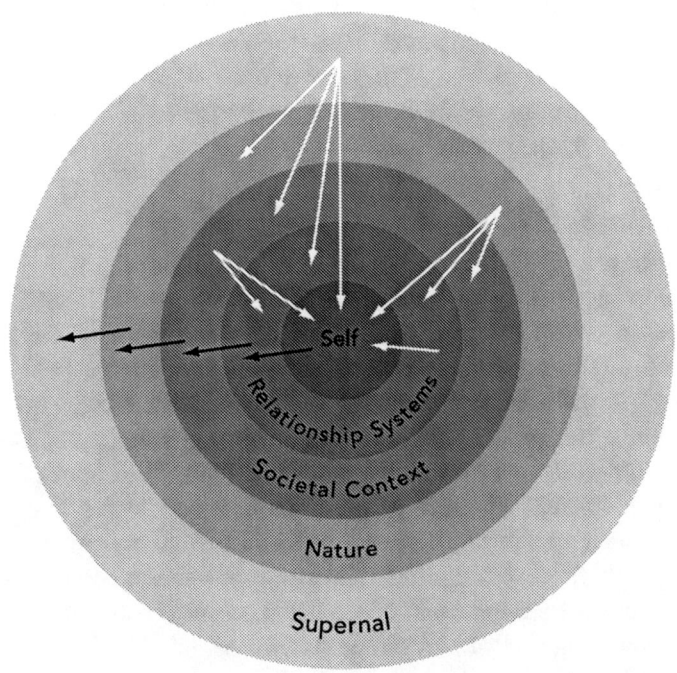

The black arrows show that if one is working from the inside circle out, each bourn only has influence over its next closest neighbour. So:

➤ Self may influence relationship systems,
➤ Relationship systems may influence the societal context,
➤ Societal context may influence nature, and
➤ Nature may influence the supernal.

However, if one is working from the outside or largest circle in (represented by the white arrows), then each bourn may influence any of the bourns in circles smaller than itself. This means that:

➤ The supernal may exert influence over every other bourn.
➤ Nature may influence societal context, relationship systems and self (you).
➤ Societal context may influence relationship systems and self.
➤ Relationship systems may influence self.

If it's easer, you may think of the bourns as floors in an apartment building. Self is the ground floor, the supernal is the top floor. Every floor's elevator only goes up *one* floor, but it will go all the way down. So the bourn of the supernal can get to every floor, as can the bourn of nature (because its elevator goes up one floor, and down all the way).

The Path of Change

This book is about your desire to bring about change, which is only possible when you take leadership in your own life (the bourn of self), and within the relationship systems within which you have some sort of influence. It is impossible for any bourn to begin the process of change without first changing itself. If the supernal were to change the course of nature, societies, families or even individuals, the supernal would first have to change itself. The supernal does not just act randomly. Nature doesn't either. Both the supernal and nature (who have a reciprocity) behave in predictable ways. So far. If either one of them decides to change itself, there will be an influence on the other. But there cannot be an influence on the other if one does not first change itself.

It's easier to comprehend that the societal context cannot change nature without first changing itself (i.e., its belief systems or "laws"). First, the context has to start to "think" differently. Only then will the universe be perceived differently and then change. Societal context must obviously change itself before any change can be seen in smaller groups or communities of people. When I say "change," I really mean *grow*. Society can change its laws or its morals, but if this is not a change based on real spiritual growth, the influence on the people it governs will be minimal or nonexistent. People may behave differently, that is, "comply," but they will not *be* different.

Relationship systems have influence over the individuals within them, but the same rule applies: they have to experience true growth in order to evoke any real change in individuals. Families who seek only to change one member, without any growth taking place within the rest of the family, will absolutely fail. So will individuals who try to change a family member, rather than changing themselves.

The heart of the matter is this: it is not possible for *you*, who is reading this book, to change anyone or anything but yourself. While change in you (in the form of spiritual growth) will *evoke change* in your closest relationships, you cannot have, as a primary goal, the changing of others. If you impose your will upon others forcefully, you may see temporary change in others, but it will not last, and there is a high risk it will backfire. Exerting power and control over others will not bring any real change into their lives, and it can serve to make both you and them utterly miserable.

Since you can only change yourself, there is no point in "skipping over" bourns by running off to "change the world." There is also no point in one individual praying diligently for the supernal to be significantly different, or to behave differently in a different kind of universe. You can only change yourself. You cannot change the world without experiencing the kind of spiritual growth that will bring change first of all to those with whom you are in closest relationship.

World leaders who have made the most difference are the ones who fully understood this nature of change. They are often not heads of state or brilliant scientists. Many have been great religious figures who have welcomed the supernal power into their lives and worked on their own "selves." By doing so, they increased their capacity to love, thus adding to the growth of the supernal. It is only when the supernal grows that any real change to the whole world happens.

This leadership journey is essentially a painful spiritual path. As such, it rarely enters the minds of politicians, psychologists or scientists to embark upon it. In 2004, his Holiness the 14th Dalai Lama visited Vancouver, British Columbia, and joined international visionary thinkers at a conference at the University of British Columbia. Among them were Archbishop Desmond Tutu,

Rabbi Zalman Schachter-Shalomi and Dr. Jo-Ann Archibald of Canada's First Nations community. A little over a month later, a G8 Summit was held with some of the most powerful political leaders in the world, including George W. Bush, Tony Blair and Jean Chrétien. Ironically, the tape of the religious leaders' conference and the coverage of the summit aired on local television at about the same time. If you flipped back and forth between channels (as I did), it was glaringly obvious who the most extraordinary, thoughtful, visionary and integrated individuals were. The spiritual leaders astonished their audience with their incredible, awe-inspiring wisdom. The politicians in this bizarre juxtaposition came across as shallow and self-absorbed if not downright slimy.

Just because you consider yourself "religious" or even "spiritual" does not mean that you have evoked real change in the bourns of self or relationship systems. Many religious or spiritual people seek *only* a relationship with the supernal in hopes that this will bring change to their closest relationships or to the societal context. They wish that the pattern of change would skip over a number of bourns, and they carry on throughout their lives as if this were true. They fail to see how the supernal is bidding them to grow, to heal themselves and their closest relationships, and that by doing this, they will become closer to the supernal and feel less pain and more joy. Extraordinary, world-changing leaders are always spiritual people, but spiritual people are not necessarily extraordinary world-changing leaders.

Skipping over bourns to change the world often takes the form of praying for the supernal to change the course of history. Do we really think this is possible? However, what if everyone on the planet prayed simultaneously to change the course of history or to end disease? Would not nature be affected somehow and then, in turn, the supernal itself? Sounds crazy, I suppose. But what if it isn't?

You may be wondering about now if there is any point in praying for peace or an end to disease and human suffering. My congregation prays for these things every Sunday. Many of the people in the room (but not all) actually believe in the power of prayer while they're praying. I tell people that there is always a reason for such prayer, even though we may never see the results, because one day perhaps we will all pray together and we will all mean it. So we faithfully continue, including always in our prayers our wish for the rest of the world to have the kind of conviction that transforms and endures.

The Beginning and End

Taking leadership in your own life (spiritual growth) is what evokes real change. The next chapter will give you a greater understanding of the nature of leadership itself. Parts Two and Three of this book are devoted to an understanding of self and an understanding of how your closest relationships—living systems—work. It is from within these two bourns that you have the power to take leadership and bring about change. This change may one day become the yeast of *shalom*.[15]

---

[15] See footnote 7.

Chapter 4:
The Leadership Trinity

When in doubt, don't just do something—stand there.
—Murray Bowen

Systems theory provides exceptional insight into how bourns are connected with one another and thus how change takes place. As a human organism, you are a *living system*. Your various cells and organs work together and influence one another. Change in one part of you will necessarily bring change to another. Check this out by having a few stiff drinks and see how that affects your ability to wiggle your toes or keep down your supper.

All groups of humans who live, work, play, meet or otherwise interact together are also living systems. A system functions in a particular way, intricately linking all of its participants together. There are no "problem people" within systems. There are problems with the systems themselves, and they show up in people. There was no problem with your toes a few minutes ago after those beers; there was a problem with the way your whole body reacted to the alcohol, and it showed up in your toes.

Within any system, you will respond with behaviour and according to roles that are often predetermined by the way you function emotionally in the most natural system you belong to—your own family. Once I began to learn more about a systems approach to leadership, I realized that the best way I could lead was to improve my own functioning within the system (in the bourn of self). This meant that in order to affect the systems I was leading, I had to know how to affect my own family system as well as affect *myself* as a living organism. All systems need good leadership in order to change. There is no difference between being a good leader in any system and being a good leader within your own life. Good leadership is all-encompassing.

Defining Leadership

The amount of literature out there these days on leadership is quite remarkable. A lot of it describes what I would call *gifted leadership*. By this, I mean the qualities that very gifted leaders often possess—things that may appear to bring quick or temporary change. Gifted leadership is not necessarily *good leadership*. Good leadership is what gives rise to real and lasting change. *Extraordinary leadership* necessarily combines the two.

You do not need to be an extraordinary leader. You may possess exceptional gifts, but you may not, and there is no need to be discouraged if you don't. It would serve us well to embrace extraordinary leaders and learn as much as we can from them. But you do not need to possess all or any of their giftedness in order to take leadership and evoke change. You do need to understand the difference between giftedness and good leadership. Let's take a closer look at those concepts now.

I begin all of my workshops by asking the group to assemble a list of words that denote good leadership. It's a trick question, and so I generally get a list of the qualities of gifted leadership instead. The most common words or phrases are usually something like the following.

Words that Describe Gifted Leadership:

- Enthusiastic
- Challenger
- Empowerer
- Inspirer
- Coach
- Motivator
- Seeks win-win
- Vision/visionary
- Big-ideas person
- Adventurous
- Risk taker
- Passionate
- Charismatic
- Has followers

- Upbeat
- Good listener
- Skilled or knowledgeable
- Has integrity
- Genuine
- Collegial
- Team player
- Empathetic
- Compassionate
- Owns a golden retriever

After the group carefully develops such a list, I usually take a black marker and put a big "X" through the whole thing. This list denotes the qualities necessary for *gifted* leadership, but gifted leaders aren't necessarily good leaders. Gifted leaders are always at risk of falling victim to conflict or downright mutiny (perceived as a failure of the leader). If this does not happen, it is usually impossible to ever replace a gifted leader by anyone else (perceived to be a failure of the people).

It is easier to list concepts that should be avoided in the definition of good leadership, things that reflect the abuse of power. Let's call this *offensive leadership*. Here are some words and phrases that describe it:

Words that Describe Offensive Leadership:

- "Anyone who tries to take over your money, your body or your will"[16]
- Insincere
- Dishonest
- Reactive
- Takes things personally
- Lacks integrity
- Rages

---

[16] A Buddhist monk, whose name I cannot remember, whom I met at an interfaith event, provided me with this excellent definition of the abuse of power.

- Forces
- Coerces
- Manipulates
- Controls
- Railroads
- Abuses
- Harasses
- Owns a reptile
- Is a reptile

Just the idea of taking over one's will seems strong. And yet any situation where the leader has a good idea or even a great vision and he tries to get others to "catch it" must somehow involve imposing the will, even if it's touted as "empowerment," "collegial learning" or "leading from behind." It is the attempt to transfer one's values to another. Imposition of the will is also referred to as "strong leadership," which some experts propose is called for in certain situations. But strength in leadership by itself is not necessarily good leadership.

Words like "convince," "persuade" or "assert" often find their way onto either list. These words involve imposing one's will upon another, and therefore I am not willing to include them in the definition of good leadership.

Good Leadership

There are three imperatives to good leadership, and they cannot be placed on any sort of list or even displayed in linear form for they are held in a delicate, *equitable relationship* with one another. I have named this relationship the "leadership trinity."

If it were not for a lot of baggage with the word "trinity," I would have made *The Leadership Trinity* the title of this book. The word comes from the Latin "trinitas" meaning simply "three." Both Christians and Hindus have a theory of the trinity. For Christians, although God is one, God is expressed in terms of three "persons": Father, Son and Holy Spirit. All are equal, and all are in relationship with one another. Similarly, the Hindu trinity of Brahma, Vishnu and Shiva represents the Divine in a three-fold nature and function. I do not wish to attach any religious characteristic whatsoever to the term "leadership trinity." I have coined it to convey only the equality and relational nature of the three concepts.

The first two concepts (self-definition and emotional intelligence) exist in the bourn of self, and the third (meaningful connection) exists between the bourn of self and the bourn of relationship systems. I will describe each concept briefly in this chapter and then devote three major sections (within Part Two of this book) to a further full discussion of them.

Self-Definition

Self-defined leaders know who they are and what they believe; they have an opinion. They have good ideas and are not afraid to support the good ideas of others. They know what they will or will not do in most situations. They operate out of their well-thought-out core values. They are acutely aware of their emotions (able to name each emotion and how it can be identified in their own body) and can clearly understand the difference between emotion and rational ideas or facts. This is known as *self-definition*.

Perhaps it seems obvious that the leaders most perceive as "good" know what they think, yet a multitude of them do not know what they think. They take up a point of view only to be swayed by the reactivity of others who may disagree with them.

Good leaders are not rigid or stubborn about their beliefs, however, for it is not possible to be both meaningfully connected and rigid. Poor leaders are anxious that if they change their mind on a matter, someone will emotionally react to the change (for instance, with angry or personal criticism). Good leaders are open to change what they think, but only because of logical, rational, new information and never because of the emotional reactivity of another. They understand that as long as they behave with compassion and integrity, they are not responsible for other people's emotional reactions.

Emotional Intelligence[17]

In order to be clearly self-defined, it is necessary to be emotionally mature, which allows the leader to remain calm or "maintain a non-anxious presence"[18] in the face of the (immature) emotional reactivity of others. This also seems obvious. Everyone knows they do not want a leader who is shouting, crying or silently pouting. However, many leaders (even great leaders) *look calm* but are not calm. Inside they are anxious; their hearts may be beating faster, they feel nauseous, or they are overwhelmed with feelings of dread, guilt, fear or rage. Granted, it is better to fake calm than to run from the room screaming. Nevertheless, this façade has been claimed by many a poor leader as "a non-anxious presence." When humans are anxious, they cannot think as clearly, and they cannot fake clear thinking. Coming to the place where you can truly maintain a non-anxious presence is a spiritual journey. It is to "have your act together." It is to be emotionally aware and spiritually mature.

True emotional maturity is the commitment to a never-ending journey of increasing one's own emotional awareness and intelligence. "Emotional intelligence" is the ability to know what emotion is operating in the body at any given time, its triggers and probable origins. It is also the solid commitment to the ongoing work of healing those emotions that are maladaptive to the self.

---

[17] The term "emotional intelligence" was first coined by Peter Salovey and J. D. Mayer in a 1990 article for *Imagination, Cognition and Personality*. It was later made popular by the book with the same name by Daniel Goleman (1995).

[18] Edwin Friedman, *Generation to Generation*, 27, 208–210. This term of Friedman's has been picked up by many leaders–who have given his work a superficial reading–as if it is the one and only component of good leadership.

Meaningful Connection

The third component of good leadership is *staying meaningfully connected*. Simply put, it's easy to hold a clear point of view and be non-anxious if you don't talk to anyone. This was my worst error as a young minister. If someone disagreed with my ideas, I just ignored them or somehow deked around them.

Meaningful connection means deeply listening to our opponents, searching for new information or insights that may help inform your own views and opinions. It does *not* mean succumbing to them when they are emotionally reactive, often veiled as "compromise." Neither does it mean arguing with them, trying to force your point of view upon them. This is not necessary. Leaders who are competent in their roles do not need to convince others to change their minds. This would be an example of imposing the will, which good leadership seeks to avoid.

Extraordinary Leadership

Extraordinary leadership is the marriage of gifted leadership with the foundational principles of the leadership trinity. Extraordinary leaders are exceedingly gifted individuals and adventurous, enthusiastic visionaries. They are caring, kind-hearted people who are also charismatic, having the ability to inspire and challenge others to new and exciting goals, forms of organization or programs. They are usually highly intelligent and educated, possessing a wealth of knowledge and skill. They brim with ideas, visions and passions. They are always willing to take risks, but calculated risks, for calculation comes easy to them. People naturally want to follow them because they are so brilliant and so full of human compassion. A zeal for their work just shines out of them. As self-defined, emotionally mature people, they don't take themselves too seriously. They understand that they will have both worshippers and enemies, and they don't concern themselves much over either.

This book is not about extraordinary or gifted leadership. Good leaders who are also talented and gifted are rare, but wherever they are found, it is the solid grounding in the leadership trinity that sets them apart. This grounding is a foundation accessible to all.

Part Two

The Bourn of Self

Self-Definition

Chapter 5:

Self

Love your neighbour as yourself.
—*Jesus, quoting Leviticus 19*

What exactly are we talking about when we use the term "self"? Philosophers, theologians and neuroscientists have been trying to answer that question for centuries. Most commonly, we think of the self as the brain, or something in the brain. Joseph LeDoux, a neuroscientist, attempted to demonstrate in his book, *The Synaptic Self: How Our Brains Become Who We Are,* that the self lies within the synapses of our brains. Deciding what we mean by self involves what we mean by consciousness. I am conscious of the fact that I exist. But who is the "I" that is conscious of it? Self is not a simple idea.

Try to imagine everything that makes you, *you*. Imagine placing all these things into a large clear bubble: your personality, your childhood experiences, your knowledge, your skills, your education, your career, your family connections, your likes and dislikes, your emotions, your body and body image, your ideas, thoughts, dreams, your goals and visions, your core values. All of these things are inside the bubble now. Everything that is you is in there. The bubble is you. But who is looking at the bubble? Better said, who is *perceiving* it? Whoever, whatever it is, it is the true *self*. It is also known as the "witnessing consciousness."

Since this kind of talk makes one's brain hurt (even mine), please exhale in relief when I tell you that you may evoke change in yourself, in others and in the world by concerning yourself with the stuff *in* the bubble. For the purposes of this work, we are going to call all that stuff *self*.

As a human being, you are an animal—a mammal, in fact. As an animal, you know instinctively, even within your cells, what is "self" and what is not. Unfortunately, years of societal conditioning have squelched this instinct in humans to the point where it is very difficult to define self simply or clearly.

Because your brain will tell you that you are in some sort of "danger" if you do, you may often be afraid to say what you think or to truly *be who you are*. Instead, you decide to be something or someone else, and put on a mask that shows a different you.

You may reject the idea of being "fake," so instead you will arrogantly announce to others "who you are" or what you think because at some level you fear what will happen in a close intimate relationship that involves listening to others' opinions as well. If you are in relationship with and listen to others, you may need to change what you think. This frightens many people because change entails work. It is the work of *adaptation*, and we humans, although highly adaptable creatures, don't like to do it. We would much rather fight to keep things the way they are. It is an exercise in spiritual growth, therefore, to be able to define self, to say "This is who I am," or "This is what I believe," while maintaining a good relationship with others.

In my leadership classes, I give people a little card that many have found helpful. It's called the "Self/Not Self" card. Some put it on their refrigerator. Others carry it around in their wallets. I suggest you memorize the components and then spend most of your lifetime trying to figure out what it means to live them.

"Self" means:

- Who I am
- What I believe
- What my core values are
- What my core operating principles are
- What I am willing to do
- What I am not willing to do
- What I *feel*
    - Owning those feelings as mine alone
    - Knowing how to identify them clearly, and locate them in my body
    - Fully understanding where they came from in my previous experience
- What my goals are
- What my vision/destiny is

- ➤ Where I need to *grow* (change, question, rewrite my mission, values, principles)
- ➤ Wherein I am imperfect/challenged/uneducated
- ➤ What gifts, strengths and knowledge I have
- ➤ *Clarity* on all of the above

"Not Self" means:
- ➤ What others (should) think, believe, feel, behave like
- ➤ Path/goals/destiny of others
- ➤ What others think/say about me
- ➤ Projected emotions onto others
- ➤ Blame of others/the world/circumstances
- ➤ Feeling threatened, envious, or inferior to others
- ➤ Being anxious—worried, fretting, angry, troubled—about a problem of another
- ➤ Being invested in the outcome of problems/challenges/events that involve others
- ➤ Rigidity in beliefs/values/map of reality, stubbornness
- ➤ Belief that the dysfunction of others is about me
- ➤ Feeling the feelings of another
- ➤ Desire to take on or solve another's problems, to give advice
- ➤ Desire to fix another
- ➤ Having no idea what I *feel*
- ➤ Having no knowledge of the origin of my feelings
- ➤ *No clarity* on the "Self" list

For the rest of this chapter, we'll look at each attribute of defining *self* in more depth.

Who I Am and What I Believe

It doesn't matter if one is taking leadership in a corporation, a country, the local soccer club or one's own marriage. If you cannot *define yourself*, there will be trouble. Think about it: how much time do you spend trying to respond to the reactivity of others compared to the amount of time you spend deciding what you think? When you do know what you think, how easy is it for someone else to have an emotional reaction, or criticize your thinking, spurring an emotional reaction in you, which then causes you to change what you think? Do you believe you could evoke any real change in yourself or others without knowing what you believe? Would you want a leader who doesn't know who she is and what she thinks?

Rudy Giuliani, former mayor of New York City, was interviewed on *The Oprah Winfrey Show* after his term in office. Oprah asked him what the most important thing was in leadership. He said, "Do your homework." I take this to mean, "Know what you think" about everything to do with the topic you are dealing with. If you are the chair of the property committee of the church, *do you think* going into debt for a new furnace is a good idea? What time *do you think* is reasonable for a teenager to come home, despite what your spouse believes? And if you are running for prime minister, *what do you think* about social programming or going to war? Chances are, if you're afraid to say what you think for fear of not being elected, either you won't be elected anyway, or if you are, you will be a terrible prime minister.

Knowing what you think or believe *is not the same thing* as projecting this belief onto others, forcing (or even expecting, or schmoozing) others to believe what you believe or arrogantly announcing what you believe to those in your organization or family. It is just *knowing it,* figuring it out. Listening to others, educating yourself and connecting in a meaningful way to people who disagree with you so that you ensure your beliefs are reasonable. This is the essence of self-definition.

Core Values and Operating Principles

It is a good idea to come up with a list of your core values. What are the things that you value at the very heart of life? Here is a list of 15 core values held by virtually everyone, but in differing orders of importance. The list is in alphabetical order.

Core Values:

- Faith
- Family
- Freedom
- Fun
- Health
- Honesty
- Integrity
- Justice
- Legacy
- Money
- Precision
- Responsibility
- Safety
- Success
- Work

Try choosing just five from the list and put them in priority order.

My top five core values are:

1. _____

2. _____

3. _____

4. _____

5. _____

Now ask your significant other, or even a co-worker, to do the same and compare your lists. Make it a game! There is no point in arguing for the choices or the priorities of another. It is perfectly acceptable to hold any of these values in any order, but you may notice how difficult it is simply to define yourself and to resist the temptation to define the other person. Imagine the amusement in my house when my daughter chose honesty, integrity and responsibility as her top three, while her partner selected family, freedom and fun. Some interesting insights and conversation ensued!

An operating principle is more specific than a core value. It is a written statement (for yourself only) of how you will operate in any given set of circumstances. For example, one of my core operating principles is that I am unwilling to discuss anything I have said in a workshop, leadership class or sermon with someone who was not there. I have on occasion had people come up to me angrily, saying, "I heard you said such-and-so, and I'd like to take issue with it." If they did not hear it for themselves, then I am unwilling to enter into the conversation. Another one of my operating principles is that if I ever have to choose between responding to a long-time church member in crisis or a stranger in crisis, I will choose the stranger (the one who has no relationship with a Christian community, or other spiritual resources from which to draw).

Take a few moments now to write out some of your operating principles. You may add to the list at any time. Are you willing to define yourself clearly around these principles and not waver on them despite how others may react? (This is an ultimate goal of good leadership.)

My operating principles include:

➢ _____

➢ _____

➢ _____

➢ _____

➢ _____

➢ _____

What I Am or Am Not Willing to Do

Knowing what you will or will not do is perhaps one of the most central qualities of good leadership in terms of defining a self. It's fine for you to say to someone else, "*You* are not allowed to do such and such." But the other person may be automatically thinking, "Or what?" This is one of the biggest mistakes in parenting: telling the child/teenager what he will or will not do, instead of telling him what *you* will or will not do.[19] What you are willing to do may change over time as you acquire more skills, knowledge or insight. Rigidity or stubbornness and self-definition are not the same thing.

It is very powerful to say, "Now that I understand *x*, I am no longer willing to do *y*." You have to mean it. Often you may need to be clearer about your willingness or lack of it by adding a statement of what the consequence will be. The magic word here is the word "if." "*If* you do *x*, I will do *y*." And you must follow through.

What I Feel

Part of defining self is knowing the difference between what you *think* and what you feel. Although experts on emotion vary in their definitions, I define feeling as the conscious awareness in the body of an emotional response within the brain. A large portion of this book is devoted to "emotional intelligence," which is the skill of understanding your emotions, acknowledging them and seeking, if necessary, to process or change them. At this point, it is sufficient to express that knowing what you feel, and not only what you think, is part of defining self. The two principles (defining self and being emotionally intelligent) are intricately connected, which is why the leadership trinity is diagrammed as it is.

---

[19] Michael Kerr and Murray Bowen, *Family Evaluation*, 217.

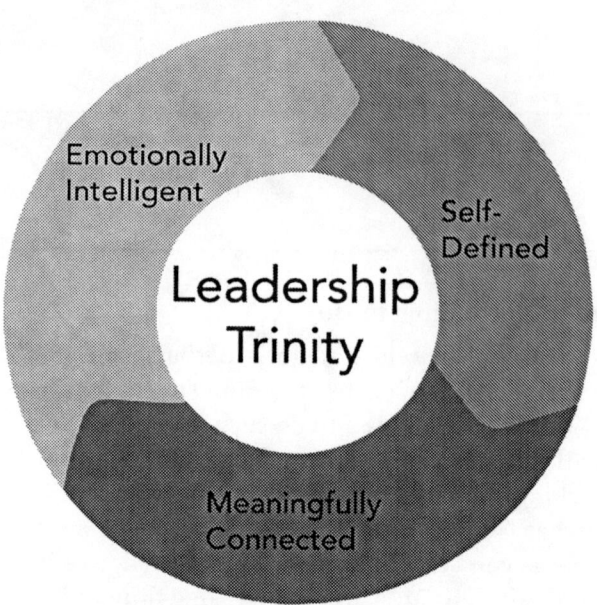

Goals/Vision/Destiny

Stephen Covey has an excellent chapter in his book *The 7 Habits of Highly Effective People* called "Begin with the End in Mind."[20] "How can you start out to build a house," he asks, "without a blueprint?" Is not building a life more valuable than building a house? Our lives need a blueprint or "mission statement." Covey suggests that you engage in an exercise imagining what you would hope people say about you at your funeral. Do you hope they say you spent most of your time at the office? Or that you were a great father? Do you hope your children say, "She always got us to obey her" or "She was always happy to see us when we walked in the door"? Your response will be reflective of the goals that you value most for your life. I suggest that you take some time now to write out what you believe your purpose in life is, what your goals are, what you envision for yourself, and/or what you desire your destiny to be. Once you do this, it will be easier to make decisions, because you will always choose the thing that relates to your mission and its explicit or implicit values.

---

[20] Stephen Covey, *The 7 Habits of Highly Effective People*, 96–144.

My purpose in life/destiny is:

_____

_____

_____

_____

My life goals are:

➢ _____

➢ _____

➢ _____

➢ _____

➢ _____

Where I Need to Grow, Change, Question, Learn

Knowing where you need to grow is one of the greatest assets any leader has. After you finish reading this book, you will perhaps know more about that! I once had a woman in one of my seminary summer school classes ask me very early in the course, "Is there anything wrong with getting to a certain stage in your life and saying, 'I'm just good enough'?" Um, yes. That was all I could answer. I probably could have thought of something cleverer, but the question took me completely by surprise. She dropped my class quite early on in the program.

Good leaders know what they don't know. They understand wherein they are imperfect, challenged or lacking in knowledge. They don't feel bad about themselves in light of these imperfections or challenges; they just understand them and are willing to admit them. Good leaders are committed to lifelong learning, even though they know they will never live long enough to learn everything they need to know. Any leader who doesn't think she needs to know more about the subject she's leading in is a fool. And anyone who believes he doesn't need to grow any more will be severely limited in the leadership he can display in all of his closest relationships.

Where I need to grow:

➢ _____

➢ _____

➢ _____

➢ _____

➢ _____

➢ _____

My Gifts, Strengths and Knowledge

It is just as important to know what you *do* know, as well as what you don't. What are your gifts, strengths, skills and knowledge? Go beyond the regular résumé and write yourself a résumé that lists all of the gifts you have. Don't worry; no one needs to see it but you. If you are telling *yourself* that you're not worth much, how on earth will you evoke meaningful change, and how will you take leadership as a mother or life partner? Deep down, our pain comes from a belief that we may be worthless at some level, but this belief should not permeate every level of our being.

My strengths, gifts, and knowledge areas include:

➢ _____

➢ _____

➢ _____

➢ _____

➢ _____

➢ _____

I-Statements

Whenever one is defining a self, the I-statement is key. Children in schools all over the country, couples in therapy, and business teams are learning and finding value in the I-statement. When you use I-statements, you own your feelings or ideas, rather than project ideas or feelings onto others. It is the best way to communicate with anyone—a partner, co-worker, team member or a child. Taking an "I-position" means that you can think for yourself. You are self-defined. It also means being able to hold that position, calmly, in the face of others' reactivity to it. When you use "you-statements," you seek to define others, rather than self. "You-statements" project blame onto others or seek to impose one's will onto another.

You-Statement	I-Statement
1. You make me so angry.	1. I am angry.
2. You don't care about me.	2. I don't feel cared for.
3. You don't respect me.	3. I don't feel respected.
4. You hurt my feelings.	4. My feelings are hurt.
5. You are so lazy!	5. I am very frustrated (or angry) that I have to do all this myself.
6. You were bad (or, "it was bad") to crayon on the walls.	6. Crayon ruins the walls. I'm very upset now, because I have to clean all the walls.
7. We have to stop spending money.	7. I have to stop spending money.
8. We both neglect the yard work.	8. I neglect the yard work.
9. You're not a team player.	9. As a member of this team, I don't feel appreciated (or supported).

Note that "we-statements" are a weak excuse for "I-statements" because they contain the word "you." ("We" literally means you + I.) So the next time you're tempted to say "we," just leave out the "you" part of it. You'll probably discover precisely how much you were projecting onto the other in your "we-statement."

Knowing what constitutes self is imperative in the quest for clearer and better self-definition. It can therefore also be helpful to discover these truths by examining what is *not* self.

Chapter 6:
Not Self

No one can drive us crazy unless we give them the keys.
—Doug Horton

Things that are "not self" belong in the bourn of your relationship systems. It is imperative that you understand the clear line between this bourn and the bourn of self, because you only have the power to define yourself. *Defining others will not change them.* The ability to separate yourself and the qualities you possess, either physically or emotionally, from those which someone else possesses, is called having clear *boundaries*. The concept of boundaries will be discussed more fully in relation to systems theory in chapter 22; however, a simple definition is in order at this point to grasp the idea of self/not self.

We have great physical boundaries, because it is completely obvious which body parts belong to us and which belong to someone else. But our emotional boundaries are more like liquid than solid, so they can virtually flow into another person. Having good boundaries means you know where you end and someone else begins as an emotional unit. If you're thinking about yourself and feeling your own feelings, this is self. Once you start thinking in terms of another, and *feeling* in terms of another, you have ceased to be able to define self. It is as though you have no boundary, and so you are emotionally stuck together with the other or *fused*. While it may not be possible to stop being emotionally stuck together with others completely, it is possible to be more *aware of it* and work toward defining your boundaries more clearly.

Believing you know how other people should think, feel or behave is the first indicator of a poor leader. Remarkably, this has often been touted as strong leadership. Osama bin Laden, the Ku Klux Klan and a variety of cult leaders also know what everyone should think, feel or do. In fact, it's impossible for something to be defined as a terrorist group or even a cult *unless* the leader imposes what he believes on the others. Although there is more to the definition than this, if the group you belong to allows you to have freedom to believe what you want, then it is not a cult.

Impose-your-will thinking is most pronounced in the military. It only makes sense that military leaders force their ideas upon their followers to the point that the follower cannot think for himself but must obey orders like a machine. But this is not *good* leadership, it is only *military* leadership. This kind of leadership evokes no positive change in the system anywhere outside of the military. Religious groups, particularly Christian, have tried to impose their will upon others ("saving souls" or "making converts") for centuries. It has not resulted in even a majority of people becoming Christian. In Canada, less than 40 per cent of the population attend religious services monthly or more. This number has not changed much since 1975.[21] Yet many Christians continue to implement methods of evangelization that impose a belief system upon others. What was that definition of insanity again?

Let us take a few moments to go through, one by one, the various characteristics of what I am calling "not self." It is a valuable exercise, for much can be learned about defining self by also discovering what is not self. You can go a long way toward evoking change by not allowing yourself to waste time with things that are outside of your own bourn. Here are some elements that are clearly not self.

The Journey, Path, Destiny, Values, Principles and Goals of Others

Attempting to change others is of no concern to a good leader. This is especially true in families when you are raising children. The most fundamental flaw of parenting occurs whenever the parent tries to impose her will upon her children. Two parents presenting a "unified front" is even worse. (It's fine if both of you genuinely feel the same way about an issue, but one parent imposing her will on both the child and her partner will eventually backfire.)

If you concern yourself with what they should think, do or believe, either your children, much like your employees, parishioners, team members or clients, will comply without thinking for themselves, or they will rebel against you. Who wants either? I do not want children who willingly comply with the most powerful person in the room. If I raise them that way, my daughters might grow up and comply with a date rapist, or my son might join Al Qaeda. Give me a kid who argues with me intelligently any day. I should know, I've got three of them. The only hope I have for my children is that I have equipped them well

---

[21] Reginald W. Bibby, "Religious Services Attendance Trends" (Press Release), University of Lethbridge, November 25, 2004.

to make their own moral decisions. I may or may not agree with their decisions, but I will be able to trust that they made them wisely. And more importantly, I will always have a close and meaningful relationship with them.

What Others Think/Say about Me

There is no point in dwelling on what others think of you. The only thing worse is dwelling on what someone else says someone else said about you. Never mind dwelling; don't spend any life energy on it at all. Deal with people one-on-one. It is poor leadership to operate out of what others may think of you or what others may say about you. A lot of what people say to or about leaders, *especially* good leaders, is more suggestive of their own emotional reactivity than it is of anything else. This is most true with criticism and particularly true of criticism with an emotional reaction attached to it. Such criticism is not about you. It is about their projecting of emotion onto you, recognizable in "you statements." There is nothing wrong with constructive criticism. The most helpful kind would be delivered in the form of a description of what you've done, along with "I-statements" depicting how your behaviour has affected them. Emotionally charged you-statements fired at you say more about them than they do about you.

I often give people a little business card that simply reads:

INAM

The letters stand for "it's not about me." Whenever someone becomes very emotionally reactive—angry, shouting or critical, you can just pull out the card from your wallet and look at it. Whatever she's saying or doing is about *her*— her issues, her projection of emotion, her reactivity. Whenever someone tries to redefine you, she is defining herself.

Sometimes you-statements, when you hear them, can be turned around to be heard as "I-statements". I had a client with a rare anxiety disorder whose partner absolutely did not understand it. When she panicked, her partner would say things like, "Why don't you get over it? You're ruining our lives with this. You're just being ridiculous. It's all in your head. Why can't you just snap out of it and stop being so stupid?" These comments distressed her greatly. Her main focus in the session was on fixing her partner, so he would "understand" and stop saying these things. She wanted some printed information about her specific disorder to give to him to read. I didn't think there was much hope for the guy, at least not as far as understanding was concerned. I did, however, coach her to hear the comments differently. She needed to hear them as I-statements, even though he was not capable of forming I-statements. She might have heard something like this: "I can't stand it that you have this phobia. It's messing with my life. I want a more normal girlfriend. I want to be in control. I feel so helpless! I can't fix it when you're like this! Do something so that I feel better!" Once she was able to "hear" his accusations more as I-statements, she was able to understand him better and talk about his own worries. She expressed to me in a later session that when she did this, for the first time, she began to feel less anxiety!

Blame of Others/the World/Circumstances

Blame is a complete waste of time. People invested in blame can squander their entire lives. While it may be true that other people are fools, and the world is an unjust, unforgiving place, nevertheless, you have no control over it. You are wandering out of your own bourn and into another's. Psychologist and popular TV host Dr. Phil McGraw often remarks to his guests, "Do you want to be right, or do you want a good relationship?" These are very wise words. Yes, it is true that other people can be idiots. Yes, it is true that the world just sucks sometimes. You are correct. You win the prize for astute observation. Now what? You cannot change others or the world. You can only change yourself in relation to others. You can only change yourself in relation to the world.

Feeling Threatened, Envious, or Inferior

While it is true that we often *feel* inferior, it is best if we can identify the feeling and accept that it is a feeling, rather than believing it as fact. We often dwell on the accomplishments, skill or knowledge of others around us, rather than focusing on self and our spiritual growth.

There is enough fame and glory to go around. It's not a pie that other people are grabbing pieces of before you get there. *Everyone can excel.* There is room enough in this world for every person to succeed and be recognized. The best recognition you get is when you are emotionally mature and committed to your own growth. Mature people who graciously give way to the success of others are ultimately respected and admired. And they are always successful because it is only the emotionally immature who will not work with them or for them. So their organizations fill up with mature, gifted people. Every stalk of wheat soars to the sun and bears a harvest a hundredfold. The chaff falls inevitably to the threshing floor and is thrown into the fire.

It doesn't matter how "good" other people are, you are you, and that's all that matters. You are not inferior to anyone. You are a unique combination of gifts, skills, talents, passions, personality traits and abilities. You may not be a scholar or a movie star or even wealthy, but you contribute to a world that has scholarship, entertainment and abundance. What difference does it make, really, if you write a thousand words or clean a thousand ovens? There is no need to be jealous of another's success. You will always be a part of the success of the whole human race.

Investment in the Outcome
Fretting about things you have no control over is another waste of time and particularly of life energy. Many leaders spend far too much energy fretting and worrying. Good leadership requires, instead, a journey toward one's own growth. There is no need to fret or to be invested in the outcome of anything because you have no power to change the world or nature or the operations of the supernal, anyway. I often ask people in therapy who worry excessively: "What's the worst thing that can happen?" I call it the "what if" game. Here's a summary of one such conversation:

Client: Ever since 9–11, I'm worried about flying.
Therapist: What's the worst thing that could happen?
Client: I'd get blown up and die.
Therapist: And then what?
Client: Well, I'd go to heaven, I suppose. But my kids would have no father. I grew up with no father—that's no good.
Therapist: It was difficult growing up without a father.
Client: Ya. I guess I turned out okay, though.
Therapist: It contributed to your character, somehow.
Client: I suppose so. I guess if my kids didn't have a dad, they'd be all right.
Therapist In the grand scheme of things, all right.
Client: I really wanted to do something for this world before I die, though. Make some sort of a difference.
Therapist: If you died in a plane crash, you would die in vain.
Client: If I did, it's like my life has no purpose.
Therapist: People need to leave a legacy.
Client: I guess my kids are my legacy. I guess all the people I've influenced.
Therapist: Perhaps you can't save the whole world before you die.

Client: (laughing) I guess not. I guess that's up to God.
Therapist: Indeed.
Client: So I suppose if I died in a plane crash, everything would be okay.
Therapist: I suppose so.
Client: Of course it would be. I'm being silly. The universe is in good hands. God doesn't need me alive to make it all work for future generations. There are lots of people left to do that.

If people arrive at the idea that the universe is in God's hands, or at least *out of their hands,* they can often let go of their worry. There is no reason to be "invested in the outcome," for nature and the supernal have that covered.

Sometimes I play another little game with people that they absolutely hate. I call it the "it doesn't matter" game. I find it to be a good exercise for reducing meaningless worry. But it only works if you are on a spiritual journey that you take seriously. My friend, Ian, played it with me one year when I was fretting over being the chairperson of the nominations committee for our denomination's judicatory. I couldn't get anyone to chair the camp committee for that fall, and I was worried sick. Ian sat in the muggy warmth of my living room one August night and cracked open a second can of beer. "It doesn't matter," he said.

"What are you talking about, it doesn't matter? If I can't get anyone to chair the committee, then the committee can't even meet!"

"It doesn't matter."

"The whole camp committee will fall apart."

"It doesn't matter."

"They can't run the camp next season without a well-functioning committee!"

"It doesn't matter."

"But this camp's been going for 60 years. All of a sudden, we don't run a camp?"

"It doesn't matter."

"What about all those kids?"

"You think if they don't go to camp, they're all going to go to hell or something? So we don't run a camp anymore. Camps can't last forever. Maybe this is the year that this one ends. God's in charge of those children's souls, Anna. *It doesn't matter.*"

I went to the meeting of the judicatory in September and announced that I could not find a chair for the camp committee. The previous chair, who had declared he would not serve another term no matter what, stated with a sniff, "Well I guess I'll have to continue chairing it. We can't go without a camp."

His investment in the outcome was greater than mine; he took the stress and anxiety, and he overworked for another year!

Not being invested in the outcome is not the same thing as not caring. Ian did not convince me not to care about the camp. He only convinced me to let go of my fretting and worrying and trust more in the supernal to evoke change. There are lots of people who slough off on their jobs and don't give a damn about anyone but themselves. These people will never evoke true change. But there is a difference between *caring* and being *anxiously invested*. I care about my children and the choices they make in life. If they make poor choices, I am disappointed, sometimes sad and sometimes fearful. But I am not anxiously invested in my children's choices, working overtime for them or imposing my will upon them so that they define themselves exactly as I would. There is a huge difference. I was not willing to wake up my teenagers in the morning if they slept in and missed work. If they did that, they would be yelled at by their bosses, or they would be fired. If this were to happen, I would be disappointed. To date, I have refused to be invested in their lives in this way, and all three of them are responsible young adults who have never failed at anything nor been fired by anyone.

You picked up this book to read it because you want your life to make a difference; you are already a good and moral person who cares about other people. There is no chance that by letting go of your anxious investment you will become uncaring and immoral, accomplishing nothing. Those kinds of people don't read books like this.

Rigidity

It is tricky, but necessary, to avoid rigidly clinging to your values or beliefs and refusing to integrate new information. Rigidity or stubbornness is not the same thing as self-definition. Many who give these concepts a superficial read mistake the two. I have taught a number of students who've come to me proudly announcing they have "defined themselves" with their bosses, wives, children, parishioners or parents. Whenever I hear it, I have one eyebrow up. I want to hear more. "What did you learn from them?" I often ask. It's usually met with a blank stare. But if you have not listened to the other's point of view, even if he has been trying to define you, then you have not learned anything. You are rigidly holding onto your belief without *thinking* about it. Without listening, learning, evaluating or being interested.

"I'm very stubborn" is nothing to be proud of. The word "stubborn" comes from the same root as "stillborn." It means your mind is dead and incapable of growth. Poor leaders can become anxious when they receive new information that makes sense. They may feel ashamed of their original point of view, or they may be too lazy to adapt to the new way. So, rather than rethink their mission, goals or values, they cling to the view of the world just as they like it.

"Defining self" rigidly comes across as conceited and superior. People don't want to be part of a group led by an ass. A good measure of whether your self-defining effort has been successful is this: when you defined yourself with others, did they leave the room feeling respected, listened to and cared for? Lots of times people will leave the room in complete disagreement with you. But the point is: Did they feel like you listened to them? Did they get the idea that you treated their opinion with great respect, even though you did not agree with it? And did they feel as if you cared about them, despite the fact that you cannot change your viewpoint? This is the mark of a good leader.

As a good leader, you may be *accused of being stubborn*. Often those who define themselves clearly are accused of stubbornness when nothing could be farther from the truth.

Feeling the Feelings of Another

This one is probably the most imperative, and many people don't get it. Some folks are downright outraged at this notion. "What do you mean, it's wrong to feel another's feelings? Only a cold, uncaring person wouldn't!" Nothing could be farther from the truth. It is utterly unhealthy to feel someone's feelings other than your own. It is a symptom of being emotionally "stuck together" with another person, as though you are a glob of glue. The only way you can sincerely care for another is if there is some space to allow for the light of day between you. If you are a more solid individual, you will be more effective in caring for another. Your "solidity" is a stance from which to care.

A glob of glue is just one more glob of bad feelings, now stuck to the other person who felt bad enough in the first place. Think about it. If you had a huge, ominous decision to make, would you also want to be burdened with other people's worry? When a child becomes sick or is diagnosed with a learning disability, his parents' worry is one more thing he now has to deal with. I know it's easier said than done—especially when it comes to our children. But the more we can work in that direction, the healthier it will be for everyone involved.

Some people are so hopelessly fused with others that they cannot imagine a life without feeling the feelings of others. It is possible, and quite liberating, I might add. As a former "feeling addict," I can tell you that I only have to fall off the wagon for one day to remember how unpleasant it is, and to see first-hand how *un*helpful feeling others' feelings really is for both them and me.

Myrtle's best friend, Krista, lost her husband in a tragic accident when he was just 36 years of age. Myrtle was severely affected; she cried for weeks. This is not an example of feeling her friend's feelings: Myrtle was experiencing her own sadness. It was sad for her to see Krista and her children so sad, horrified and devastated. It was sad that a man could die so young, and that it could have been Myrtle's own husband. As time went on, Myrtle's grief healed—a lot quicker than Krista's (of course). When Krista got worried about finances, Myrtle did not get worried. Myrtle cared. But she did not worry. For that would have been *Krista's* worry, and not hers (Myrtle's finances were just fine). It takes a lifetime of working on emotional maturity before we are ever able to strictly "disengage" from feeling another's feelings altogether. But it is a journey worth taking. It is the journey of good leadership.

Desire to Fix Another's Problems

Wishing, let alone trying to fix someone else's problem, is similar to feeling someone else's feelings. In fact, if you can learn to stop feeling anyone's feelings but your own, you can learn to stop trying to fix other people. When others we love or care about get into a jam, it is human instinct to want to help them. However, we cannot help anyone but ourselves, unless they are small children. Even older children can deal with their own problems better than most of us give them credit for. Whenever we fix other people's problems, we give them a bigger problem: powerlessness. We render them helpless, as though they are children. They may come across that way because they have been rendered helpless all their lives, but that is not relevant. They are not helpless. If they are adults, they can solve their own problems.

A husband who was overweight continually whined to his family that he needed "help" in dieting. Someone had to help him shop and count calories and go to the gym with him. The whole rest of the family had to "diet" as well, in order to "help" him not be tempted to cheat. This is ridiculous. He was a grown-up and didn't need anybody's help to feed himself properly. What is worse, his insistence that he needed help was suggestive of his emotional stuck-togetherness with the rest of the family. Helping him was the worst thing they could have done, for he would never discover his inner strength and commitment to his own goals with this sort of continual "help."

The childlike cry for help is often disguised in the phrase "I need your *support*." Grown-ups do not need support; they can stand up on their own. (Think of the word "support" in an engineering sense.) People likewise do not need your advice. If they ask for it, by all means give it to them. However, most human beings can make their own decisions without advice. What people do need, instead of help, support, advice or agreement with their position is human relationships and human compassion. They need your presence, your concern, your assurance that you care. In the church and in the palliative care ward, we call this "the ministry of being there."

What may be helpful to people who are experiencing a problem or crisis is assisting them to separate what they are thinking from what they are experiencing. This can be done by deeply listening to them and identifying what you think they are saying as either fact, assumption or feeling.

Usually when people sort these three out and have someone validate their experience without advice or judgment, they can easily find the most workable solution to their own problems. The people you care about are not helpless fools! Therapists have known this little secret for years. Every parent, partner and leader of a group would be well advised to learn some good reflective listening techniques. It is the most help you can be to another. A more in-depth treatment of effective listening will be discussed in chapter 20.

No Clarity

Defining self is being clear without any doubt. It does not mean faking it, bluffing or making idle threats. That is emotional reactivity, not self-definition. Unless you are clear on what you believe and what you will or will not do, you are not defining yourself. You are adding to the problem—yours and the group you are leading.

A Change in Self

Once you are clear about who you are, what you think and believe, and what you will or will not do, in order to evoke change, you must learn more about your inevitable emotional reaction when:

- Someone you care about reacts emotionally to your beliefs
- You react emotionally when someone challenges your beliefs
- You learn new information and revise or give up a belief you once held

In any of these situations, emotional intelligence is imperative. Fully comprehending your own emotional systems is such an important component to spiritual growth and good leadership that the largest section of this book is dedicated to it. An understanding of how change happens both in your closest relationships and in the world is dependent upon an understanding of yourself as an emotional being.

Emotional Intelligence

Chapter 7:

The Healing of Self

If you try to look, but you don't touch, then you won't touch, but you'll never feel, and if you don't feel, you'll never cry, and if you don't cry, then you'll never heal.
—Harry Chapin

Defining yourself is an important yet small part of taking leadership within the bourn of self. It is the easy part, in fact. Real change in this bourn (a necessary step before change can occur in your relationship systems) comes through emotional intelligence, which means, among other things, *knowing yourself fully, deeply and intimately*. The first step toward this self-knowledge is the awareness, understanding and progressive healing of your pain.

No matter how normal, loving or happy your family life was or is, you will have emerged from your childhood in a certain amount of pain. From a theological perspective, this reminds each of us that we have not yet reached the level of the supernal, but rather we are human—fallen, imperfect and wounded. Healing our pain is what the supernal "force" beckons us to do. It is the path of our spiritual growth. We are not called to make a difference in the world. We are called to make a difference in ourselves. The path of spiritual growth, that less-traveled road, is the path to our own healing.

As long as you are on *this* path and not the most common one—denial of pain and the pursuit of "happiness"—you will find *ultimate* happiness, which is *shalom*. The more you grow, the more you experience shalom and the more shalom spreads to all your human relationships, to the societal context in which you live and work together as a human family, to the universe and eventually to the supernal.

People on the path to their own healing are the true leaders in this world. They are the ones who make a real difference, by following this path. Other outwardly "successful" people are flashes in the pan. Their leadership may appear exciting, life transforming, institution transforming or world transforming. But in the end, these leaders become irreplaceable, and after their inevitable departure, the systems they lead return to old, comfortable ways. This is true in families, churches, corporations, soccer clubs, governments and world religions. Good leadership will eventually bring real change to the world because it begins with the healing of self, a healing that inevitably infects all human life that it touches. In case you've forgotten, you may not be alive to see this real change in the world. But you will most certainly be alive to see it in yourself.

The Three Faces of Pain

At the root of your pain is the belief that somehow you are either *flawed*, *helpless* or *worthless*. You may experience these "faces of pain" to varying degrees, depending on your early experience in childhood. If you have a history of sexual abuse, you may easily identify with feelings of helplessness. If you were physically abused, bullied, felt unattractive or were made to feel intellectually inferior, you may come to believe you are fundamentally flawed. Others describe themselves, in some form or another, at the very root of their pain, as "I am worthless." You may be encumbered with a "combo" of any two or all three of these beliefs.

Some people have feelings of worthlessness that they can express immediately. I had one 40-year-old man present with anxiety attacks whenever he would go out in public. For two or three sessions, he described a childhood of physical abuse. Then he outright asked me: "Do you think that I'm just so…*damaged*… that I can never really expect much more from this life?"

Some people come across as perfectly confident, strong and in control of their lives. But the pain lurks somewhere down deep. When someone comes in for therapy, it usually takes less than three sessions to "get to the bottom of it." Hitting the bottom can look something like this:

Client: I think my dad always favoured my sister more than me.
Therapist: That sounds like a tough way to grow up.
Client: It was okay…
Therapist: The times you would get that feeling—of your dad favouring your sister more—what were you telling yourself about *you*?
Client: (after much thought) I don't know. Maybe that I just don't measure up somehow.
Therapist: [thinking] BINGO!

I once had a high-powered business executive come to see me when he was "downsized" out of a job at 55 years of age. This man was a stable, happy, goal-directed individual with a good marriage, a lovely family and lots of friends. He eventually described the feeling he had that day as similar to the time when a teacher caught him cheating on a test in grade one. (Apparently, he hadn't understood that what he was doing was "cheating" or wrong.) The teacher called his parents, and the whole thing was explained and supposedly forgotten. However, the man sat there in my office 50 years later and said, "I felt like I was a completely worthless human being—a liar, a fraud…I have never cheated at anything again my whole life. But sometimes I still feel like if I don't watch out, someone's going to *find out*."

"Find out what?" I asked.

"That I'm really just a good-for-nothing *cheat*."

Many people have a "core narrative" such as this—a story from childhood that becomes the snapshot of the root of their pain. It can be a horrific story, or it can be a simple story. One woman I spoke with briefly remembers going to a friend's birthday party at age six only to discover she wasn't invited. After being turned away at the door, she walked past a downstairs window and peered in at all the other children laughing and playing games. She said to me, "I always feel like I'm the one left out, like I'm just on the outside of everything, looking in."

What I am proposing is quite different from the idea that your core narrative is the *cause* of your feelings of worthlessness. It is often not the cause at all, even when it is a dramatic tale of trauma. People with stories of being abandoned by their parents on the side of a road (clearly a trauma) and people with stories like this woman's—of feeling abandoned by others—often present with exactly the same problems or symptoms. The core narrative is a snapshot. There is no *one cause* of pain. It is multi-faceted, and many things contribute to it over time.

The source of some people's pain seems blatantly obvious. His father told him every day of his life, "You are so stupid." Each time he did not understand some concept that seemed simple to his dad, the dad remarked at the child's stupidity. The worst day of this child's life was report-card day, when a list of Ds, Fs and Not Satisfactorys underscored both his dad's and his own belief that he was stupid. By the time he reached adulthood, this person's feelings of worthlessness were high. Thirty years later, he's a business executive sitting in the boardroom awaiting feedback on his presentation. Someone gives a fairly harmless critique such as, "I'm not so sure that idea will work." All the unresolved feelings of worthlessness from childhood come flooding back at that moment, the critic "becomes" Dad, and the business executive blows up in anger, leaving the critic wondering what on earth just happened.

Perhaps the critic was once a child whose parents told her every day how brilliant she was. She would therefore have no idea why the business executive was angry and yelling. If someone were ever to say to her, "I'm not so sure that idea will work," it would simply be received as interesting information. However, a comment about her shoes made by a co-worker that morning may have triggered feelings of being flawed related to the fact that she didn't have the pretty little feet of her sister: the size 10s meant she was fat and ugly.

People whose core narrative is one of abuse, perhaps even an incident as a child of molestation by another (older) child, are the most likely to present with root feelings of helplessness. In their childhood experience they were innocent—completely blameless and unable to help themselves out of the situation. Adults with these core narratives often go to great lengths to avoid feelings of helplessness ever again. The high-functioning people may be strikingly confident, even domineering. Those functioning at the lowest levels with more dramatic core narratives may dissolve in a sea of helplessness, having to be committed to institutions for life.

The belief that one is flawed, helpless or worthless is triggered so easily in some people that we cannot understand the huge emotional reaction they have to the smallest, simplest thing. For others (those in less pain) the feeling will still be triggered somehow, someway. Your pain probably is triggered often and you are not aware of it. But one thing is for sure, which has huge ramifications for leadership: when someone's pain is triggered, he will behave badly. The people you lead will behave badly, and you will behave badly too. This is the reason that awareness of our pain ("emotional intelligence") is so important for leadership.

It is common to believe that feelings of helplessness, worthlessness or being flawed are not shared by all humans—surely there must be many people out there who are not *in* pain and who think nothing but well of themselves right down to the foundation of their being. Because we believe this may be true of others (but not ourselves), our pain is a huge secret *of ours* that we must cover up at all costs. We think that we must either seek to avoid situations or behaviour that triggers our feelings of worthlessness/helplessness/being flawed (hence our pain) or we must change the behaviour and belief systems of others, by somehow *imposing our will upon them*, so our own painful feelings do not ever, *ever* get triggered. People spend an inordinate amount of time and energy in this life in both of these futile exercises: avoidance of pain and imposing their will upon others.

Projection

When your pain gets triggered, you may lash out at someone, or begin treating them differently than you did before (perhaps by clamming up, distancing yourself, quitting the group or never speaking to them again—without telling them why). Unresolved pain is very often projected onto others. The business critic who had to endure the executive's extreme anger was a recipient of *projected pain*. The executive projected his own anger, from his unresolved pain, onto her. He tried to make it her problem, demanding an apology or that she change her behaviour or words, so that his pain would not be triggered again. Rather than looking *inward*, this executive did what many people do: sought to change the other. Inward work heals your pain; outward projection makes your pain worse.

Projected pain may (and often does) trigger the pain of others, causing *their* feelings of worthlessness to come flooding back. Since this feeling is uncomfortable, they will seek to project it outward as well, often snapping back at the first "projector." This is a "hot potato" or "electric" process where the pain of two humans is tossed or zapped back and forth in a highly charged emotional interchange.[22] Figure 6 shows two examples of one person's projection onto another, and the feedback loops created.[23]

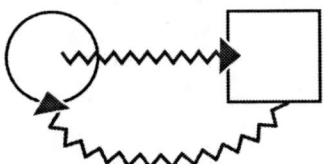 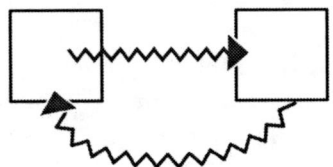

---

[22] Roberta Gilbert used the analogy of the "hot potato" game to illustrate emotional process in *Extraordinary Relationships: A New Way of Thinking About Human Interactions*, 40.

[23] In this book, circles represent females and squares represent males. This is customary diagramming in Family Systems Theory.

Perhaps the person receiving the projected pain just goes silent, retreating to another place to seethe, or feels victimized, or tells someone else how horrible the first "projector" is. She may harbour anger for another time when it becomes too much, or she may become depressed, even bursting into tears. All this behaviour is indicative of the same axiom—projected pain—manifested in different ways. It is an *emotional process*. In addition to continually working on healing their own pain, effective leaders also understand the emotional process within their relationship systems *and their own role in it*. More will be said about emotional process in chapters 24 and 25.

It is a human instinct to project your pain or distance yourself ("fight or flight"). Because you likely think these behaviours protect you, you must continually fight an uphill battle against your own instincts. The "road less traveled" is straight uphill and hard work. It is always easier to soothe your pain temporarily or protect yourself from feeling it by blowing up at someone or running away, rather than seeking to heal yourself of the pain permanently.

The Scale

People are in pain to various degrees. This seems obvious, yet it is an often-misunderstood phenomenon, especially by those who are not in very much pain. Lots of educated, intelligent, church-going people judge by their own standards those in this world who are in a hundred times more pain than they are. They assume that these poor unfortunates could and should just address life the way they do, and they would achieve similar results (cheer up, get a job, make a plan, go to therapy, stop whining, get motivated, find someone to love). The fact is that our level of functioning is related to the degree to which we *experience* the core, human belief of our own worthlessness, and thus our level of pain. "Strategies" to relieve or deny pain by those who are not *in* a lot of pain will not work for those who suffer exceedingly. (They don't work for anyone, but people who aren't in as much pain may appear as though they've found a strategy for their life that has made a difference.)

Since people are in pain to various degrees, there is no such thing as "normal" or "abnormal," "healthy families" or "dysfunctional" ones. People and families fall along a *scale*. Family Systems theorist and therapist Murray Bowen developed a scale of "differentiation of self."[24] He expressed it as theoretically ranging from 0–100. Although Bowen was a scientist, he could not prove his

---

[24] Murray Bowen, *Family Therapy in Clinical Practice*, 472–475. For Bowen, "differentiation" refers, among other things, to the degree to which we are fused into the family system, and thus reactive to the emotions of others. It is also the degree to which we are able to distinguish what we think from what we feel.

scale, nor could he develop any sort of test for it. He said that one cannot determine scientifically where a person falls upon the scale; one always has to rely on subjective evidence and observation. Bowen believed that most people fall around the 50 mark on a scale of 0–100. A few people may have a base number as high as 60 or 70, but beyond that are only "mythical creatures." Bowen also believed that one could only move up a few points in a lifetime. This idea, that real spiritual growth is just not possible, is unequivocal nonsense.

Many theorists have expressed the human condition in terms of various other scales such as a "scale of maturity" or a "scale of overall health" including physical, emotional and spiritual health. Although Bowen's scale may have some problems, the idea of a scale is a helpful one, and using numbers from 0–100 is a simple way of considering it. The main problem with Bowen's scale is that the points are not high enough; everyone ends up feeling bad about themselves. (I mean, really, who wants to get a score of only 50 on anything?)

I believe that the scale is one of "integrated wisdom," reflective of our ability to persistently tolerate pain, work toward healing it and thus be able to love. As we grow, we integrate our knowledge of our own emotions and pain, sense better the emotions of others and come to learn the emotional process with and among others. We also integrate our knowledge of the supernal and knowledge of the world. When I say "knowledge," I do not mean merely an intellectual understanding, but a deep, life-changing awareness.

Figure 7 shows my Scale of Integrated Wisdom. (I will hereafter refer to it as the Scale—capital "S".) It is only for the purposes of reference. It is entirely subjective and cannot be proven or even tested. I offer it merely as reference in our discussion of spiritual growth.

Scale of Integrated Wisdom

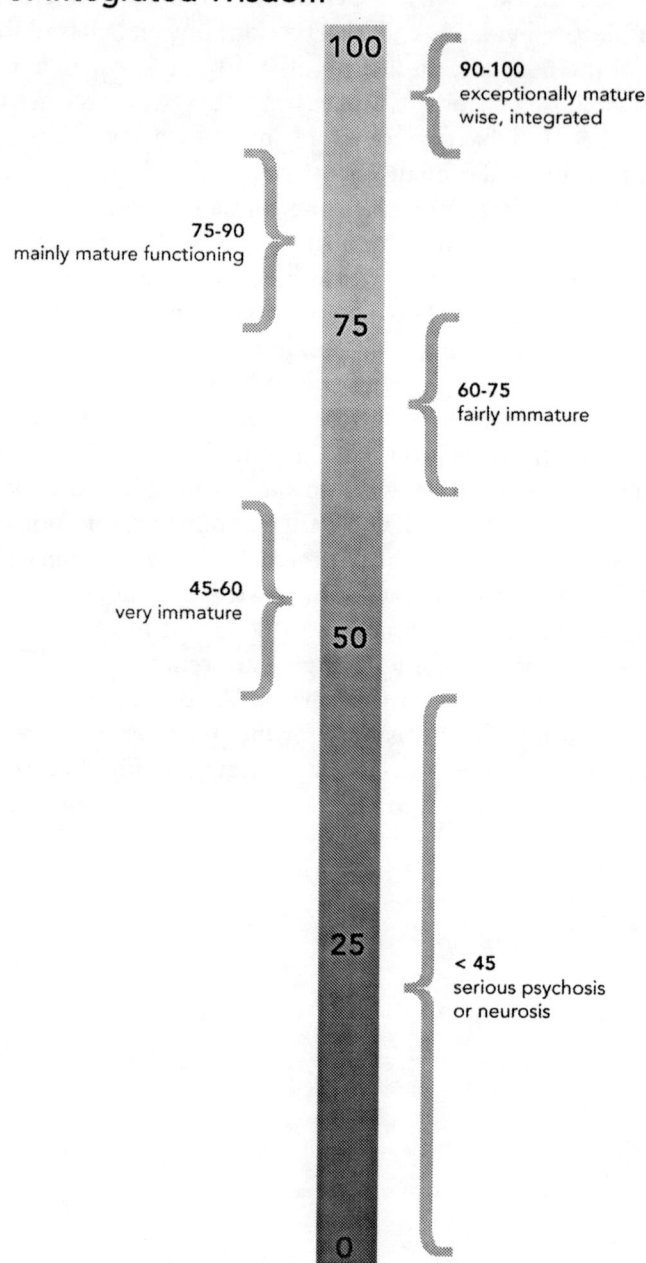

Exceptionally wise, integrated humans are rare. One hundred on the Scale is akin to setting your compass to the North Star. You will not reach the star, but knowing where it is will always point you in the right direction on your journey. Most people who function fairly well in life fall between 75 and 90. The growth you can achieve from here is quite remarkable. Those who are between 60 and 75 are stable, functioning people who are nevertheless immature with a fair bit of unresolved pain; either they or the people in their emotional systems may suffer from depression, anxiety, addiction or rage and may occasionally seek professional help. Very immature, low-functioning people (between 45 and 60) contribute to others' pain in their emotional systems. They project nearly 100 per cent of their pain somehow. Either they or others around them will have diagnosable symptoms of mental illness, abusiveness, violence, severe addiction or chronic physical illnesses. Those who fall on the Scale under 45 have diagnosable psychoses or neuroses that render them helpless, incarcerated or institutionalized.

Where you fall along the Scale points to your level of unresolved pain. Moving up the Scale through spiritual growth is not only possible, it is the very essence of the meaning of life. The best leaders are the people who have moved up the Scale the most and refuse to accept that there is no more room yet to grow. These leaders may be bishops, world rulers or CEOs, or they may be serving tables, toiling in coal mines or pounding grain in huts.

Moving up the Scale, through spiritual growth, is difficult for everyone but much more difficult the lower *or higher* you are on the Scale to begin with. It is certainly possible to grow from 40 to 100, but not very probable. It is also most common for human beings who emerge from childhood as high as 80 to sit there the rest of their lives and never move a notch.

If we were to grow all the way to 100, we would become one with the supernal, and be of the same essence as the supernal. We would be said to reach "enlightenment" or "divinity." This is possible because the supernal is the primary player in our spiritual growth, the One who beckons us toward this goal. As a Christian, I believe that Jesus of Nazareth reached this supernal, achieving equality with the essence and substance of God. I therefore look to the life of Jesus as a model for my own spiritual striving. I am sure that however we discover the supernal—the Buddha, Torah, Mohammed or Brahmin— its force or power bids us to grow. People who possess this wisdom are true leaders in this world. Their journey of healing will be an integration of their knowledge, experience and awareness. Closer to the supernal themselves, they become agents of real change, the results of which they may never see in their own lifetime. This knowledge will not cause them to fall into despair. It may bring them more pain, but they will gladly experience the pain.

Those who grow higher on the Scale are not "better people" in the sense that we should judge those who don't. Of course, it is better to be more mature, integrated and wise; if it were not, then no one would strive for it. But so much of where you fall on the Scale has to do with where you were born, what circumstances you were born into and what your family was like that it is hardly a reflection on *you*. Those who were born into less pain often do not believe they are in any pain at all and make no attempt to grow. Similarly, many people born into a great deal of pain grow a fair bit, but it may not be noticeable because they were so far down the Scale to begin with.

If your experience of the supernal is a God who loves and cherishes every human being as a precious child, then it will be self-evident to you that where one falls on the Scale is irrelevant to one's worth. No one person is more deserving of reward or of more value than any other. The supernal equally values those high up on the Scale, those who have no intention of growing spiritually, and those who live their entire lives out of their pain. It calls all of us, equally, to grow more.

Love, love.

Back in chapter 2, I described the supernal as a "force of Love" in the universe, and distinguished capital-L Love from the lower-case variety love. This chapter is about understanding yourself deeply in order to grow, change and heal your particular manifestation of *pain*. A further discussion is necessary of Love and love and how these work within our lives either to mess us up or move us forward toward more growth. Let's begin by reviewing Scott Peck's excellent definition of Love:

> I define love thus: The will to extend one's self for the purpose of nurturing one's own or another's spiritual growth.[25]

The degree to which we experience the core belief of our own worthlessness and thus our pain relates directly to the degree to which our parents were able to demonstrate true Love toward us.

Love is neither a feeling nor the reaction to a feeling. It is the will to extend oneself (endure pain) for another's spiritual growth. Love is therefore not the same as feeling another's feelings. We must feel only our own feelings, but often

---

[25] M. Scott Peck, *The Road Less Traveled*, 81.

they are so painful that we refuse to do so. We give up and feel others' feelings instead and call it Love. But this is not Love. Love is an action, meaning if you Love someone, you will act in ways toward him and make decisions regarding him that promote his spiritual growth.

The feeling of love may be sexual attraction or emotional hunger—the need for another to soothe your pain. Sometimes this soothing is achieved through your actions toward others. You mistake your actions toward others for Love, when all you are doing is meeting your own needs and soothing your own pain. In its extreme form, these mistaken acts become an illness of codependence or as the Al-Anon group (partners of alcoholics) are well aware, "enabling." By this, they mean that the "love" or "kindness" of the partner essentially enables the alcoholic to continue to drink.

I don't know about other religions, but I see the unhealthy kind of love running rampant in the Christian church, especially by those who mistake Jesus's command for us to Love one another as a call to some form of chronic niceness or codependence. Clergy and lay people alike cater to toxic individuals, low on the Scale, believing that this is Love. It is not. It does not bid the other to grow but rather allows the other to continue to behave out of his pain. This shielding of others from the natural consequences of their behaviour (which would encourage their growth) is not only *not Love*, it is an unconscious form of cruelty.

Parents are human, therefore they are neither perfect nor divine and cannot possibly Love completely. Their love will be, at the very most:

> - Fragmented
> - Intermittent
> - Conditional
> - Incomplete

You may be a parent yourself and take exception to this. You may say, "That is ridiculous. I love my children as much as I possibly can." If you are thinking this, then you are referring to love, not Love. You are referring to the feeling of love, which of course you could not possibly possess in any greater quantity toward your children than you already do. The feeling of love is seldom stronger than it is toward our own children. We love our children, but we cannot possibly Love them 100 per cent of the time, nor to the fullest degree. Our capacity to Love is related to the Scale, and thus to the sum of the amount our parents Loved us added to our own spiritual growth.

74 EVOKING CHANGE

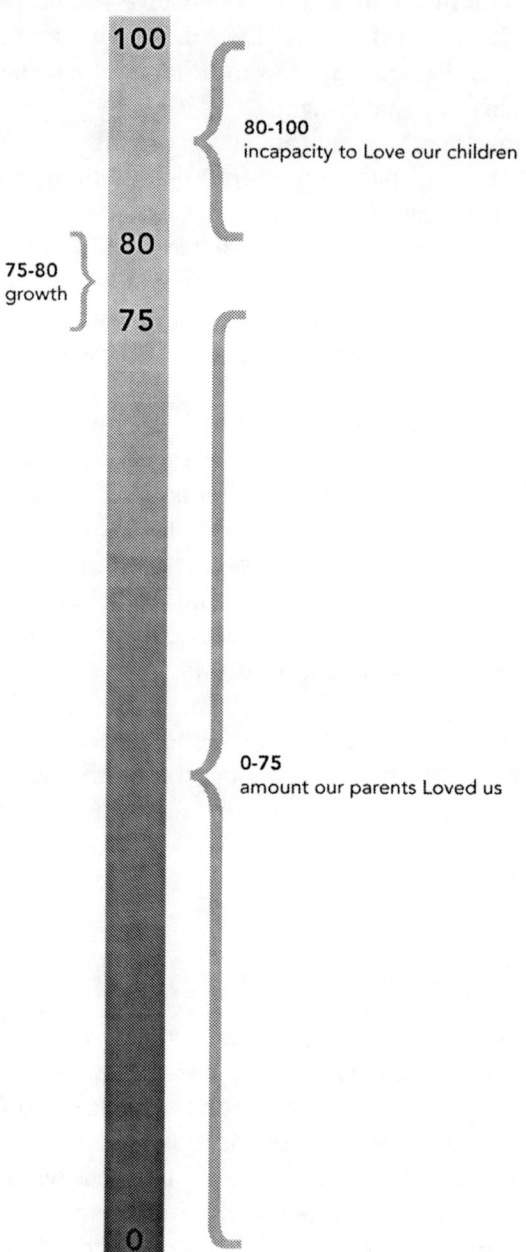

If you enter into adulthood at the 75 mark, and even grow to 90 (inordinately high for a human being), nevertheless, you still have 10 "units" of *incapacity* to Love your children or anyone else for spiritual growth. Thus, unless a child is born to two parents who are *divine*, they will grow up with at least some measure of unresolved pain.

People who emerge from childhood low on the Scale and have not yet grown often present with emotional symptoms from which they cannot seem to recover (anxiety, depression, rage or even psychosis). Although part of this may be pathology (body/brain construction, based on "heredity"), pathology seldom accounts for much more than 50 per cent of it. The truth is, their parents had minimal capacity to Love them. Without substantial growth, they will have minimal capacity to Love their own children. Children who were victims of violence becoming abusive parents themselves is the most obvious example.

Farther up the Scale, people become unaware of this incapacity to Love and generally take exception to it. They assume they are being accused of being "bad parents." They are not "bad parents," because parenting, like everything else, cannot be described in terms of "good" or "bad" but is relational and falls along the Scale. Nevertheless, they are imperfect parents—we all are. And this imperfection shows only their imperfect capacity to Love. The higher up the Scale we are from birth, the less aware we are of our lack of Love—what we did not receive from our parents and what we are incapable of giving to our children. This lack of awareness is at the heart of our pain.

The supernal, as a force of goodness and Love, draws us toward healing and wholeness, toward the *shalom* of our own lives. You are being called to grow into leadership to function at a much higher level than you ever thought you could. This is an awesome, ominous calling, for you are being called to experience that which frightens you more than anything else: your pain.

Chapter 8:
Leviathan

If you are going through hell, keep going.
—Sir Winston Churchill

No matter how much pain you are in, you will naturally view the pain as a horrible, terrifying monster. You will somehow believe that you must do everything in your power to avoid this pain or it will be so overwhelming that something mysteriously awful will happen to you. Whatever that is, you will not be able to tolerate it. This awful thing is often dreaded more than death. It is a huge, demon-like monster of pain. It is Leviathan.[26]

---

[26] Leviathan, meaning "coiled one," is the name for a terrifying, mythical, dragonlike monster recorded in various biblical texts (Isaiah, Job, Psalms). Leviathan lurks beneath the sea, and when it surfaces, it breathes fire. The concept of Leviathan appears in Canaanite texts, as well, and has parallels in Iranian beliefs.

In order to avoid Leviathan we will go to a great deal of trouble. Convincing ourselves, and often others, that we are not in pain of any kind is *avoiding* Leviathan. We shove Leviathan as far down as possible into our being and slam shut a heavy trap door over this monster so that it cannot possibly "come up" and affect us in our day-to-day life. Then we cruise merrily along as though we have "dealt with" our pain.

If we ever have any trouble, we seek the assistance of a good cognitive therapist who helps convince us that our pain (anxiety, depression, rage) is not rational. This can temporarily be quite helpful to us because it provides us with some nails to pound into the trap door so that it can never possibly be opened again. Nevertheless, Leviathan lies in wait, banging its ghastly head against the boards of the door, weakening the hinges little by little. When the stress in our lives goes up, we feel the ominous vibration below and we freeze in terror or scramble about to find a better dead bolt, fastener or honking-big spike to drive into that door.

Leviathan lurks within everyone, because no one comes out of his family of origin much higher than 75 on the Scale. If you're above 75, you had to grow to get there. Many people balk at this. They believe their childhoods were great and their families were just fine. Surely they are higher on the Scale than 75—why that's not even an A! My experience with hundreds of families and thousands of people over the years, very few of whom would ever show up in therapy, tells me something different.

I have heard numerous clients and parishioners speak of their "perfect" families. But their behaviour tells another story: they may be prone to angry outbursts at church meetings, they may cry easily or they may distance themselves from others.

I have known people who appear completely balanced and well-adjusted, but they cannot stand up in a church court and speak to an issue they feel passionate about without tears welling up in their eyes. Others suffer from anxiety in the form of stress or burnout at work. Their marriages fail, they can't hold a job or they're just plain unhappy. All these things have their roots somewhere. Those missing 25 points on the Scale are directly related to their parents' inability to Love them completely. The trapdoor may not have a lot under it in these individuals, but it is there nonetheless, visible in the antics that some of them will resort to in order to avoid opening it.

Even if your family were completely loving, supportive and joyful (although never "perfect"), you may have had troubling experiences at school or with playmates, babysitters or other adult guardians. Perhaps you were made fun of by your classmates because you stumbled once while giving a speech. Speaking in front of others then brings on feelings of shame that are intolerable. Soon, the very idea of standing up in public becomes Leviathan. If this is your story, it is also very likely that your parents were either dismissive of your feelings around the experience, rather than validating, or they added to your anxiety by being anxious about you, or it, themselves. Whatever happened to you in childhood, no matter how seemingly "mild," it is human nature to avoid the pain of it, to shove Leviathan down deep and slam the trap door shut so that you never have to feel this feeling again.

Of course, some folks know darn well they have a gigantic monster dwelling under their trap doors. They have been victims of crime, abuse, death of a parent, critical illness, accident, war or natural disaster. If you get enough overwhelming stuff under the trap door, Leviathan becomes huge and menacing, and it is as if the trap door moves up higher and higher until you're "up to your neck" with it. When this is your reality, you'll believe the door must be double-locked, nailed down and glued.

Most self-help books and many therapy techniques reinforce the bolts on the trap door, providing little more than rationalization of our pain. This is not a bad thing, but it is not healing. It is not the ultimate peace and happiness that is possible. It is not *shalom*.

Some people are low enough on the Scale (under 50) that their trap doors cannot even close. They exist in the midst of Leviathan all the time. These people may be exceptionally angry and intolerant, terrified to leave home, addicted to drugs or alcohol, hardened criminals or institutionalized with emotional illnesses such as severe depression or psychoses. Regardless of how a person's life with Leviathan is expressed, he is deserving of nothing less than our patience, understanding and the warmth of our human compassion.

Figure 11 shows how the trap door moves up and down in relation to the Scale.

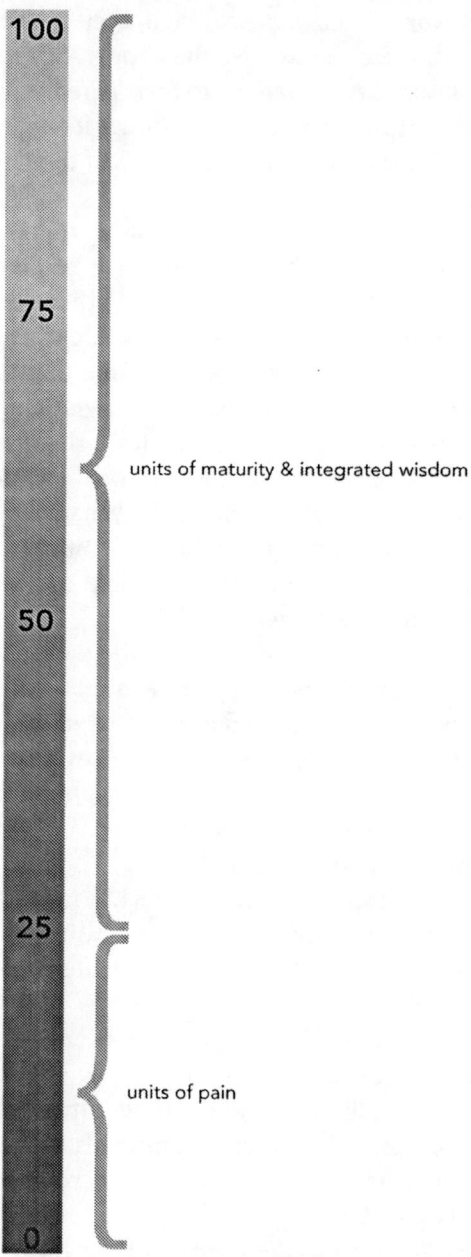

I have said that the majority of people in society who are functioning well (are in relationships, have jobs, enjoy friends and hobbies) are at around 75. This means they still have 25 "units" of monster under the door. If you are as high as 80, you are probably very wise, integrated and calm most of the time. It would take a lot to make your trap door fly open. This is a curse as well as a blessing, for people at this level often believe there is nothing wrong with them and they have no need to grow. But even if you are at 90, admired and respected by most of humanity, perhaps even a great world figure, you will still have 10 "units" of pain, and this pain can rise up and bite you in the bum at the most inopportune times. No matter where you fall on the Scale, there is always work to be done. Unless you spend a lifetime dedicated to your spiritual growth, Leviathan is in there, somewhere.

To some extent, everyone on the planet lives with the fear that, given enough stress or a trauma, this door will certainly fly open and Leviathan will come screaming out. In every case, if there are things in your past that you absolutely do not want to talk about or think about, then you are working with a trap door shut. The fear is that if you do begin to talk about or think about whatever it is, the emotions will be so intense and terrible that you will be completely consumed by them. Whatever "it" is that you'd rather forget, you've made it into Leviathan.

You can live your entire life creating a zillion clever ways to keep the trap door shut. But the problem with these emotional trap doors is that it seems they're made of slats of wood, so they have cracks. Despite your best efforts, stuff will ooze out of these cracks all the time, and you will never be sure exactly how much pressure it will take to pop it right open and have all hell break loose.

The Case of Ellie

"Ellie" was a person who seemed happy all the time: joyful, upbeat and smiling. And always giving. She gave and gave and gave, always doing for others unselfishly. I worked with Ellie's family which was completely devastated when she just up and left them one day after 30 years of marriage. She ran off to Vegas with the fellow who owned the fruit market. She flipped her lid completely, and all sorts of anger came out toward her husband and four grown children—30 years of pent-up stuff, all shoved under the trap door. You never know about a person from her appearance *above* the trap door. Especially if it's you.

In some cases, the door is bolted down so well it stays shut forever. These "Ellies" don't flip their lids, but what is underneath festers, making them chronically ill. We often think that our troubling childhood experiences can make us emotionally ill, but we don't often consider the possibility that they could contribute to our physical illness as well. Our bodies usually work hard to manage the emotional stress we have, and keep us stable and well. But occasionally our bodies succumb to it and give up. It is as though the physical pain (or chronic illness or even cancer) is signalling the soul through the body: "Help me! I'm in pain!" But often the soul does not hear, and so the body is overwhelmed with disease. The worst thing about this theory is that no one can prove it, because it doesn't happen to everyone.

Of course, illness is also related to things like genetics and viruses and toxins and diet, a subject that I discuss in more detail in chapter 9. We do not yet have a fail-proof explanation as to why some people with similar diets, the same genes, equal exposure to bacteria or pesticides or even radiation get ill and others don't. The truth is that you may have a huge lurking monster under your trap door and not get ill either. Emotional or physical illness is just *one way* that "life above the trap door" may be expressed. Another might be that someone else in your family becomes ill, from the amount of stress in your household thanks to you never dealing with your "stuff." The themes of family stress and the mind-body-spirit connection will be revisited in Part Three of this book.

Ellie came from a childhood of intense physical abuse from her father. Her father beat her with wooden switches, forced her to do all the housework and demanded As in school. He constantly told her she was stupid. So she grew up vowing not to be like her angry father or "mousy" mother. Ellie was always laughing and hugging people. She baked cookies weekly and gave them to the whole office. She was generous and thoughtful, a delight to be around. Her "midlife crisis," as it was described, was a shock to everyone. Hormones were blamed—menopause gone awry. But I don't think it was hormones. I think it was a flipped lid.

You see, for Ellie to say, "I find that kind of hurtful" would be unthinkable. Unthinkable! Saying it aloud would mean she would have to re-experience the pain (Leviathan). So Ellie avoided conflict at all costs and never told anyone how she really felt. She gave to others with no regard for self because to tell someone what she needed would have been to admit she had needs and was in pain. Avoiding all confrontation meant putting more fingers in the dike than she had. One day, a leak was sprung and she was out of fingers. In a last-ditch effort, she pulled out all the fingers at once and let the dam burst forth. Unfortunately for Ellie, Leviathan was finally unavoidable. The conflict with her husband and children sent her into unimaginable pain. I hear from her occasionally. She says she's "doing a lot better now" because "time heals everything." Time heals nothing. Time is another word for big bolts to double-reinforce one's trap door.

We all suffer from the Ellie disease to varying degrees. Most people avoid conflict, which in its simplest form, can be described as anyone disagreeing with you. We avoid conflict because we fear Leviathan. If you can think of a situation where someone else might be angry with you, what would that do to you inside? How about telling a friend something that might get her angry or make her cry? Take a moment to imagine yourself in a situation like this. *Really* imagine it. If you're like most people, you will experience a physical reaction in your body. Mentally scan through your body right now and see if you can find the clues. Did your stomach drop at the very thought of that sort of confrontation? Are your muscles tighter? How are you holding your mouth and jaw? Is your heart beating faster? How quickly these feelings get triggered and how terrifying the feelings are to you is an indicator of how far up the trap door must be in order for you to keep them covered most of the time.

I don't know of anyone who would feel nothing in his body when he thinks of conflict. I do know people who are able to act in spite of their feelings, because they believe it's the right thing to do (keeping calm, trying to be reasonable and rational). This means they are fighting against their emotional responses to cope with the natural bodily feelings that come up. Some folks can sustain this for a lifetime. Ellie lasted 50 years before going completely off the deep end.

The fear response in humans elicits either fleeing *or* fighting. Angry bullies are therefore no different than those who are quivering before them. Perhaps you're one of those people who march into conflict fighting. You may admit you're an angry bully or you may just think you're "assertive." It could be that you have bought this book because people keeping telling you you're an ass and can't work with you. What may be going on is that you are unaware of your real fear and that you are dealing with your fear through aggression, which can take the form of bullying, defensiveness or just being argumentative. It's very likely that you are using these things to keep your trap door nailed shut. Underneath all these forms of aggression there is always another emotion that is painful to experience, such as sadness, fear or shame.

Once I learned that angry bullies were just as frightened as I was, I was able to feel compassion for them. If you can separate yourself and your own "triggers" from these people, you can stand back and watch them do their Tasmanian Devil[27] routine without getting upset yourself. You can even change the bully's

---

[27] Warner Brothers cartoon character, The Tasmanian Devil®, aka "Taz": "A strong murderous beast, jaws as powerful as a steel trap, has ravenous appetite, eats tigers, lions, elephants, buffaloes, donkeys, giraffes, octopuses, rhinoceroses and moose." However, this definition is only partially accurate. He also eats chickens, ducks and especially *rabbits*. Whirring around like a tornado, slicing through trees like a rotary

response by remaining calm and being curious, rather than getting sucked into it or assuming it's about you. Most times a calm, reflective reaction to the Taz routine such as, "Wow, you seem really upset. That must be very important to you," can work wonders to shift the emotional energy.

My favourite Bugs Bunny cartoon is the one when Taz throws Bugs into a pot of water and sets it over the fire. Taz growls, spits and bares his fangs as he chops up vegetables and herbs with a fury and tosses them into the pot. Bugs, calmly chomping on one of the carrots in the pot, asks, "Ehhh, what's up, Doc?" It is as if he's saying, "You may think I'm in hot water, but I *know* that I am in no danger at all." Bugs Bunny is one of the best metaphors of personal leadership I have ever found.

Soothing Our Pain

Either the supernal, the bourn of nature, the societal context or some combination of the above may provide us with temporary joys to alleviate our pain. Although we are all in pain, it is not as if we never smile or laugh or have fun. Temporary joys that soothe us can be good things like relationships, laughter, good food or a nice 1998 Burrowing Owl Cabernet Sauvignon. If you are a religious person, then developing your relationship with God may be soothing in itself. This relationship alone may not be the same as healing, but it feels good nevertheless. When you nurture a relationship with God through worship, prayer and the practice of spiritual disciplines, you may get a *glimpse* of what life at the top of the Scale would be like: a glimpse of peace, a glimpse of joy, a glimpse of the euphoric connection with the divine.

It seems as if the temporary joys of this life, in moderation at least, are some sort of "foretaste of glory divine.[28]" They are a glimpse, but only a glimpse, into real joy, which is permanent—a joy that cannot be attained by soothing things but only through the healing of our pain. So there are temporary joys and real joy, which is everlasting. The very wise and integrated cannot have their real joy extinguished even when they are completely lacking in soothing things. Consider the lives of Viktor Frankl, Nelson Mandela, Martin Luther King Jr., Mahatma Gandhi or the Apostle Paul—all truly great individuals who were

---

saw and feasting on an entire ecosystem of jungle creatures, this carnivorous native of Tasmania has the power to devour everything and anything in a single gulp. When this furry, salivating beast comes a-runnin', giraffes scurry for their lives, alligators turn themselves into luggage to hide and sharks literally leap out of the water." (www. looneytunes.warnerbros.com)

[28] From the hymn, *"Blessed Assurance,"* by Fanny Crosby (public domain).

wrongfully imprisoned and endured unspeakable hardship, injustice and even torture. Yet they were still capable of experiencing real joy.

The more we heal, the more real joy we experience, little by little, until it envelops us completely, and we are no longer in need of soothing. Our real joy is complete.[29] Without this healing, we are only allowed a peek into the treasure chest, when what we long for is to run our fingers through the incredible riches of *shalom*.

The Trap Door and Psychotherapy

Too much of a good thing can lead to disaster: too much of that 1998 Burrowing Owl, too much food, sex, gambling—even too much religion. Those who succumb to the "too much" problem as well as those who are burdened under the weight of anxiety or depression may need someone to help. When all attempts to keep the trap door shut don't work anymore, millions turn to psychotherapists for help. Unfortunately, in this new millennium, many therapists are paid by health care insurance. Insurance companies only want to pay for six to eight hours of therapy and insist that therapists use short-term techniques with their clients. People either legitimately cannot afford private therapy or they don't want to pay for it because their own emotional health is lower on their priority list than owning a car or a TV set.

Cognitive and behavioural therapy is considered the norm. Courses and group sessions on "anger management" and "behaviour management" are encouraged. Television psychologists diagnose the problem in 10 minutes: this is how you are behaving; stop doing that.

I do not mean to be critical of all cognitive and behavioural therapy. As a theory, it is immensely helpful to people who present with particular symptoms—generally anxiety or depression. I have been the beneficiary of cognitive-behavioural therapy myself and have used its various techniques with my own clients. Although it can be an excellent way to relieve symptoms, it never really helps people get under the trap door. Long-term therapy, especially methods that focus on emotion, is a different story. It takes a commitment to tolerating your pain for a number of sessions for a fairly healthy person, and many more for anyone presenting with more severe symptoms.

We cannot hold therapists or insurance companies to blame completely. Many people have come to me for therapy and, although I offered them

---

[29] Jesus said: "I have told you this so that my joy may be in you and that your joy may be complete. My instruction to you is this: love one another as I have loved you." John 15: 10–12.

unlimited sessions at no cost, most quit when they were no longer sad, anxious or fighting with their partners. In other words, once the trap door was sufficiently closed *again*, they returned to their old ways of functioning.

Despite the fact that I am writing this in the 21st century, there is still some stigma involved with going to a therapist, as if working on one's own spiritual growth implies some sort of weakness. In the majority of cases, the people who say they don't "need" a therapist or who want to "fix the problem themselves" are in reality people who are so fearful of their own pain, so terrified of the trap door opening, that they will not set foot in a therapist's office. Those who refuse to spend one hour a week on their emotional health could be better described as "weak" than "strong." The same is true for those who vow to be "strong" at funerals by avoiding their grief.

I recently saw on television a very troubled celebrity who had abandoned her husband and children, and was arrested for shoplifting and possession of cocaine. She stated, "I know I need help. I've gotten help. I *actually* went to see a psychologist once." It was the way she said "actually" that struck me. As though she were saying, "It's true folks. Even *me*. As sane and together as I am, unbelievably, I *actually* had to go see someone. And for a whole hour!"

I don't know how many times I've heard someone say, "Therapy can become a crutch." Quite often, it is a client of mine seeking to end therapy just when we're getting down to the really good stuff. This is a strange expression to me: a *crutch*. What are crutches for? I assume they help you walk when you have a broken leg or a sprained ankle. And I further assume that if you were no longer in pain, the last thing you would want to do is to continue using the crutches. I bollocksed my ankle once and spent two weeks on crutches. I couldn't wait to get rid of the damn things. The idea that people continue in therapy when they no longer "need it" is preposterous. For if anyone were completely healed of his pain, and spiritually healthy and mature, he would still welcome the opportunity to talk with someone wiser than he (if he could find such a therapist) so that he could continue to learn and grow. On the flip side of the astoundingly immature celebrity I saw on TV are the people who have no presenting issues to speak of—no emotional illness, depression, anxiety or "problems"—but they see a therapist to receive guidance and thoughtful reflection about their continual journey of spiritual growth.

Therapy is hard work, it takes time and it is expensive. It seems counterintuitive. You take an hour out of your week to pay someone to help you to *not* avoid pain. You agree to open your trap door and welcome your pain, and then sit in it for a while so that you can slowly learn to live with the trap door open all the time. It can be unbelievable anguish. I have a colleague who, for similar reasons, goes on silent spiritual retreats. She sits in silence, except for meeting with her spiritual director, for up to 40 days at a time. Unbelievably painful—and difficult.

People who are willing to do this personal work are some of the most gifted and brilliant leaders in our culture. They are not necessarily famous. They are often quietly wise, wonderfully integrated human beings whom others look up to and admire. Sometimes they are such phenomenal people that it's hard to understand them. It is a common flaw of the immature leader to be under the mistaken impression that it is enough to imitate the way these great people speak, behave, address issues or solve problems. Nothing could be farther from the truth. In order to reach a similar destination, you must take a similar path.

Spiritual Healing

Although many people use their relationship with God as little more than soothing, and many even adhere to rigorous religious doctrines and practices to reinforce the trap door, it is still possible to heal completely through spiritual means alone. I know some very wise, integrated leaders who have never seen a therapist, or read a self-help book, but they have committed themselves to a life of spiritual discipline and self-examination. In every case, however, they were willing to enter into and re-experience their pain. Interestingly, although the people I speak of are Christians, Buddhists and Jews, they are all clergy. Perhaps that is because this kind of commitment takes years of study, prayer, meditation or other forms of the spiritual disciplines and a clergyperson's "job" allows them this time. But there is no reason why lay people, if committed to the healing journey, could not achieve excellent results, especially if they are guided by a competent spiritual director or companion.

Most people who believe in God are not even willing to open the trap door and let God in to heal what's under there. Instead, they use God *only* for soothing (which is perfectly acceptable, but does not result in healing and growth). Sometimes the prayers of the average person are little more than, "Oh God, please keep this trap door *shut*." For some reason, God seems to work better with it open, however, and these prayers are seldom answered to people's satisfaction.

Drugs

For those who are quite low on the Scale, and whose pain is particularly severe, prescription drugs may be in order. Although I never used any drug therapy in my own healing, and I fully believe that it is *possible* to heal without it, I am not opposed to using drug therapies and often recommend them to my clients and parishioners. If you are so anxious that you cannot even come to my office or cannot sit there without panicking virtually the whole time, or if you are so depressed that you cannot even get out of bed, then you may need the help of pharmaceuticals. Once your condition stabilizes under the care of a psychiatrist, therapy will be more helpful. You may be able to work hard enough and long enough to go off the drugs, but I do not generally encourage this.

If you're doing better taking drugs, then it is only reasonable to assume you'll do worse if you stop taking them. "Not taking drugs" is a ridiculous life goal. No one expects it of a diabetic or someone with heart disease, so why would anyone expect it of someone suffering from anxiety or depression? For whatever reason, your brain has sustained some pretty impressive harm over the years. You may not have enough hours in a week or year to spend in therapy to make up for that harm.

For some, Leviathan is so huge—the trap door so high up—it's hard to believe they could possibly live long enough to heal everything that's under it. When I worked on skid row in a suburb of Vancouver, I met dozens of drug addicts and heard their personal stories. I stopped wondering why everyone didn't open their trap door and try to heal. I also stopped wondering why they had turned to drugs. Moreover, taking a pill or injecting oneself with something to end that horrible pain, even temporarily, seemed a pretty sane idea.

Although I have never taken any sort of drug to help with my emotional pain, nor have I ever tried an illegal drug of any kind, I did have an incident with opiates once. It was at the same time as I was working on skid row, so it was a most eye-opening experience. I had what turned out to be an infected tooth and sinus. Since the roots of my teeth were imbedded in the sinus cavity, I kept getting shuffled back and forth between my doctor and dentist until the whole side of my head swelled up like a balloon. By this time, the pain was so excruciating, even shots of morphine barely made a dent in it. I was given a prescription for an opiate so powerful my doctor called it "heroin in pill form." I took one of them every four hours for three days. On the fourth day, I walked into the kitchen to talk to my husband, Charlie. The scene is still vivid in my memory, some 12 years later. "Everything is okay," I said.

"What are you talking about?" he asked.

"I don't know how to describe it. It's just that *everything* is all right."

The weird thing was that I did not feel "drugged." I didn't feel dopey or floaty or anything. I felt normal: clear-headed, completely sane and capable. But when I said, "Everything is okay," I really meant *everything*: everything in my life, in my past, my present, my future. Everything in the universe. It was absolute euphoria, and I have never felt anything like it to this day. Vancouver psychologist Dr. Geoffrey Carr holds a doctorate in neuropharmacology as well as clinical psychology. He says that the euphoric feeling that opiates imitate in the brain is matched only by the feeling a baby has, safe in her mother's arms.

Although it was one of the most insightful experiences of my life, when the drug wore off four hours later, I threw the rest of the bottle down the toilet. I was no longer in pain, anyway; the antibiotics had obviously worked. And just the thought of having access to that wonderful feeling in a bottle of pills scared the dickens out of me.

From that point on, when I heard the tragic life stories of street junkies, I began to imagine the feeling they must have had when they took their drug of choice for the first time. Leviathan would have miraculously disappeared. I could completely understand that once the effects of this "high" wore off, they would want nothing more than to go to any means to duplicate the experience.

If medical science could come up with a drug that would eradicate emotional pain forever, we wouldn't have addicts. The problem with street drugs (or even the "drug" of sex, overeating, or shopping) is, of course, that once you start using it, you need more and more to get the same effect. Eventually, you're using it just because you're addicted. Leviathan then reappears, and on top of being in horrible emotional pain, you're now an addict.

"Street drug therapy" doesn't work for very long, and you end up worse than when you started. This is due to the addictive nature of the drugs themselves. It doesn't matter who you are or what the circumstances. Rats, if given heroin, will all become addicted, and will keep choosing to take heroin until they die from the effects. The rat does not have a "gene" for addiction. Dr. Avram Goldstein, professor emeritus of pharmacology at Stanford University, writes: "A rat addicted to heroin is not rebelling against society, is not a victim of socioeconomic circumstances, is not a product of a dysfunctional family, and is not a criminal."[30]

I'm not suggesting anyone take drugs, but I do understand how easily one might be fooled into thinking that they could help. Society makes it sound so simple: Just get off drugs. Drugs are the problem. Declare war on drugs, say no to drugs. But you know what? If addicts get off drugs, they have to deal with Leviathan. For them, it is so huge and menacing that the trap door must always be shut over it. It rages and terrorizes every aspect of life. "Just say no to drugs" are easy words for those sitting high on the Scale. Where I sit on the Scale now, a few minutes of prayer in the afternoon will bring me relief from my suffering.

---

[30] A. Goldstein, *Neurobiology of Heroin Addiction and of Methadone Treatment*, Delivered to the U.S. National Methadone Conference, April, 1997.

For most people on skid row, hundreds of milligrams of heroin a day won't even make a dent in it.

If we cannot, or should not, close a trap door over Leviathan, then what do we do? Denial, soothing ourselves or even cognitive therapy are not optimal solutions. But healing this pain, this fear of our Leviathan, seems critical. Perhaps we need to spend a little more time with this creature. But before we invite him up for tea, let's look at what factors led him to lurk down there in the first place.

Chapter 9:
Leviathan: Nature or Nurture?

If it's not one thing, it's your mother.
—Murray Bowen

The discussion of nature versus nurture has been going on in scientific circles for decades. What experts most differ on is the *degree* to which factors other than genetics or pathology contribute to diseases or disorders. The whole debate came to a head in an amusing way in 1997 when John Stossel of ABC's *20/20* aired a new special entitled "The Mystery of Happiness." Among other factors, Stossel reported that "studies involving identical twins raised in different environments and cross-cultural population statistics suggest that there is a strong genetic component specifying one's capacity for happiness." Did you catch that? Supposedly there is a gene for *happiness*.

In the same year, T. J. Bouchard, director of the Minnesota Center for Twin and Adoption Research, published a paper entitled "Whenever the Twain Shall Meet."[31] Bouchard stated that "for all their striking findings, twin studies do not explain how genes influence personality, intelligence or social attitudes," and he also concluded that twin studies refute *both* "biological and environmental determinism." His conclusion? "We are an integral part of a complex biological world." No kidding.

Finally, in October of 1997, Robert Sapolsky, professor of biological sciences at Stanford Brain Research Institute, published a layperson-friendly article entitled, "A Gene for Nothing."[32] Sapolsky says that despite research into cloning and twin studies, even those with identical genes do not behave identically. "If an identical twin is schizophrenic, the sibling, with the identical 'schizophrenia

---

[31] in *The Sciences*, 37, 5, 52–57 (1997).
[32] in *Discover*, 18, 10, 40–46 (1997).

gene' has only about a 50 per cent chance of having the disease." He adds that "identical twins with their identical genes never have identical brains." There are few who disagree with Sapolsky's conclusion: "You can't talk meaningfully about nature or nurture, only about their interaction…there are genetic vulnerabilities, tendencies, predispositions, but rarely genetic inevitabilities." It seems that no matter what the era or age, what scientists discover, whether they are researching brain neurology, genetics, disease, psychology or family therapy, they all eventually agree that either genes or genetics accounts for only about half the problem.

Despite all of these findings, there is an alarming trend sweeping through our culture: the idea that every problem we have is due to nature, meaning it is "genetic" or "pathological." We believe there is a gene for addiction, a gene for obesity, a gene for anxiety, a gene for anger, sexual dysfunction, depression, cancer, tooth decay and the ability to appreciate country & western music. It stuns me to think that blaming our genes is an attractive concept to people, that we are the way we are because we were born that way, and there is nothing that can be done about it. The fact is, as of this writing, a gene has been found for very little of what is generally thought to be genetic—alcoholism, depression, anxiety or even schizophrenia. Although there are differences in the appearance of the brains of schizophrenics, it is not known what causes, leads to or contributes to these abnormalities—or whether they were there at birth.

Genetics is a complicated field, and I will make a fool of myself if I try to do anything but provide some broad general statements—as comedian, Arsenio Hall, might remark—things that make you say, "'Hmmmm,' as in the following:

> - If you do possess a gene for something, it will not necessarily be "turned on" without other factors coming into play.

> - Not only can genes be "activated," but they can also be "deactivated" by other factors in the environment.

> - Even when a disease is clearly linked to chromosomes, such as Down's syndrome, there are still variables in how "affected" people are who have it. Some Down's syndrome patients live independently, have jobs and play sports. Others are helpless and confined to institutions. What makes the difference?

> - Some diseases are "strongly genetic" such as breast cancer in women with the gene BRCA1 or BRCA2. But women possessing these genes only have, at most, an 80 per cent chance of developing the disease in

their lifetime. Why is it not 100 per cent? What is different about the small percentage of women who don't get cancer?

- If schizophrenia is "genetic," and since schizophrenics reproduce remarkably less than the general population, why, rather than becoming extinct over time, is schizophrenia on the rise?
- Does the fact that something is in your family history necessarily mean it's in your genes?
- Since people with deep emotional problems can come from "nice families," and often "nice families" have only one "troubled" family member, what if it is not a problem with the family's genes but a problem with the family's "niceness"?
- If we all agree that stress can lead to a body breaking down, what if there are more factors contributing to stress than we are consciously aware of?
  - What is the role of our pain in our overall stress level?
  - What if the stress from our unhealed pain is more of a factor in the stress level and health of someone in our family than it is to us—our partner or children, for example?
  - What if our stress about someone else's health is more harmful to them than their genes? What if it affects their genes?
- If addiction really is a disease, why is there not one shred of scientific evidence that can be tested for or seen under a microscope to back this up?
- What if everything that happens to us is a "perfect storm,"[33] and it takes much more than genetics or pathogens to affect us with anything?
- What if we have more control over our psychological and even physical health than we ever dreamed?

---

[33] The term a "perfect storm" has been used to refer to the Halloween nor'easter of 1991, subsequently the subject and title of a best-selling book by Sebastian Junger (Little, Brown & Company, 1997) and later a popular motion picture (Warner Bros., 2000). A "perfect storm" requires several atmospheric conditions to come together at once. If any one of the factors is absent, the storm will not develop. When they are all present, however, the result is frightening and deadly.

Almost as popular as blaming our genes is the idea that if something is wrong with us, if it is not genetic, then it is wholly pathological,[34] meaning it is some "disease" or "disorder," often with an unknown cause. In the case of mental or emotional illness, it is said to be a defect in the brain or a "chemical imbalance." This trend is driven in part by corporate drug companies and the gargantuan industry, which includes medical personnel, research institutes, medical-supply manufacturers/merchants, and most alarmingly, universities. There is big money invested in making you think that you need a pill, an operation or a procedure of some kind to fix whatever is wrong with you—and that all these "treatments" need to be preceded by very expensive tests. This industry is also invested in ensuring that you think you cannot possibly do anything about your problem yourself. Research and literature about "mind-body-spirit connection" abounds, yet if you're like most, as soon as something goes wrong in your life, you are most likely to run to members of the scientific/medical community first ("body" people), therapists second ("mind" people) and clergypersons or spiritual directors absolutely last.

Despite the fact that the scientific research community cannot substantiate everything it concludes about the nature of our physical and emotional disorders, we as a culture are invested more in the media attention on genes and pathogens as the "cause" of our problems than we ever have been before. There are a number of reasons for this, as I outline below.

Laziness

If I am the way I am because of a gene, there is nothing I can do about it. I cannot alter my DNA. This excuse is very convenient, for it seems easier to do nothing and be a "victim" one's entire life than it is to grow. Spiritual growth is very difficult, painful and time-consuming. It involves educating oneself, a commitment of time and energy and usually the help of some professional, which costs money. Why would I want to do that if I can avoid it? Better to wait around until someone invents a better pill for my anxiety, depression, addiction or even physical illness and blame my genes.

While genetic research has done little to help those who suffer from addiction, the 12-step program has worked wonders. Thanks to the 12 steps, alcoholism is one of the few disorders that has seen positive outcome studies. It

---

[34] Pathology. (n.d.). *Merriam-Webster's Medical Dictionary*. Retrieved February 26, 2007, from Dictionary.com website: http://dictionary.reference.com/browse/pathology: refers to the anatomic and physiological deviations from the normal that constitute disease or characterize a particular disease.

is no coincidence that the success of the 12 steps is related to the program being a very well-thought-through path to spiritual growth.

Although it seems easier to temporarily avoid painful feelings, they do lurk under the trap door, and jump up to bite you when you least expect it, or more likely, when you have other stressors in your life or in your family that are high. This is the worst possible moment for them to show up, I might add, and is the time when you are the most vulnerable.

Self-Blame

It is appealing to think that a gene caused the problem in your life, if for a long time you blamed yourself for your problems. Self-blame never helps anyone to grow. It merely paralyzes you in a feedback loop of guilt. One thing I learned early on as a preacher is that when people feel tremendously guilty, they go home and do nothing. It's almost as if their subconscious is saying, "I've done something. I've *felt guilty*. There is nothing more I can do. There is nothing more *to* do."

Blaming yourself is not the same thing as taking responsibility for yourself, however. To blame yourself would be to confirm the foundation of your pain: I am worthless, helpless or flawed. But it is this belief that is at the core of your dysfunction, and it is the same with all humans. It is a "critical inner voice" [35] that reinforces the belief in your mind that something is terribly wrong with you *that is not wrong with everyone else*.

While most of us know logically that we are not perfect, and we make mistakes and we are "only human," often we only give lip service to this logical belief and don't integrate it into our lives. Once you come to understand deeply that *nobody* is perfect, *everyone* is human, and *everyone* makes mistakes, you can start to look at yourself and how you may have contributed to, and keep contributing to, your own problems. After all, if your car breaks down, it's not the car's "fault." Perhaps it was manufactured imperfectly; perhaps it's just wear and tear; perhaps the driver did something foolish; perhaps the car was the "victim" of an accident. Blaming the car would be ridiculous. Assuming the car is either fundamentally flawed or that there is nothing wrong with it at all, thus never taking it to the repair shop, is equally ridiculous.

---

[35] Robert Firestone, Lisa Firestone, Joyce Catlett, and Pat Love, *Conquer Your Critical Inner Voice*, (Oakland, CA: New Harbinger, 2002), 146.

Blaming the Family

Blaming your family can be another way of sloughing off responsibility for growth. A very immature person may say something like, "My family did this to me. I was abused as a child. That's why I have this problem. It's just the way I am. Oh yes, and by the way, because I am like this now, *you* have to adapt to *me*."

It is just as unhelpful to blame your family as it is to blame yourself. But there is another posture to take in response to your problems that is neither blaming yourself, your genes or your family: it is simply to acknowledge that your family may be *responsible* for your past and your present, and to "get real" about the fact that *you* are responsible for your future.

I think of my (neglectful) mother in this way: she is *responsible* for contributing to the anxiety disorder that destroyed my life for almost 40 years. However, she is not *to blame*. There is a huge difference. If I *blame* her, I may assume there is nothing I can do myself. I believe that she must change in order for me to feel better. (Then, when she never does, I assume I never can.) If, however, I can acknowledge that she was *responsible,* then I can understand my current problems better and work toward healing them myself. It is not necessary that I talk to my mother about her responsibility for, or role in, my adult problems. Just because she is responsible does not mean she did not do the best she could given the maturity level and skills that she had.

Many people are not willing to even consider the possibility that their family's emotional process may have contributed to their problems, because they believe that this is the same thing as blame. It is easier to blame your mother's genes than your mother because the genes will not blow up at the dinner table or run out of the room crying. I have been astounded to sit with counselees whose parents sexually and physically abused them, and yet they would refuse to even entertain the fact that this might have had something to do with their presenting anxiety, depression, addiction or sexual dysfunction. "You can't blame parents for everything," they'll say. I had one fellow sit in my office for about a hundred hours before he was even willing to think about the fact that his dead father might have contributed to his sexual problems by sexually assaulting him at age nine. He was even afraid to "think bad thoughts" about his father, lest he hurt Dad's feelings (Dad, who was now "looking down from heaven"). I once blurted out something like this to him, "Now let me get this straight. You are responsible for the feelings *of the dead*?" Once he was able to shift from focusing on his dead father's feelings and could acknowledge that his father was responsible, without blaming him, his sexual dysfunction disappeared.

Clients who are Christian often have a particularly difficult time separating blame from responsibility. After all, blame, even if you call it responsibility, just isn't Christian. Forgiveness is. The truth is that they are not mutually exclusive. Once we are able, in a calm and mature manner, to see that perhaps there *were* factors in our family life that contributed to the way we are now, we are able to shift responsibility away from ourselves, give up the idea that it is genetic and there is nothing we can do about it, and still not *blame* anyone.

Forgiveness is meaningless, if not impossible, as long as you are still in pain. Since we are often unaware of our pain, or the degree of it, we don't understand why we can't bring ourselves to forgive someone. When your pain is healed, forgiveness is effortless. If you cannot find it within yourself to forgive someone, more likely than not, you are still in pain.

Common Sense

I am not suggesting that you ignore medical science and never go for your annual checkups. That would be foolish. I am saying that there are several factors that contribute to your problems in life, even physical ones, and perhaps you should look at attacking your problems on all fronts. I speak from personal experience.

When I was diagnosed with cancer at age 37, the first thing I did was march into a hospital and have the thing cut out of there. Then I happily let them nuke it into oblivion so that it would never come back. Somewhat more reluctantly, I endured months of having my body poisoned, my entire immune system killed off as a "preventative" measure. But I didn't stop there. I went to counselling weekly and worked hard at the arising issues of fear and grief over the loss of my health at such a young age. I read dozens of books on nutrition and changed my diet significantly. I took vitamin supplements, shark cartilage and drank some nasty rotting water that a giant mushroom had been growing in. I prayed intensely and purposefully and was prayed for. I took part in a liturgical healing. I began looking at the emotional process in my own family and worked to become more of an observer of it than a participant in it. I meditated and used guided imagery to imagine the cancer cells being destroyed. Ten years later, I still do some of the things on this list. So in the end, I have no idea what "cured" my cancer or what kept me healthier during cancer treatments than I had ever been in my lifetime. But I can tell you one thing: out of everything I tried and everything I changed, the most benefit I received in my life was that which came from the discovery and healing of my emotional pain.

A Call for Hope

The biggest problem with believing that your problems are 100 per cent genetic or pathological is that it is hopeless. Woe is me! I cannot change my genes, my brain chemicals or every virus in the world. There is no hope; I am doomed to suffer with this forever.

I fail to see why people so easily jump to the conclusion that they can do nothing about their problems. Sometimes you can almost see a sigh of relief when they tell you the diagnosis: "Anxiety is hereditary. My mother had it." The implication is that it is therefore hopeless. If not for the fear or unwillingness to endure pain and grow, no one would be relieved to hear that his problem is genetic.

If only part of your problem or tendency toward a problem is genetic or pathological, and there are other factors as well, including the degree of your pain and the emotional process within your family, there is something you can do about that. You can begin to understand it. You can learn more about family process and how to approach your family differently so that you will begin to heal. You can become more emotionally intelligent; you can discover how your early experience now triggers particular emotions and how you might work to heal them. This gives you an incredible amount of *power*. All you have to do is to be able to tolerate pain! This means stopping your avoidance behaviour and all the accompanying excuses. The more pain you are willing to tolerate (in small doses, of course, and very gradually), the more you will be able to heal. To heal is to literally change the "wiring" and "chemicals" in your brain. In order to do that, it is necessary to have at least a simple understanding of how your brain works.

Chapter 10:
The Brain Made Easy

Brain: an apparatus with which we think that we think.
—Ambrose Bierce

The noted neuroscientist Joseph LeDoux, in his book *The Synaptic Self*, argues that the true "self" resides in the synaptic connections in our brains. We have *trillions*[36] of these synaptic connections, and the patterns of impulses firing across them numbers almost as large. Whether or not LeDoux has been successful in locating the self in these electrical connections, it is impossible to imagine the concept of "self" apart from our brains. This is problematic, because the human brain is the most complicated single entity in the universe.

Our bodies are made up of trillions of cells. The special cells of the nervous system are called "neurons." They carry messages to and from the brain and communicate with each other within the brain through a process that is both "electrical" and "chemical." The brain has approximately 100 billion neurons.

As you can see in Figure 12, a neuron has tentacle-like arms or strings extending from it called "dendrites."

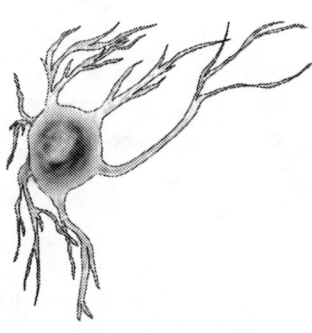

---

[36] A trillion is a difficult number to comprehend. Think of it this way: if you had a million dollars to just "blow," you could spend about $274 a day every day for 10 years. But if you had a trillion dollars, you would have $274 to spend every day for 10 *million* years!

Between each neuron there is a space or gap known as a "synapse." Information travels along neural pathways and from one neuron to another across these synapses in the form of electrical impulses and a flow of chemicals called "neurotransmitters." When the message reaches the next neuron, it sort of clicks into a "slot" and, depending on the slot, is either passed onto the next neuron or it stops. If it continues on, it is said that this neuron "fires."

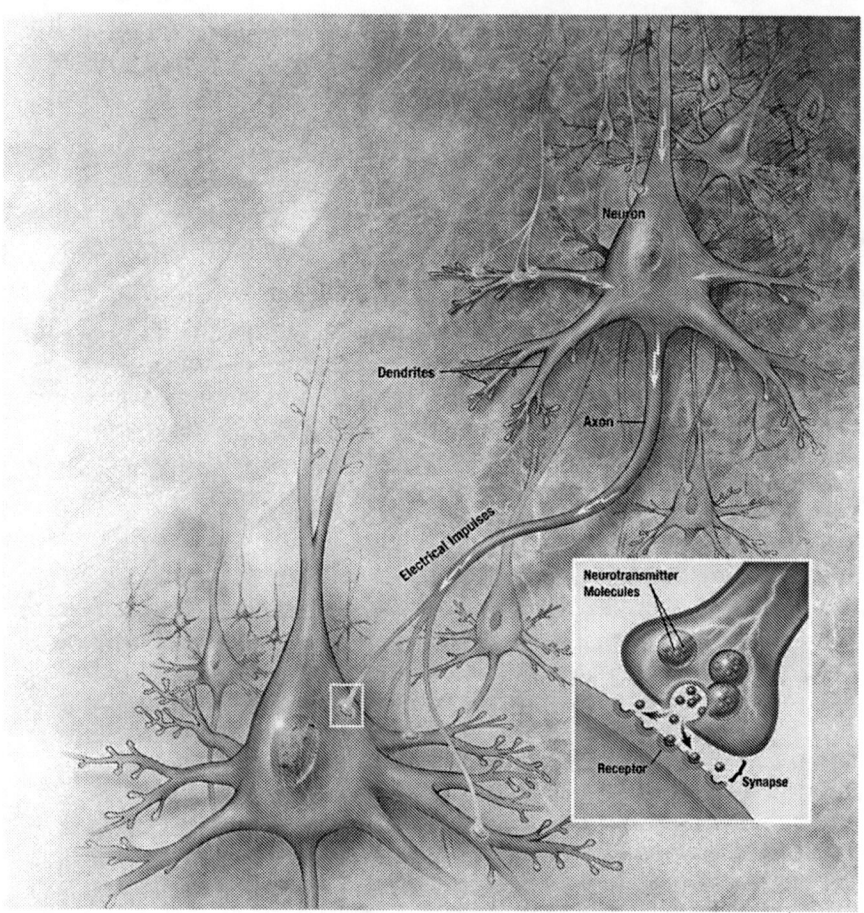

Messages pass from one neuron to the next in a particular pathway that is unique to each person. The major pathways are wired up in utero, and life experience contributes a fine-tuning of the connections. This fine-tuning has a profound effect on our emotional experience in later life. The pathways are built like complicated freeway systems with cloverleafs, roundabouts, exit lanes and merges. Once neurons fire together, they wire together[37] (building the freeway system). This wiring together of neurons means that if any stimulus sends a particular message down a particular pathway in the brain, that stimulus will usually send the same message down the same pathway until a new one is "built."

The brain has been compared to a computer, which may be puzzling enough for someone who knows virtually nothing about them. But even if you do, the brain is not only "wires" or electrical connections like a computer; the brain is *wet*, made up of blood, tissue and chemicals, and it needs oxygen to survive. So in order to fully understand the brain, you need to be a combination of an electrical engineer, computer scientist and chemist.

The brain is unbelievably vast and complex, and, unlike computers, each brain is infinitely different from all the rest. Every second of every hour of the day, our brains receive and process thousands of pieces of information. We are consciously aware of very few of them, yet they all go "in there" somewhere, somehow. When our brains are still forming in infancy, many trillions of these pieces of information are affecting us. Our brains "remember" each one of them, even if "we" don't.

Most people think of their brains as being only an organ in their heads, but for the purpose of developing emotional intelligence, it is perhaps more helpful to think of your whole body as your brain. One way to look at it is that the brain extends down the back of your neck into your spinal cord, which in turn extends out to your limbs and into your organs as your central nervous system. Although your brain receives information *from* your body, it also sends both electrical and chemical information out *to* your body. And this happens so instantly that one could quite safely say that your brain and body are "one."

---

[37] Donald Hebb introduced this concept now more commonly referred to as "Hebbian theory." The theory states, "When an axon of cell A is near enough to excite cell B and repeatedly or persistently takes part in firing it, some growth process or metabolic change takes place in one or both cells such that A's efficiency, as one of the cells firing B, is increased." (*The Organization of Behaviour*, New York: Wiley, 1949) This is often paraphrased as "neurons that fire together wire together."

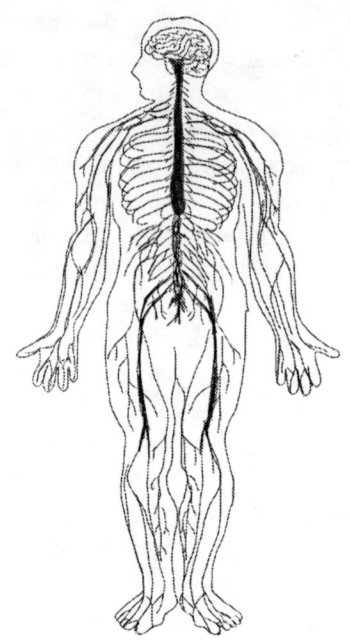

Although we all have essentially similar brains, each of our individual "wiring" and "chemicals" is immensely different, based on our life experiences. Even identical twins, who have exactly the same DNA or genes, have dissimilar brains, as it is impossible to expose them to precisely the same environment, experiences or even foods. Even though twins have the same parents, those parents do not interact with them in exactly the same way. Imagine for a moment two new parents who are about to take their identical twins home from the hospital. Mommy dresses one of them in a new outfit, and he begins to fuss. She says, "There, there, my love. Are you cold? Let Mommy wrap you up tight in this blanket." She does just that, and holds him close. He stops fussing and settles in to sleep. Meanwhile, Daddy is dressing the other one, who also begins to fuss. "You're all right," he says. "Come on now. We're going in the car seat." Dad attempts to put the baby in the seat, but soon he is screaming uncontrollably. Dad gingerly picks him up and hands him over to Mom, switching for the baby who's asleep. "That one's going to be trouble," he remarks.

The amazing thing about being human is that before these twins are even home from the hospital, if we were to remove their brains and examine them with microscopic exactness, we would find differences. You see, the brain is all about different kinds of *memory*. When you have a particular experience, such as these twins did, your brain processes the information both by the release or regulation of chemicals and by the forming of connections or pathways from one brain cell to another (synaptic connections). This is a type of "memory" because the next time the one twin is in a similar situation, his brain will expect a similar outcome; his brain "remembers" the process from the time before. In fact, each baby has "learned" something about life that the other hasn't yet. And they have learned it in a particular way and at a particular age.

The baby that Daddy dressed has been under stress, perceiving himself to be in danger, whereas the baby that Mommy dressed has not. Never mind the fact that Daddy's baby may now come to be labelled as "the fussy one," and treated differently for the next 20 years. If one turns out to be a doctor and the other a poorly functioning dropout who can't hold down a job, it is nonsense to say, "Well, we raised them the same, so it can't be their upbringing. It must be something genetic."

Despite the fact that our brains develop differently, they all have the same basic structure, chemicals and capabilities. Knowledge of these basics is helpful to anyone who is interested in spiritual growth. If you've ever tried to read anything about brains before or seen labelled drawings of them, you may already be confused. Some neuroscientists use different names for the various parts, depending on what they're trying to illustrate! To add to your confusion, no one has succeeded in mapping the trillions of cells, connections and chemical paths/functions of the brain—an exercise that will take scientists working diligently (which they don't have funding for) about a hundred more years. So no one knows everything, and those who know some things confuse the rest of us. Nevertheless, it is a magnificent field of study, to which many have contributed a great deal of knowledge that is helpful. Researchers have ascertained their current knowledge of the brain by:

1. Studying animals whose brains are similar to ours, especially rats and cats. It has been said that there are two ways to study a cat's brain: dissect and label or put down a mouse and watch. Both methods are used. Scientists also find locations in animal brains that contribute to certain emotions or behaviours and electrically stimulate them with "electrodes." They then study the animal's reaction. Rats are also injected with every sort of chemical you can imagine, and their subsequent behaviour is observed and documented.

2. Studying the behaviour of humans who have had certain parts of their brains removed due to tumours, or damage from an accident. There is a famous story of a man as far back as 1848 whose frontal cortex (the part of the brain unique to humans) was damaged from a steel rod

penetrating his forehead after an explosion. At first, the man seemed completely normal. But he was not at all normal, for all his inhibition was gone. He became rude, extravagant and anti-social. Alcohol has this effect on the brain, too, but not to such a great extent and not without other obvious symptoms. This guy said *literally* everything that was on his mind. (Can you imagine his poor wife asking him, "How do I look in these pants?"?)

3. Observing human behaviour in various circumstances and at various stages of life—particularly infancy—when our brains are not fully developed yet. This may involve certain experiments with a variety of stimuli. For instance, Jerome Kagan, a Harvard University researcher, took 16-week-old babies and dangled a mobile in front of them that they'd never seen before. He not only observed their reaction at the time, but categorized the babies based on their reactions and followed the groups for over 20 years.[38] Other brain observation experiments may include hooking people up to equipment that measures such things as heart rate, skin/sweat reactions, respiration and brain activity or "waves."

4. Looking at the brain's physical structure, characteristics and health through the use of very sophisticated equipment such as CAT[39] scans, PET[40] scans and MRIs.[41]

The Triune Brain

A brain researcher named Paul MacLean attempted to make the brain easier to understand by dividing it into three parts. MacLean believed that each part represents a distinct evolutionary layer that has formed upon the older layer before it. His "triune brain" theory was generally accepted until fairly recently.

---

[38] I heard Jerome Kagan in 2006 at a seminar in Vancouver, and was privileged to be able to chat with him afterward for a couple of hours at a cocktail party.

[39] "Computed Axial Tomography" is the process of using computers to generate a three-dimensional image from flat (i.e., two-dimensional) X-ray pictures. The brain can be viewed in pieces akin to "slices" this way.

[40] "Positron Emission Tomography" is a nuclear medicine imaging technique that produces a three-dimensional "map" of body processes.

[41] "Magnetic Resonance Imaging" is a complicated technology using a powerful magnet to make a two-dimensional or three-dimensional image of the body, capable of examining, among other things, exactly what kind of tissue is present at any given point.

Although MacLean's idea that the brain has three distinct sections or centres is oversimplified, even more recent researchers agree that it is a simplification that at least points us in the right direction.[42]

MacLean identifies three sections of the brain as illustrated in Figure 15: the *reptilian brain* or brain stem, the *limbic system* or midbrain, and the *neocortex*.

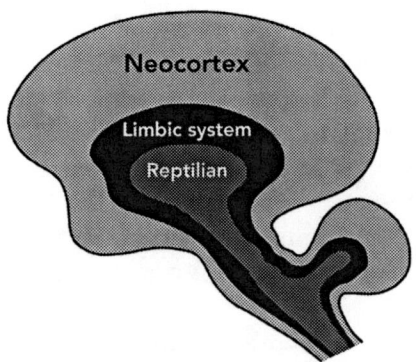

- ➢ The brain stem, also known as the "reptilian" or "lower" brain, is thought to be the oldest part, from an evolutionary perspective. It is responsible for basic and automatic things often known as the "four Fs": feeding, fleeing, fighting and sex.
- ➢ The limbic system, or the "emotional brain," also known as the midbrain, is responsible for things other than emotion such as regulation of body functions. It includes a small but powerful part called the *amygdala*.
- ➢ The cerebral, or neocortex, or the "thinking" brain, is thought to be the "highest" part of the brain and the "newest" from an evolutionary perspective.

While this triune idea is an oversimplification, it is true that the brain is hierarchical; there are higher and lower brain functions. Let us now consider each of them more closely.

The Reptilian Brain

MacLean calls the brain stem "reptilian" because it is thought to be the "oldest" part of our brain from an evolutionary perspective. (Reptiles evolved long before

---

[42] Jaak Panksepp, *Affective Neuroscience: The Foundations of Human and Animal Emotions*, 70.

humans.) Reptiles still have brains very similar to our brain stems. Reptiles do virtually nothing but sleep, bask in the sun, have sex and kill things to eat before they are killed and eaten. Every once in a while, you meet a human being with similar life goals. I think I may have dated one when I was an undergraduate.

The Limbic System

The middle section of MacLean's triune brain, the *limbic system*, is the system we have in common with other mammals. The limbic system or, midbrain, is the "feeling centre" and is responsible for a variety of emotional responses, memory and maintaining calm, regular "balance" in our bodies (blood pressure, temperature, sugar levels, immune system). It also regulates hunger, thirst, sexual arousal and our sleep/wake cycle. The limbic system includes the amygdala, which is the most important part of the brain to understand for the purposes of this book. For reference, it is pronounced:

uh-MIG-duh-la

The term literally means "almond," as the amygdala is made up of two small almond-shaped pieces buried within the midbrain. Some neuroscientists believe the amygdala may be even "older," and so they include it in the reptilian brain.[43] Either way, the amygdala has the power to bring out the reptile in us.

Your amygdala is very handy to have. It keeps you alive and keeps you from being eaten. Whenever there is even the slightest hint of a threat to you, the amygdala kicks into action. It fires off a **DANGER!** message to the rest of your brain *and* to your body so quickly that you are not even aware of it—in about 1/5000th of a second.[44] As such, it is the great guard dog of the trap door, flying into action at the slightest stirring of trouble. It will spur you to flee or fight—whatever it takes to keep the trap door shut or to slam it shut again if it's been inadvertently opened.

As soon as the amygdala is activated and sends its **DANGER!** message, your body momentarily freezes and then prepares for either "fight" or "flight." This can trigger either anger or panic, which you become consciously aware of. Even though you may become aware of a panic response, if it is strong enough, your brain systems for logic or reason may not be quick enough or strong enough to

---

[43] Panksepp, *Affective Neuroscience*, 70.
[44] C. L. Larson et al, "Fear Is Fast in Phobic Individuals: Amygdala Activation in Response to Fear-Relevant Stimuli," *Biological Psychiatry*, 15 August 2006 (Vol. 60, Issue 4, 410–417).

"tell you" that there is no danger. That's because your amygdala will be activated over and over in very rapid succession.

In order to fight or flee, your body needs adrenalin, oxygen, blood flow and tense muscles. The amygdala arranges for all of these, in a flash. Your heart rate and breathing dramatically increase, you may feel the surge of adrenalin as a "bang" sensation in your midsection, a mild version of which is often described as "my stomach dropped." Adrenalin may lead to shaking, a tingling sensation in your extremities, dizziness, light-headedness or nausea. Your muscles will become very tense; you may sweat or experience clamminess in your hands due to increased blood flow and heat to your muscles—designed for fighting or running away. Your digestive system will shut down temporarily, which is why in a state of panic (rather than just "nervousness"), a human being may feel nauseous but will not vomit. There are other bodily responses that can help us drop a bit of weight in quick preparation for fleeing. This is the subject of such expressions as, "Excuse me, but I believe I must retire to another room and change my underpants."

If you feel any of these things happening in your body, even in the mildest way, then you know that the amygdala has been activated. This is important information because the amygdala not only works quicker than "higher" brain functions, but once it is engaged, it slows down or completely shuts down reasonable, rational thought processes in order to protect the organism. If a crocodile jumps out of the water and starts chasing you, it's best if you don't stand there and start thinking about crocodiles, crocodile activity or the latest article you read about reptiles in the *Globe and Mail*. While you are thinking, you will be eaten. Your only hope is to run like mad and figure it out on the way, and your brain knows this instinctively.

Unfortunately, it is very difficult to switch that pesky amygdala off when you don't find it necessary anymore. Ask a 50-year-old man why his heart rate increases when he talks to his angry mother on the phone. I mean, is he in some sort of *danger*? What could his mother possibly do to harm him?

Whenever you make a hasty decision at work, fight with your partner, put your "foot in our mouth" or freeze in an exam; whenever a car goes out of control or a plane crashes due to pilot error, the amygdala is the culprit every time. The amygdala is, according to Daniel Goleman in *Emotional Intelligence*, responsible for an "emotional hijacking."[45] It is, without a doubt, the most powerful part of our brain, capable of overriding every other emotional system

---

[45] Daniel Goleman, *Emotional Intelligence*, 13–14.

as well as the systems for logic, reason and creativity. It also acts at lightning speed—thousands of times faster than other systems.

It takes many other parts of the brain to identify the danger, assess it and send a message back to the amygdala to calm it down. During whatever time it takes for the brain to carry out these other "executive" functions, the body may temporarily "freeze." You may have seen a famous videotape of people calmly eating in an outdoor café when a bomb goes off. The tape shows that as soon as the bomb explodes, *everyone*, without exception, freezes momentarily—then they all run like blazes.

In the brain of a phobic or post-traumatic stress disorder sufferer, for some reason, the amygdala keeps firing **DANGER!** despite the "logical" part of the brain attempting to send messages back to stop it. It is therefore ridiculous to try to *reason* with someone who is having a post-traumatic flash back, or whose severe phobia has been triggered. The reasonable parts of the person's brain know darn well there's no real danger. But the amygdala persists, and it is very difficult to shut it off. I once suffered from a severe phobia and had to endure several incompetent therapists before I found one who actually helped me beat the thing. One rather boorish cognitive therapist explained to me, quite rudely, that I had nothing to fear. This was immensely frustrating because as an intelligent, educated person I *knew* that I had nothing to fear, I just couldn't stop the horrible, terrifying panic response in my body. It was as if she was trying to convince me to jump out of a plane without a parachute. "Tell it to my amygdala," I said, and left without paying the bill. When I finally found a therapist who actually listened to what I was saying, I was successfully treated for the phobia.

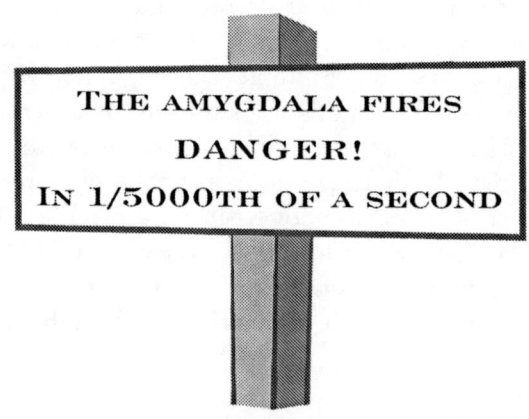

Phobias and other anxiety disorders have multiple factors contributing to their development, but in every case, the amygdala has gone haywire. This is partly due to the amygdala having the best "memory" of any other part of the brain. If you have ever been in a situation that sent your body into a panic, even if, or should I say especially if, this was very early in childhood, then it is almost inevitable that you will be sent into a panic again every time there are similar circumstances to that very first experience. This is a pain in the ass, especially when you can't even remember what sent you into the panic originally because you were younger than three years old. Your amygdala "remembers" what you do not.

That amygdala can wreak havoc in so many aspects of your life, I swear I thought about having mine removed. Unfortunately, since this little almond-shaped piece of trouble has such a good "memory," the brain uses it for nearly all forms of memory. I once read about a woman whose amygdala was removed due to disease. Following the surgery, she described absolutely no sensation of fear in any form. She said she could have been dangling from a cliff, logically knowing that if she fell, she'd die, but still could not feel afraid. The only problem was, she wasn't able to function in a lot of other areas. Her short-term memory was severely compromised. She couldn't work at any sort of job or function properly in everyday life. So we need this "guard dog" and we are cursed by it at the same time. But there is good news; the dog can be trained and even tamed.

The Neocortex

The "highest" part of the brain, according to MacLean, is the neocortex or "thinking" brain. It is located literally at the top and front of our heads. It has also been labelled the cerebral cortex. "Neo" means "new," and from an evolutionary perspective, this part of our brains is new. The neocortex is responsible for "executive" functions like reasoning, logic, solving problems, organizing, memorizing and learning. It is the "place" where our beliefs, values and principles—everything listed as "self"—is held.

No other mammal has a sophisticated neocortex as humans do. Although chimpanzees and dolphins are highly intelligent animals, there are some things they just can't manage. For one thing, they don't have the capacity to develop *original* language, nor do they have our intricate problem-solving capabilities.

The neocortex is not as smart as it seems. It is very slow to receive information, process it and react, especially compared to that quick-triggered sharpshooter, the amygdala. The amygdala is more than ten thousand times faster than the neocortex. It sends to your body one unmistakably clear message: **DANGER!**

Then…run! If you can't run, fight like hell! Despite all reason put forward by the tortoise of a neocortex, the amygdala *keeps* sending the **DANGER!** message, flooding the neocortex with more information than it can handle. The neocortex slowly and methodically sends "logic" messages to your body in an attempt to calm the amygdala down. But it usually starts off wasting a good deal of time by trying to figure out what's going on, rather than responding to it. "Why?" your neocortex asks. "Why am I afraid?" "Did something happen to me in childhood?" If the amygdala is active enough and the stimulus powerful enough, your neocortex doesn't have a hope of coming up with an answer that will satisfy it quickly.

In some situations that are fearful enough, the neocortex shuts down completely, and you actually become *stupid*. Try reasoning with a phobic or someone with a rage disorder whose amygdala has been triggered—good luck! Phobics and people with rage disorders, as well as "normal" individuals caught in dangerous situations, often report that they feel in a "fog" or a "black hole." Even vision and hearing can be compromised. We call this *dissociation from reality*, and it is a temporary phenomenon where the neocortex completely stops processing thought until the fear stimulus is removed. Unfortunately, four billion years has not quite been long enough for us to evolve to a place where our amygdala and corresponding body systems automatically obey the reason and logic of the neocortex. A few billion years from now this may be so, and humans will live peaceably and joyfully in relationship with one another purely because they know that it is "rational" to do so.

The good news for us in the 21st century, barely evolved from cave people, is that the neocortex, although slow and "weak," can become faster and stronger with training. Even someone with a severe phobia, if he works with the perseverance of an Olympian, can train his neocortex in such a way as to alter his perception of the world so that the things that trigger the amygdala come to be interpreted as less dangerous. *This is key to good leadership*. How much training it takes to do this depends on how strong the synaptic connections are in your brain and how long they've been there. Under stress, the brain will want to go back to its old wiring, at least in part. A newly trained brain, however, like a once-trained body, will never go back to being as bad as it was before, and it will take less effort the next time around to get it into shape again. It is just as important to continue one's neocortex "training" throughout life as it is to adapt an ongoing lifestyle of healthy eating and regular exercise.

The Brain and the Stress Response

No book about evoking change within oneself and taking leadership would be complete without some discussion about how stress factors into our ability to do so. Stress literally means "imbalance." Every living system, whether it is an amoeba, a forest, a family or the Hindu students association, maintains itself in a comfortable balance or equilibrium. More will be said about this state of balance or "homeostasis" in a subsequent chapter. All that is necessary to be aware of at this point is that when this balance is thrown off through any type of change, problem or threat, it is said that the organism is "stressed" until such time as the system *adapts* to the factor(s) contributing to the stress and creates a new state of balance.

Humans are remarkably adaptable as a species. But despite this fact, like all other organisms, we will try everything in our power *not* to adapt, if we possibly can. The first thing we humans do, rather than adapt (learn, grow, change) is to mount a *stress response*. Stress is therefore a reaction to any of the following:

- Temperature change
- Illness—presence of viruses, bacteria
- Accident (being wounded physically in any way, which includes surgery)
- Any real *or perceived* threat or trauma
- Any real or perceived threat to the family or social group (the more closely "related" you are to those people, the greater the sense of threat)
- Chemicals or other toxins introduced to or present in the body
- Pain
- Fatigue
- Malnutrition or dehydration

Each of the factors listed above somehow threatens the delicate balance that the body is maintaining at all times. When this balance is in jeopardy or disrupted, the first thing that kicks in is an amygdala response: **DANGER!** By now, you know what happens when the amygdala is in charge; the neocortex or logic centre slows down or even shuts down. The amygdala then hooks up with other brain systems that scramble chemically and electronically to restore the balance. When the brain is not able to do this, either the organism *adapts* (permanently changes) or it completely breaks down, which is known commonly as *disease*.

There is no doubt in the minds of a huge majority of the medical/scientific research community that the mind and the body are intricately linked and so, therefore, is the stress response and disease. This is not to say that stress *causes* disease, for there are a variety of other contributing factors. The more stress, the less other factors are needed for the body to break down.

There is good news for leaders wishing to address the stress in their lives. Since stress begins with an amygdala response, then any personal "growth" work that you do emotionally and in your family of origin will help you to recognize when the amygdala is having an electrical storm within you and help you address it. This knowledge, journey of learning and subsequent spiritual growth will then "spill over" and have a positive effect on *all* amygdala-response situations, including stress.

Many people involved in research on stress suggest a "technical" approach to addressing it. By technical, I mean that they propose certain techniques such as breathing, relaxation tapes, yoga, prayer, meditation. There is nothing wrong with these ideas, and in the end, any technique may become an integral part of a healthy human life. However, if they are viewed from the perspective of "solution" alone or even "quick fix," they will fall short, and you will be disappointed in their effectiveness or lack thereof. While these techniques do have the power and potential to calm down the amygdala and its subsequent connecting brain systems, the amygdala can continue to fire instantaneously and continually, despite any relaxation techniques that are being implemented.

Although you may listen to a guided imagery tape and relax your whole body, the moment you "think" of the encroaching board meeting, your amygdala will fire *again*, 1/5,000th of a second later. This restarts the process of tensing your body again. If, however, you take the time and put in the effort to identify, address and process the underlying emotion that leads you to fear the board meeting in the first place ("emotional intelligence"), then it is definitely possible to calm down the amygdala/stress response entirely. As I have said, this takes time and effort, an opening of the trap door, and a re-experiencing of your pain, something that most people are far less likely to do than to sign up for a yoga class. If you take the time to do some research on yoga (or meditation, or prayer, or breath therapy) you will find that these things are based on the same principles as is emotional intelligence.

In Summary

It is easy to imagine the brain as "triune," although contemporary researchers have discovered that it is actually made up of a number of intricate systems using both electrical wiring and chemicals. These systems are responsible for various emotions and functions, none of which are wholly located geographically in "centres."

It is true that the neocortex or "higher" brain is responsible for thinking, but in order to think, and especially remember, it needs to use other parts, such as the amygdala, and even those as "low" as the reptilian functions. Each emotion that we experience or "feel" is a *process* involving many parts of the brain, often including the lower amygdala and higher neocortex.

So the brain is complicated—complicated, but not completely impossible to understand. What is important for anyone who is striving to take leadership in any emotional/relational system is this:

1. The amygdala is not your friend. It is the guard dog of your trap door, and if catered to, may severely inhibit your spiritual growth.
2. It is imperative in leadership to become aware of when your amygdala is activated, even mildly, so that you are not "hijacked" by it.
3. Number one, above, does not apply if you meet a bear in the woods or a large spider drops on you in the carport. This is the time when your amygdala is your best buddy.
4. The amygdala can be "tamed" by:
    a. training the neocortex;
    b. becoming aware of other emotional systems, what they feel like *in your body* and how they work (emotional intelligence); and
    c. being willing to re-experience difficult emotions (your pain) and therefore *process them through the neocortex* so that they are no longer feared.

In order to accomplish #4, above, it is necessary to become as emotionally intelligent as possible, which begins with acquiring knowledge of how the attunement and attachment processes work, and affect amygdalan responses.

Chapter 11:

Attunement and Attachment

A mother is not a person to lean on but a person to make leaning unnecessary.
—*Dorothy Canfield Fisher*

We are not born with our brains. Well, okay, we are born *with* brains, but they are not fully formed or developed at birth. Some theorists even go so far as to say that humans may originally have been inside the womb for 18 months, but when we began to walk upright our pelvises changed so that it was no longer possible to birth a child that large. If this is true, then the first nine months of our lives we are basically still "part of our mothers." Like teaspoon-sized baby kangaroos or pandas in a pouch, humans are meant to be in their mother's arms at least until they can move around some, as well as eat something other than mother's milk.[46]

Mother is not merely a source of food; more importantly, she is the means by which the infant's brain develops properly in a process called "attunement." She also helps the infant develop language skills through a variation of this process. Although the process begins in utero, mother—and to some extent father and significant others—plays an integral part in a child's emotional brain development through a process called *attachment*. It is within the attunement and attachment processes that the amygdala is trained to send out **DANGER!**

---

[46] Infant development and psychology is a larger field of study, and so I apologize for oversimplification for the purposes of this work. I also wish to acknowledge that prenatal psychology is a growing field and to simplify this even more, many factors including the health and stress responses of the mother contribute to the formation of a child's brain in utero, including synaptic connections and chemicals.

signals.[47] Wiring is literally *created* within the brain that is permanent or "hard-wired."[48] Although new wiring can be created later, the wiring created through our earliest experiences remains there for life. It is important to know something about attunement and attachment because your best hope of creating new wiring later on is if you can discover the nature and origin of your original wiring, what it is now that triggers the electrical responses, and what that feels like in your body. In this way, you can "rewire" by experiencing (in small, tolerable doses) the emotions that involve fear and anger so that they can be processed through your neocortex, where they are interpreted more logically.

Attunement[49]

Although it is the 21st century and both mothers and fathers are involved in childrearing, as well as other relatives, nevertheless, a child forms an attachment primarily to one person. This person is the *primary caregiver*. Even today, most of the time, this is mother. Sometimes as time goes on, the child transfers his or her primary attachment to someone else.

Attachment theory was first developed in the 1950s by a psychiatrist named John Bowlby. He worked with James Robertson, who assisted in producing some of the most important original research on the subject. Bowlby also worked closely with Harry Harlow who studied rhesus monkeys, one of our closest animal "relatives." Mary Ainsworth, who studied hundreds of babies and their particular attachments to their primary caregivers, later refined the topic of attachment. The summary below is but a brief overview of the profound contributions of these researchers.

During the "second" nine months of life (the first nine being in utero), a baby's mother is his emotional window on the world. Babies are less interested in looking around at what's happening and far more interested in looking at Mom and what she thinks of it. And this is serious stuff, folks; a child is dependent on its mother for proper emotional development. Of course, every mother falls

---

[47] Some current research supports that this process may also begin in utero.

[48] These references to "hard-wiring" are merely an analogy for the sake of simplicity. They can be misleading. Although new neural connections do get formed, a lot of experience-based change is due to the strength of the neural connections because of the increased number of synapses and increased receptors for neurotransmitters. So the memory depends not on new neural fibers ("wires") but the contact of one to the other. (I am indebted to neuroscientist Dr. Geoffrey Carr, PhD for this footnote to my original manuscript.)

[49] This section is attributed largely to A. N. Schore (1994), *Affect Regulation and the Origin of the Self: The Neurobiology of Emotional Development*.

short of perfect attunement because, after all, she's only human. But the infant human *needs* to see and experience his own emotional state through the "eyes" of a primary caregiver who attunes or "mimics" the child's emotional state.

Your adorable little baby smiles for the first time—what do you do? Smile back! When she is sad or distressed, and pouts with a quivering lower lip, you automatically give her back virtually the same look. You might say something like, "Oh, poor baby's *sad*." When the baby looks at you in a confused, quizzical manner, the chances are that you will return the same look. You usually add words to it as well, like "Ya, what *is* that thing?" It is also true that when a baby shows fear about something that is to be legitimately feared (like an oncoming car), Mother will also show fear in her face and in her body. If a baby shows fear in regard to something he need not fear (such as Grandma or a house pet), Mom will instinctively mimic the fear for a second, then demonstrate calm and happiness. With a smile, Mom will say, "It's okay! It's Grandma!" And she will hold her baby close so that he feels nice and secure. Depending on his age, he will normally stop crying, ponder the situation for a moment, look at Grandma, check back with Mom and calm down. He may even smile along with Mom. Unfortunately, anxious mothers may mimic fear in a baby's face when there is nothing to be afraid of, making for an anxious baby. Anxious babies usually turn into very anxious and fearful adults.

Attunement means that the baby is learning based on Mother's actual emotional state. This is impossible to "fake," and babies are far more perceptive than adults. We can fake a tone to our voice and fake words, but the attunement process is much more subtle than that. Babies are sensitive to very delicate facial expressions that almost always go unnoticed with adults. Even though Mother is smiling with her mouth, her eyes do not smile unless she is smiling on the inside. There are other subtleties to her face, as well. Emotion researcher Paul Ekman did research and experiments on "facial coding"—videotaping and magnifying the face—where he observed and noted thousands of distinct and predictable muscle changes and movements for each emotion.[50] It could well be that the reason some people are more "intuitive" than others is that they are better able to perceive subtle facial changes and therefore know if someone's words are genuine or not.

It could be that Mom may also have a certain smell to her when she is experiencing one emotion or another. As early as a week old, babies can already

---

[50] Paul Ekman, "Facial Expressions of Emotion: New Findings, New Questions" in *Psychological Science* 3, 1992, 34–38.

distinguish the smell of Mother from the smell of other women. If she is afraid, she will also sweat and breathe differently. The muscles in her body will be tenser. All of these things can be "picked up" by the baby. According to physician and author Gabor Maté:

> A loving parent who is feeling depressed or anxious may try to hide the fact from the infant, but the effort is futile. In fact, it is much easier to fool an adult with forced emotion than a baby. The emotional sensory radar of the infant has not yet been scrambled. It reads feelings clearly. They cannot be hidden from the infant behind a screen of words, or camouflaged by well-meant but forced gestures. It is unfortunate but true that we grow far more stupid than that by the time we reach adulthood.[51]

I always find it amusing and sad when couples tell me they never fight in front of the kids or Dad never drinks in front of the kids, so the ulcers their child has, or his phobias or headaches, can't possibly be related to the overall stress in the house.

Babies *know*, and children are pretty damn sure. Mother may say there's no reason to be afraid of a spider, because she doesn't want her child to develop her phobia, but if *she's* afraid of the spider, the child will pick up her anxiety in a millisecond. Unfortunately, it's not so simple as to conclude that the child will also grow up with a spider phobia. She may not. But she will grow up with something, and the severity of it will be directly related to the degree of anxiety the mother is *experiencing* (not necessarily feeling, or being aware of, or displaying). I recently had a client with a severe germ phobia and obsessive-compulsive disorder (OCD). His mother had no diagnosable mental illness, but the client described her as "very overprotective." Translation: anxious.

If mothers keep their faces expressionless when the infant is interacting with them, the infant will become upset. Depressed mothers don't appear to have the energy for attunement and cannot muster up the corresponding emotions of the baby. These children may grow up with a variety of problems, which can include attention deficit hyperactivity disorder (ADHD) or learning disabilities.[52]

---

[51] Gabor Maté, *Scattered Minds*, 73.
[52] National Institute of Child Health and Human Development, *Maternal Depression Linked with Social and Language Development, School Readiness: Maternal Sensitivity Helps These Children Fare Better*, 1999.

Interesting experiments with mothers and babies demonstrate the attunement process[53]:

> - A baby is observed interacting with mother on a closed-circuit TV. Mom mimics the baby's facial expressions, and baby is happy to interact with Mom's image on the TV.
> - Mom is on the same closed-circuit TV but is unable to see the baby and attune to what he is doing or feeling. Even though the baby can see Mom, and she is talking to him the way she normally does, the baby's face registers absolute confusion and eventually the baby becomes distressed.

A baby needs her primary caregiver to respond to her emotional states appropriately. Some mothers are very good at this, and babies grow up fairly emotionally healthy. Some mothers are severely depressed, anxious, neglectful or even abusive, and their children grow up with emotional problems that vary to great degree, depending on the other early experience of the child and the family in general.

No matter how "good" Mother is at attunement, no one is perfectly attuned all the time. For one thing, sooner or later, baby does something that Mother does not approve of. He pulls himself up on the coffee table and grabs the prized figurine with a look of great delight on his face. But Mother does not "attune" to this. She has a look of shock, disapproval or even anger. She may speak sternly to the baby and come and take the object away. He starts to cry. He feels this "out-of-attunement feeling"; we call it *shame*. Shame appears to be a uniquely human emotion, at least in the way we experience it. In our earliest experience, shame is the way we learn what appropriate and inappropriate social behaviour is. It is a *relational* emotion. Because shame is an "out-of-attunement-with-mother" emotion, it feels truly horrible. A baby out of tune with Mom fears for his life: What if Mom rejects me? How could I live? I will die! **DANGER!** Infants and adults alike will go to great lengths to avoid the pain of this cold, isolated, fearful emotion called shame.

In a perfect family upbringing, our feelings of shame are minimal. But they are never non-existent because we need the experience of shame, to some degree, in order to learn socially acceptable behaviour. When shame gets out of control, or there is any sort of trauma or continual abuse, neglect, anxiety or even disinterest by our parents, the seeds of Leviathan are planted, fertilized and watered.

---

[53] Gabor Maté, *Scattered Minds*, 72.

Attachment

The attunement process is only part of a larger phenomenon known as attachment. Being attached is not something we do wilfully, nor is it something we can easily shut off when we grow up. We are attached to important people throughout our lives, but the first few years of life we are particularly attached to our primary caregivers. Attachment extends to other people important to us, but usually there is one person for whom the attachment is strongest, and 99 per cent of the time that is Mother.

Human beings have an emotional system in their brains for attachment.[54] The attachment system involves the amygdala, and therefore it has panic associated with it. The very idea of losing someone we are attached to will instil panic in anyone from a grade schooler to a heavy-weight boxer. When this system is properly developed in childhood, our panic response slows throughout life. We fear loss of significant others, but not to the degree that it debilitates us. If, however, the normal development of the attachment process is interrupted in early years, we may find ourselves completely disabled with a panic disorder, unable to lead a normal life. (There are other factors, which contribute to panic disorders, but problems with the attachment process are almost always a major contributing factor.)

John Bowlby spent most of his psychiatric career researching and writing about attachment. Bowlby's research was remarkable because, instead of psychoanalytical "introspection" (thinking about one's early experience, trying to bring it out from one's subconscious), Bowlby scientifically observed babies and small children.

Bowlby began his scientific study with the examination of other animals with attachment instincts. The most obvious species with an attachment instinct is geese, along with some other birds, which begin to follow their mother *or anyone else* they see shortly after birth. Their migration cycles are closely linked with this instinct. However, human beings are not birds; in reality, we have very little in common with birds. Most mammals are attached for a short period of time, but (usually once weaned) no longer exhibit attachment behaviour. Some mammals do, however, specifically gerbils, female sheep and dogs. Female sheep follow their mothers, who follow their mothers in the flock all the way up the line to the oldest female. Dogs differ from cats, for instance, in that they have an attachment instinct for life. An animal experiment that brings a smile is one where a litter of puppies was raised never having seen a human being. At about six weeks of

---

[54] Some scholars refer to this emotion as "nurture," others "panic" and still others use the inconceivably complex word "love" to describe it.

age, the puppies were let loose into an enclosed pen with a human researcher sitting in the middle of it. The researcher did not move, speak or interact with the puppies at all, yet they spent *the entire time with the researcher* jumping, licking and running in circles as puppies do. Attachment in dogs may not entirely relate to the idea that you, as the master, equal the "leader of the pack." Dogs appear to have some special attachment to humans, simple as that. We don't know why, but we do know why we love them so much—because they "love" us.

Bowlby was heavily influenced by a social worker, James Robertson, whom he eventually hired to do research with young children who were separated from their mothers for one reason or another. In 1952, Robertson made the deeply moving film, *A Two-Year-Old Goes to Hospital*. A classic film now designated as "of national and historic importance," this is not a film for the faint of heart! Far from the children's hospitals of our time where parents room in with their children, these children were torn away from their mothers for well over a week. Visiting was severely restricted. These poor little preschoolers displayed a predictable pattern of clinging, then distress, then sheer indifference, which continued after their mothers returned.

Bowlby presented his early findings on attachment in 1957 to the psychoanalytic community, and was criticized. Prior to Bowlby's research, Freudian psychoanalysts believed that a child's attachment to his or her mother had more to do with her being a source of food, or the oral fixation of sucking.

Around the same time (1957), a researcher named Harry Harlow began working with rhesus monkeys. The rhesus monkey is a "close relative" of the human being, in that they share about 96 per cent of our genes (the chimpanzee is the "closest" relative, sharing 98 per cent). The rhesus is also the second most successful species on the earth after humans, in terms of survival and adaptability to the environment. The handy thing about studying the rhesus monkey is that they grow up four times as fast as a human, and their growth parallels that of humans at this rate. So instead of having to study offspring for 20 years (humans), you can study a rhesus monkey for only five years.

Harlow was particularly interested in attachment or "love," as he called it. He did not accept that mothers and children were only bonded together because of food, and he set out to do experiments on rhesus monkeys. The experiments turned out to be so dramatic that they cannot be replicated today, for it would be far too cruel. Harlow took infant monkeys away from their mothers and put them in a cage with two artificial "mothers." One was made of wire, but had a nipple connected to it and was the only source of food. The other was a cuddly, terrycloth "mother." The infant monkey spent in effect all of its time with the terrycloth monkey. Another film not for the faint of heart! The part that nearly broke me in two watching it was seeing the little baby monkey clinging to the terrycloth "mommy" and leaning over as far as he could to suck the milk from the wire monkey. Subsequent experiments showed that when put into a room and frightened by some new sound or sight, these young monkeys would run over to the terrycloth "mother" and cling to it.

Monkeys raised away from their mothers but in the company of siblings or peers were more likely to be overly aggressive. But baby monkeys with neither peer playmates nor "real" mothers were socially incompetent, unsuccessful at mating and/or neglectful or abusive toward their own offspring.

Bowlby continued to work closely with Harlow for about 10 years. In 1959, Bowlby presented a paper identifying three phases of separation response in a human infant:

1. Protest (sounds so technical but means blood-curdling screaming). The child is not able to be comforted, even by the kindest of nurses.

2. Despair (grief, mourning, sadness). This stage showed children sobbing quietly or being silent and withdrawn. It is as if they have lost all hope of mother returning.

3. Detachment (disengagement, indifference). The child seems to have "settled down." He may be responsive or sociable. However, the child no longer seeks for his mother and virtually ignores her when she returns.

A Secure Base

Bowlby discovered in further research the importance of mothers who provide "a secure base" for their infants and small children. An eight-month-old baby will naturally crawl across a new room to explore it, so long as she can stop every once in a while and look back to check that mother is still there. Small children similarly explore the world and play freely if Mother is stationary. Once she gets up and starts walking, the child's behaviour changes. He may become distressed, or he may walk right in front of her and lift his arms to be picked up. Although perfectly capable of walking, he only feels secure (much like a monkey!) in a carried position, when Mother is mobile.

This stability of Mother extends to her emotional state as well. If Mom is calm and happy, the child will be curious, interested and learning from her environment. If Mom is not "sitting still emotionally" but is anxious, worried or fretting, the child's normal learning (growth) will be compromised. He may be clingy or demanding; he may act out or freeze. Note that these are all behaviours we observe in the preschool, the monkey troop and the boardroom.

Both the experiments with monkeys and the experiments with humans showed the same thing; in order for these offspring to develop optimally, they needed a "mother" who was all of the following:

1. Attuned (not neglectful or depressed)
2. Consistently available and attentive to the child's needs (and not abusive in any way)
3. Calm (i.e., not anxious and not overly attentive to *her own perception* of the child's needs)

Any deviance from any of the above spells trouble for monkeys and humans alike, for problems with the normal development of the attachment process are the birthplace of Leviathan.

Something to Make You Say, "Hmmmm."

Attuned, consistently available, calm. That could be another way of saying meaningfully connected, self defined, emotionally intelligent. Which reminds us of this:

A good mother is the epitome of "good leadership," and perhaps the single most effective agent of change in the universe.[55]

Your Core Narrative

It is helpful in leadership to spend some time reflecting on your earliest childhood experiences and the effects an incomplete attunement or attachment process may have had on you. Again, this is not about blaming your mother. It is about gaining knowledge of self. Even a few sessions with a therapist can be tremendously helpful in getting at the root of your pain as it relates to attachment. You may already have a story or "core narrative" that encapsulates your pain: a neglectful mother, an abusive dad, a significant loss. If you do not, there is some story, however mild, there to be discovered. The value in this discovery is not to make excuses or blame others, but to understand even a portion of the way your emotional brain works and what kinds of similar situations might trigger your amygdala. This is an important component in emotional intelligence. To be oblivious to your earliest experiences is to discount a crucial one-third of the leadership trinity. As such, you will have great difficulty in evoking any meaningful change.

---

[55] I am indebted to my brilliant student, Murray Spear, for this insight.

Chapter 12:
The Nature of Emotion

There can be no knowledge without emotion. We may be aware of a truth, yet until we have felt its force, it is not ours. To the cognition of the brain must be added the experience of the soul.
—Arnold Bennett

A huge part of the activity in your brain is *emotional*. Emotion is not something you consciously do or *feel*. Nor is it a choice, particularly of those who are "weak" or aren't "rational." It is a set of processes in the brain created, shaped and influenced by our earliest experiences of attunement and attachment. Either you are aware of these processes (you "feel" them) or you are not. People who feel easily—who rage or cry—are often deemed "emotional," but they are no more emotional than any other human being; they are just more obvious about it. It may even be easier for these demonstrative "feelers" to work on emotional intelligence than for people who are completely unaware of what is going on in their brains: people who are labelled in our society as "logical," "strong," "tough," "holding it together" or even "cold."

Simply put, an awareness of your emotional processes is important information to you. It is good to be able to identify these emotions and sort them out because not all of them are helpful ("adaptive"). As you acquire more emotional intelligence, you will be able to discover which emotions help you solve problems and which ones don't. For instance, anger can be a helpful emotion in addressing certain types of problems such as being personally violated or protecting one's young. But anger can also be an automatic reaction to fear in which it covers up the fear or is "secondary" to it. It can be excessive, inappropriate and out of your control. Expressing sadness can be a significant part of a healthy grieving process *or* it can be unhealthy self-pity and wallowing. "Good" sadness, although painful, feels deep and alive, whereas "bad" sadness is dark, gloomy and self-destroying.[56] Fear serves an important purpose in your self-preservation, but fear out of control is the number one killer of good leadership. When you are afraid, you will become defensive and avoidant.

Psychologist Dr. Leslie Greenberg, a renowned teacher, author and researcher in the field of emotion, and developer of "Emotion Focused Therapy" or "EFT," differentiates emotions as "primary" or "secondary." Secondary emotions include some forms of anger and sadness as well as hopelessness, despair, panic and hurt. Greenberg lists fear, anger and joy as primary. Other researchers on emotion differ as to which are primary (normally meaning there are specific brain systems for them), which are secondary and which are merely milder or slightly different manifestations of others (e.g., jealousy as anger + fear).

Although various experts differ on the exact nature of each emotion, there is still a great deal to be learned. The more you learn about emotion in general, as well as how emotion is manifested in your body and in your behaviour, the more you will grow as a person and as a leader. You may think you don't need to know anything about emotion to be a good leader. Perhaps you adhere to one or more of the following myths:

> ➤ All I need to do is think through my problems.
> ➤ I'm very calm. I never get "emotional."
> ➤ I'm not emotional because I'm always so rational.
> ➤ I'm very intelligent, so I can think through my problems more easily than most.

I call these myths because your brain is created such that you *are* emotional, whether you describe yourself this way or not. If you are unaware of your emotions, cannot identify each one and give it a name, cannot discover to what degree it is operative, cannot determine what triggers it and what to do about it, you are not more advanced, rational or intelligent than someone who can, you are sadly lacking in the very skills needed to be a good leader and to bring change to yourself or to others around you. The current research on emotion tells us that it is impossible to be rational, in fact, unless you are aware of your emotions. *Trying* to be rational all the time can cause distress and will plunge emotional awareness farther down under the trap door. Understanding your

---

[56] Leslie Greenberg and Jeremy D. Safran, *Emotion in Psychotherapy*, 175.

emotions and not being afraid to experience them is far more beneficial in leadership than avoiding them, which can be downright harmful.[57]

Unfortunately, experts on the neuroscience of emotion cannot agree on which emotions are primary or on how many there are. All of the top 10 emotion researchers[58] list *joy, fear* and *anger*. Six list *sadness*, four *surprise*, four *disgust*, two *shame* and *guilt*, five *curiosity, interest* or *seeking*. The other obvious emotion is *love* or *compassion* or *nurture*. For the purposes of this work, we will assume that all other emotions are secondary to these. Let us now explore these primary emotions in-depth in order to begin the journey toward greater emotional intelligence.

---

[57] L. S. Greenberg, "Introduction to Emotion," Special Issue, *Clinical Psychology and Psychotherapy*, 11, 1–2 (2004).

[58] Darwin (1872), Arnold (1960), Osgood (1966), Izard (1977), Sroufe (1979), Trevarthen (1984), Johnson-Larid/Oatley (1992), Turner (1996), Panksepp (1998), Greenberg (2004).

Chapter 13:
Emotional Awareness: Fear and Anger

Boredom and fear and anger are the reasons that a gull's life is so short, and with these gone from his thought, he lived a long fine life indeed.
—Richard Bach in Jonathan Livingston Seagull

Fear

The fear systems in your brain are the "oldest" from an evolutionary perspective, and they are the most efficient. When you are in the midst of the emotion named fear, you can do little else but be afraid. Most definitely, your cognitive process (a "higher" brain function) is severely impaired.

Whenever anything remotely resembles something you were once afraid of, even a little, it triggers the fear system in your brain. The centre of this system is the amygdala—**DANGER**! So the signals are, at some level, either "run like hell, or kill it." To be sure, the amygdala and company hold the rest of your brain, and very quickly the whole body, up for ransom. *Anything* in the manner of payment, to end this feeling of fear, will do. You may do the dumbest things to stop the feelings of fear. You will go to great lengths to avoid *ever* feeling this feeling again.

Fear equals one thing: Leviathan. Your internal experience will be that Leviathan cannot, must not be let loose. Even though it is irrational, your emotional fear system is telling you through the very core of your being that if Leviathan is let loose, you will die. The feelings will be so overwhelming that you will believe you cannot tolerate them under any circumstances. Unfortunately, the avoidance of Leviathan at all costs is your downfall in every area of life and leadership.

Everything the fear system does to you makes sense if what is threatening can actually bring harm to you as an organism. If someone comes into your office pointing a gun at you, something like this will happen inside your body:

➢ Freezing: the amygdala immediately signals **DANGER!**, and the body temporarily freezes.

➤ Attentiveness: you will stare at the gun and be unable to take your eyes off it. You will not notice a pig flying by the window.

➤ Increased blood pressure, heart rate, breathing, sweating; a surge of adrenalin (which may cause dizziness or nausea or shaking); muscles tightening: all this is in order to prepare for quick flight or to fight off the danger.

➤ The sensation of horror, terror and "doom." If you have thoughts at all, they will be thoughts of sheer terror and panic, as though you are about to die at any moment, and this is the most horrible thing that could possibly happen to you.

➤ Dissociation from reality: your cognitive or "thinking" brain may eventually shut down. You will be unable to reason or think clearly. You may even feel a "floating" feeling *away from reality* or a roaring in your ears, where the words the assailant is saying just don't register. Things may appear to be in slow motion. You may feel as though you will faint or vomit, but you will do neither, for the body knows somehow that this would be dangerous to you.[59]

All of these body responses seem to make sense if someone is threatening your life with a gun. Although virtually useless against firearms, each of these body sensations would be quite helpful if you had to outrun or fight off an opponent without a weapon. The body responses are instinctive in us, and they first come into play in our lives when we perceive that something is threatening the attachment relationship we have with our primary caregiver, and, as time goes on, significant others.

If you are a baby or small child, right up until about puberty, the idea that your parents might abandon you, even "not love you" is just as frightening as someone holding a gun to your head. If your parents were to abandon you at that age, you could die (especially in ancient times when the rest of the community may not have agreed to nurture the orphan child). Children are not able to survive on their own in the forest. So when your mother first "loses it" and screams at you for coloring on the wall, the terror you feel in your body is quite

---

[59] Some people may faint or vomit with shock, but will not be capable of it when the danger level is high; I treat clients with phobias of fainting and/or vomiting (social phobia, emetophobia). Their fear levels are so high, their amygdalae so activated, that ironically they are not capable of either fainting or vomiting when they fear it most.

acute. You will probably experience every one of the body sensations described above. If your mother settles down quickly and soothes you, explaining more rationally and calmly that crayon ruins the walls, and now Mommy will have to work hard to clean them, then you will grow up relatively unscathed by this incident. But the synaptic connections have still been made in the brain. And it is possible they will hijack you at age 50 if you don't pay attention to them. On the flip side, if mother beats you for writing on the wall with crayon, or puts your hand on a hot stove to "teach you a lesson," the synaptic connections will be particularly strong, and you may be emotionally compromised for a very long time.

The problem with fear is that it is out of control in our lives. The synaptic connections are made so quickly you may do stupid things when they are triggered. You may "fight" by angrily screaming back at the person who threatens you, or you may "flee" by distancing yourself from those you love, or avoiding conflict at all costs. Both reactions are devastating in leadership. Fear that is out of control is a dangerous problem in marriage, just as it is in big business. Who wants a CEO who can't think when his fear is triggered?

It takes a great deal of training of the brain to overcome fear circuits, but it is possible. I know it is possible because I managed to overcome an extraordinarily strong anxiety disorder by working at it little by little until those triggers did not hijack me anymore. Once I was able to do that, I knew I could overcome my (much lesser) fear of angry, yelling women. Angry, yelling women triggered circuits that were formed through my experience of my angry, yelling mother. From a "logical" viewpoint, the fear response was not appropriate or proportional to the stimulus. What could a member of the Ladies' Auxiliary, who was upset that I asked for coffee to be served at the strawberry tea, really do to harm me? After time and practice, I was able to listen to the auxiliary member yell and take notice of the reactions in my body. I learned to say silently to myself, "It's all right. It's just a body reaction. You're not in any danger." *This is the process of giving ourselves what a good mother would give us.* After years of attending to this process, it was possible for me to repeat these soothing positive cognitions very quickly to myself, so that I could *think*, and then calmly define myself with the auxiliary member. I might say something like, "I think some people in this day and age might enjoy coffee and don't drink tea at all. But I am interested in your reasons for only wanting tea." And then I could listen attentively to her and try to understand. But before I gained this emotional intelligence, this response was just not possible for me.

Fear in Leadership

Fear paralyzes us in leadership. We are driven by far more fear than we ever imagine. Although the amount of fear one experiences can be related to the Scale, even those far up have little idea how much fear drives them. You may think that only "weak," "wimpy" or "skittish" people are dominated by fear. Nothing could be farther from the truth. *Everyone* is dominated by fear; it is a matter of degree. Very arrogant, rude, domineering people are in fact quite afraid. They don't show it in their tone of voice or body language, but they show it in their arrogance, rudeness and dominance. Their rigidity or stubbornness means that they are too afraid to try to think another way. Bullying, harassing, tyranny and even "strong leadership" can all be signs of fearful people. They may scream, or instead, they may immediately offer up an argument, even a very good one, to opponents. This means they are too anxious or reactive to really listen to what others are saying.

People who say they are "only logical" and are not "emotional" are merely operating out of different emotional circuits, for there is no such thing as "not emotional." Many people have learned to slam their trap door shut by "rationalizing" away the problem. This is not the same as clear thinking, although it may appear to be to an untrained eye. We are people whose emotions are at work every second. There are no "non-emotional people." There are people who are emotionally intelligent, aware of their emotions and working with them, and there are those who are oblivious to them and vulnerable to a hijacking.

Leaders who say they don't like conflict are essentially afraid of others who disagree with them, or their fear is triggered when other people are fighting or arguing. Interestingly, many leaders who say they "don't mind conflict" are also afraid. In such seemingly strong leaders, their fear response is manifested as "fight" rather than "flight." Emotionally intelligent leaders don't mind conflict either, because they are aware of their degree of fear and can think clearly through it.

Becoming a good leader means taking the time to look at how fear operates in your life and doing something about it. We are bad partners, bad parents and bad leaders in community and business because we are afraid. We are afraid of someone finding out that we are flawed, helpless or worthless. We are afraid that if x or y happens, then it will confirm that we are flawed, helpless or worthless, and Leviathan will come roaring out. Our deepest fear is that we will not be accepted or loved.

The route out of your fear is threefold:
1. Learn to identify your body response to fear (where do you feel it in your body?).
2. Learn what may trigger your fear from your earliest experience.
3. Learn how to calm your body once the fear systems are activated.

If your fear response is particularly strong, occurs often or easily or you find yourself constantly in a state of fear, this may be a sign of an anxiety disorder, and you will need to seek professional help.

Identifying the Fear Response

Psychotherapists use an 11-point scale called an SUD scale ("Subjective Units of Disturbance)[60] for research purposes and to measure (subjectively) how afraid someone is. The scale goes from 0 to 10 with 0 being no disturbance and 10 being a disturbance so fearful it cannot be tolerated. At 10 you would be in a full-blown panic attack, physically running away from the situation (if possible) and/or dissociating from reality. This is what happens in a flash back experienced by victims of post-traumatic stress disorder.

The scale is subjective, by definition. However, you may find the following number values helpful in general terms.

10   Panic. Running, screaming, dissociating from reality. Apparent to others.
7–9   Panic attack that may or may not be apparent to others. Rapid heartbeat and breathing, adrenalin burst, sweating, shaking, nausea. If your SUD level gets this high, it will probably have the effect of retraumatizing, which is not helpful in combating or eradicating your fear response.
5–6   Increased heart rate and rapid breathing or holding of one's breath. Adrenalin burst may feel like your stomach "dropped." Muscle tightness, apparent in your jaw, neck, legs and/or arms (usually in a "folding" or protective manner).
3–4   "Butterflies" in the stomach. Nervousness. Desire to avoid the situation or "snap back" in anger. Heart beating faster, holding your breath. Dry mouth. If you scan your body carefully, you will discover subtle muscle tightness.

---

[60] The SUD Scale, "Subjective Units of Disturbance" was developed by behavioural psychiatrist Joseph Wolpe in 1969.

1–2   *Very subtle* symptoms as in 3–4 or 5–6. With practice, an emotionally intelligent leader will learn to identify subtle muscle tightness, elevated heart rate or holding the breath as signs of a fear response.

Combating Fear

1. The first step in learning about emotion and growing as a person is *awareness*. Become aware of your SUD levels under various conditions. Emotionally intelligent leaders will be intimately acquainted with their own body responses to learn which they can identify most easily and quickly. If you believe you "feel nothing," you are unaware of your feelings. For beginners, the most obvious sign of fear is holding one's breath. When I discover I'm doing that, I quickly scan my body for muscle tension, and then determine the degree of fear I'm experiencing in any situation.

2. Try to remember when you've felt this way before and perhaps how old you felt then. Remembering back as far as you can to the roots of the emotional response will be helpful in automatically assuring yourself that what you are feeling is merely a body memory, and you are not really in any danger. Again, if the memories are particularly acute or troubling (such as of abuse or trauma), you may need to seek a caring professional to help you through the healthy processing of these early emotions.

3. Implement self-soothing.
    a. Breathe! Breathe deeply, fully and slowly. Deep breathing automatically slows down the heart, which triggers or "fools" the brain to switch from the symptomatic nervous response (panic) to the parasympathetic nervous response (calming).
    b. Tell yourself any one of these statements and keep breathing slowly until it sinks in:
        i.   I am perfectly safe.
        ii. I am fine.
        iii. I am in no danger.
        iv. I'm okay.
        v.   I'm afraid, but I'm all right.

    c. Scan your body and relax your jaw, neck and leg muscles.
    d. Breathe! Deeply, fully and slowly. Don't purse your lips or blow out on the exhale. Just ensure that the exhale is very *very* slow.

Yoga classes are one way to train yourself in breathing techniques. Deep abdominal breathing is also taught in singing or playing wind instruments and to some extent in public speaking and drama. Guided imagery relaxation tapes are an excellent tool to help you to learn muscle relaxation and body awareness of tension. Practice, practice, practice!

Remember that a calm leader is a good leader. A leader who is fearful, even subtly, will unwittingly whip up anxiety in the entire organization or family relationship system. This will paralyze others and will not lead to any effective change.

Fear Awareness Worksheet

My big fears are:

___

My earliest memory associated with these fears is:

___

The place(s) I feel fear in my body is/are:

___

The triggers for my fear are:

___

The amount of time I feel fear is:[61]
- ❑ Seldom, if ever
- ❑ Only if something is genuinely dangerous to me
- ❑ Anywhere from 10 to 25 per cent of the time

---

[61] The higher percentage of time you indicate, the more important it may be for you to seek professional help with your feelings of fear.

- ❏ At least 25 to 50 per cent of the time
- ❏ More than 50 per cent of the time
- ❏ I feel fearful every day

Anger

Anger and fear are quite close friends. They are both amygdala-driven emotions linked to reptilian responses. Anger, much like fear, is there for the purpose of fighting off predators. When the amygdala signals **DANGER!**, your first instinct may be to run away, but if this is not possible, you will naturally fight to protect yourself from the danger.

Psychologist and researcher Leslie Greenberg has spent an entire career researching and studying emotion. He sees emotion as the main component of human experience (rather than thinking or behaviour). Greenberg writes of two kinds of anger: maladaptive and adaptive.

Maladaptive Anger

Maladaptive anger is that which sort of "covers up" fear or emotional pain. It can take the form of resentment, seething, vengeance or "bitching." It is as if a street-fighting teenager leaps out of your psyche to your defence whenever you sense that Leviathan is near. Unfortunately, this street fighter is usually more trouble than help, for your thinking process has shut down, and you will probably project your emotion onto whoever may be in your path. Your particular street-fighter reaction may range from getting frustrated and annoyed at others and saying something sarcastic, to full-blown physical fighting or a rage disorder. The more there is under the trap door, the more maladaptive anger a person may hold and display.

Maladaptive anger is left over from our evolutionary past and is not necessary for our survival. In our society there is no need to fight someone physically when your "buttons get pushed." Protecting yourself or your family from physical predators is another thing altogether—adaptive anger, but I'm not talking about that. I'm talking about the kind of anger that rises up instantly when you're insulted (or assume/perceive that you are). Someone at work makes a joke that you take the wrong way. Someone criticizes your idea. Someone gives you constructive feedback about your behaviour. Someone calls you into her office for a "talking to." Someone is projecting his anger at you because he is not emotionally aware himself, flying into a rage about nothing.

I was once standing in a line at the toy store at Christmastime. I just joined in the line behind everyone else and partook of my favourite pastime—staring into space or at the back of someone's head. Suddenly, a store clerk stormed up to the people in the front of the line and told us all that we were standing in the wrong place, and didn't we see the chain that was across that checkout. She was very angry and started yelling at everyone. "Are you people *blind*?" she asked. The reaction of those in the line was a study in human nature. Unfortunately, it seemed to ruin everyone's day but mine. I thought it was kind of funny. But most others in the line immediately became angry. I guess they felt insulted. Perhaps they had buttons that were pushed about being "stupid." One man stormed out of the store yelling obscenities. Another woman appeared calmer and began arguing with the clerk. But you could see she was red in the face and her facial muscles and jaw were held tight. Others didn't address the clerk but muttered to others in the line, blaming everyone but themselves. There was probably someone frozen in fear. Nonetheless, it was clear we'd all made a mistake. The clerk's behaviour was unacceptable, but that didn't change the fact that we were all standing behind a checkout marked "closed."

I do not always exhibit such exemplary behaviour when it comes to maladaptive anger. I have my times. The worst is what I call "mother bear." You know how you would just never get anywhere near a mother bear with cubs, because no matter how friendly you are, she'll kill you to protect the cubs? I have all the worst qualities of mother bear. I remember one time at a board meeting, I perceived that a small group of people was "ganging up" on a pleasant fellow whose expertise I respect a great deal. I think I see gifts in him that many others don't. Unlike a bear cub, he was 40 years old, six feet tall and over 200 pounds. When the others questioned him at length, I felt the anger rising up in me, but I didn't know enough to keep my mouth shut. Chaos ensued. What came out of my mouth made little sense. I am less like this with my own children than I am with people whom I assume "need me" to stick up for them. It's ridiculous.

Adaptive Anger

Adaptive anger is quite a helpful emotion. It is the kind of anger that we need when we are *violated*, or we perceive that someone who is truly helpless (such as a child or a mentally challenged, sick or very elderly adult) is violated. When violated, you absolutely need to protect yourself one way or another. If someone violates you by entering your home in the night or physically threatening you or your loved ones, you will need the emotion of anger to fight them off. If you have been cheated or robbed, even in a work situation, you will probably need the aggressive feelings in order to take a clear stand. You may have memories of being violated by your parents in a plethora of ways ranging from their angry or humiliating words to you, right through to physical or sexual abuse or neglect. Unless and until you are able to *feel* your anger about this, you will not be able to heal. Feeling your anger means experiencing it in a safe environment or relationship and processing through it. It does not mean blaming/confronting your parents or projecting your anger back onto them. That would be a maladaptive (useless) form of anger.

In my line of work, there is a sense of violation when decisions are made that harm or exploit others such as vulnerable groups of people or children. It is adaptive anger that gives us the passion to "fight" for the rights of the poor, marginalized and oppressed.

Another form of adaptive anger is that which is experienced as part of a natural human grief response. If you have experienced a loss, you will go through several phases or "stages" of grief, one of which is anger. If you can keep your anger "pure" while grieving, meaning just "feel angry," rather than project it onto others blaming them for your loss, then it will be adaptive. You will not end up an angry, bitter person. Angry, bitter people are experiencing maladaptive anger, the kind that goes 'round and 'round as if on a hamster's wheel, accomplishing nothing but alienating the person from everyone who cares about him.

Anger is a very tricky emotion to become aware of and master. It takes a fair bit of emotional intelligence to be able to tell the difference between adaptive and maladaptive anger. I have met a number of leaders who fool themselves into thinking their anger is appropriate and justified and they are "protecting themselves" or "fighting for the underdog." Unless you have dedicated some clear quality time to sorting your anger out, it is very likely that it is the "hijacking-you" variety (maladaptive).

Legitimate adaptive anger may also trigger unresolved issues, thus maladaptive anger. This may then become all mixed up in your mind. Any "old" anger that is unresolved is festering under the trap door. In fact, everything under the trap door that has not been dealt with may have anger mixed up in it. Old anger, when triggered (even by healthy, adaptive anger) will cause the trap door to fly open. It will then be as if you and Leviathan join forces to beat the daylights out of whoever dared to open that door.

Processing Anger

Emotionally intelligent leaders will undergo a careful and thorough process of self-examination whenever they are angry. This process entails much more than only asking if the situation justifies anger. A healthy process involves the following:

1. When angry, ask yourself first how quickly the anger response kicked in. If it was instantaneous, it's probably an amygdala response and maladaptive unless it is obvious that you are being "instantly" violated such as assaulted. Adaptive anger is more thoughtful and "rises up" more slowly. When we're discussing speed and emotions, remember that we may be talking about milliseconds versus a second or two.
2. Scan your body for signs of anger that may be subtle such as:
   - A rush of adrenalin
   - Tense muscles, which could be construed as a feeling of strength (check particularly your jaws, hands and thighs)
   - Rapid heartbeat
   - Hands subtly forming fists
   - Standing up or feeling as if you want to (which is why sitting down is something you can do to try to calm yourself)
   - A "hot" feeling that may or may not be actual increased body temperature
   - A feeling of "fire," usually in the chest
   - A "rising up" from the belly to the chest, neck and face, coming to rest mainly in the chest
   - Failure to think clearly, in varying degrees

One of the things I try with my clients in therapy when they feel anger rising up is to ask them whether they can imagine taking that anger and putting it away in a box for a short time or moving it aside to a nearby shelf. "It's there if you need it," I say, "but try to put it on a shelf for a bit, and see what else is there for you." If the person is able to "shelve" the anger, it is often secondary to something else. It is quite common for a person to think about this for about one second and then become overwhelmed with either sadness or anxiety. The real emotion that underlies the anger has just been discovered.

Many people who have never spent any time exploring emotion stand up at a meeting or express themselves at work in a very passionate way and find themselves holding back tears (or unable to hold back tears). If these people could discover the underlying emotion when they speak, experience it fully, and "process it out," they would likely not cry when they speak passionately.

The only anger they would experience from then on would be purely adaptive, secondary to nothing.

Another way to know the difference, which is a bit more intellectual, is to explore the phrase "I feel violated" when angry. If you can put some meat and meaning to that phrase then perhaps your anger is adaptive. However, it is interesting to note that lots of people say "I feel violated because_____," and the sentence or concept doesn't make any sense (such as "I feel violated because my husband doesn't care about me," or "I feel violated because salesclerks are so inconsiderate.") They are experiencing maladaptive anger and disguising it as adaptive because it's eating them up so much.

It is not *wrong* to experience maladaptive anger. No emotion is ever wrong. Your emotions are your own experience, and you have a right to feel any feeling that you have. What is unhelpful in leadership, however, is to project anger onto others, especially anger that is maladaptive and all about your own "stuff." Feel it. Own it. Sit in it so that you fully experience or "process" it.

Some people are immersed in maladaptive anger. There is adaptive anger in there, but there is so much maladaptive anger surrounding and infiltrating it that it is impossible to find. These folks are often known as angry people. They fly into rages, yell, scream, rant, rave, and people avoid them whenever possible. Most people locked up in high-security prisons are quite angry. Underneath both the criminal and the business executive who turns purple several times an hour lies a wounded soul with a story that would break your heart if you could ever get close enough to him to hear it without judgment.

We often say of criminals, "Lots of people have bad childhoods, but you don't take it out in violence." Well, frankly, that's easy to say when you don't have that much to be angry about. It's also true that some people manifest their bad childhoods in anger and others in superachieving and others in debilitating anxiety or depression. We admire the superachievers, and we judge those with anxiety disorders or depression, but we don't hate them. People who have issues with anger, unfortunately, spread the poison that has been inflicted upon them onto others. It is merely a regrettable truth of our life together on this planet, however, and not true that these people are inherently worse than anyone else as human beings.

As with every other emotion that becomes maladaptive, the only way out of anger is into it. It is important to revisit the roots of your anger, sort it out and work on it. I know this from experience, as I used to be an angry person. Some may even have described me that way, although I never hit anyone or committed a crime. But I used biting arguments and sarcasm. It took me about two years of hard work to finally get through all of it to the point where I was crying and feeling the pain instead of "burning" on the inside and snapping at the people I loved.

Processing anger can be very similar to processing fear. Just as it is unhelpful to be extremely afraid (an SUD level above six), it is also unhelpful to excessively rage by breaking dishes or hitting pillows. At *lower SUD levels,* this sort of thing may be extremely helpful in processing anger, but at higher levels it will make the rage worse. Again, if you find yourself consumed with anger, you will need to seek professional help. I do not recommend "anger management" programs. Most of them seek to cover up the anger and nail the trap door tighter in 10 easy lessons. They often do not take into account the speed at which the amygdala fires (1/5000th of a second) when they make such ridiculous suggestions as "counting to 10" to calm down.

If you do not suffer from anger to an overwhelming degree, then one of the most helpful techniques to process it is to journal your anger. It's almost as if there is a finite amount of anger to be expressed. The more you write out in a notebook, the less there will be leftover for your family, friends and co-workers. The great thing about journaling is that you can write what you would never dare say to anyone. I encourage people to write the most vile, nasty things they can possibly think of. I also encourage them if "anger journaling," to burn each set of writings in the fireplace, rather than leave them lying around for anyone to find!

Often just the act of journaling will get to underlying emotions, and you will find yourself feeling either pain (most usually) or sometimes fear. This is "getting to the bottom of it," meaning slowly opening the trap door and taking a peek inside. You may be surprised at what you find.

It is an important part of your spiritual growth to be aware of, and process, as much anger as possible so that you can be an effective agent of change in whatever group you lead. While many may argue that anger is a helpful emotion so that you can be passionate and assertive, it is still true that your cognitive functioning is impaired when you are angry. An emotionally intelligent leader will have anger available to "use" when she needs to, but she will be calm and thoughtful about it rather than flying off the handle. You can access your anger easily if you are emotionally intelligent, but you will also develop the ability to shut it down when you need to think.

Anger Awareness Worksheet

The things I'm most angry about in life are:

_____

The place(s) I feel anger in my body is/are:

_____

The triggers for my anger are:

_____

My earliest memory associated with these angry feelings is:

_____

I believe that underneath my anger there is often the feeling(s) of:

_____

The amount of time I feel angry is:[62]
- ❏ Seldom, if ever
- ❏ Less than 10 per cent
- ❏ Anywhere from 10 to 25 per cent of the time
- ❏ At least 25 to 50 per cent of the time
- ❏ More than 50 per cent of the time
- ❏ At any moment, I can fly into a rage

---

[62] The higher your percentage of time, the more imperative it is for you to seek professional help with your feelings of anger.

Chapter 14:
Emotional Awareness: Shame

Shame is the lie someone told you about yourself.
—*Anais Nin*

Shame is the mother of all emotions in an emotional hijacking. Human beings are more motivated by the avoidance of shame than anything else. When I say "motivated," it is ironic, however, because shame does not motivate us to do anything except avoid certain situations and people, and often the enjoyment and fulfillment of life.

Olivia's mother was a single mom on welfare and an alcoholic. From as far back as Olivia could remember, her mother was impossible to be around unless she was drunk, when she became gooey and loving for a short time, then passed out and left Olivia to fend for herself. When her mother was not drunk, she was angry, ridiculously demanding and punitive.

Olivia was terrified of coming home from school at three o'clock because she was almost always greeted by a leather strap. Her mother would force her to do the day's household chores and prepare dinner, from as young as age seven. Olivia could never complete the chores properly to her mother's liking, and so she was strapped. She was told on almost a daily basis that she was "stupid and useless." Her mother would not begin drinking until after dinner, which, to her mother, proved she was not an alcoholic. Once her mother had a couple of hits of whiskey in her, she softened up. She would apologize to Olivia for treating her poorly and tell her she loved her more than anything. This was often followed by hugs and kisses. Then she would promise that things would be different tomorrow, and tomorrow she and Olivia would go to the park together, or the movies, or bake a cake—once she had a chance to get a good night's sleep. But the good night's sleep never came, and mother woke up the next morning angry as a bear, scaring the heck out of Olivia when she got her up in the morning to send her off to school.

As soon as Olivia was old enough to leave home, she moved as far away from her mother as she could. Of course, as the old proverb goes, when you go on a trip, you take your baggage with you. Olivia's baggage was "toxic shame."[63]

Whenever anything remotely reminded Olivia of her mother's words, actions or even her looks, the feeling of shame would come flooding back to her. Olivia's shame was intertwined with the memory of physical abuse and neglect. Her shame was triggered in any of the following situations:

➢ Saying something misinformed
➢ Not knowing an answer to a question
➢ Not understanding something (anything!)
➢ Being yelled at or spoken to harshly
➢ Being in the presence of anyone angry
➢ Experiencing someone make a promise and not keep it
➢ Being near anyone drinking
➢ Being left alone
➢ Being left out of a conversation
➢ Someone changing his mind about anything

When Olivia's shame was triggered in any of the above situations, she would become fearful and outwardly angry and defensive. Unable to recognize her own shame, she would blame others for their words or actions (projection).

The emotion of shame, and its close counterpart, guilt, is not as well researched as other emotions such as anger and fear. It is impossible to do animal research on shame. Animals do not feel guilt and shame the way we do. Now you're going to tell me that your dog feels terribly guilty when he pees on the rug, and I can go along with that to some degree because I have two dogs, and they sure look "guilty" if they pee on a rug or chew up a thousand-dollar digital camera. (I'm not bitter, really I'm not.) Their body language certainly mimics that of guilt or shame in a human: hanging their heads, looking up with their eyes, walking slowly or lying down. So while it could be true that

---

[63] John Bradshaw, *Home Coming: Reclaiming and Championing Your Inner Child*, 47–49.

dogs feel guilty and have some sort of brain system for shame and/or guilt, it is definitely not the same as the human brain system. And how would we know? It's hard to even know if an animal feels joy or pleasure, although we can surmise that it must if it keeps flipping a lever to get the same feeling over and over again. Similarly, if an animal intensely avoids a lever, an area or an object, then we can surmise that this is not pleasurable to the animal, and may induce pain, fear or both. But guilt? Shame? How could we possibly know how Fido or Fluffy feels?

Shame may be a system in the brain that involves fear as well as guilt. Shame is guilt plus helplessness. If you feel guilty about something and are helpless to do anything to fix the situation, this is shame. Helplessness is a mild form of fear, however. Helpless feelings are vulnerable feelings. If we are helpless or vulnerable, we are afraid.

Guilt, uncomplicated by shame, is a useful emotion. Guilt stops us from doing something wrong, bad, hurtful or harmful again. The sense that "this is just wrong, and I would feel *terrible* if I did it" is guilt working at its best. Properly leashed, guilt is a good guide dog. Theoretically, we would only do the same wrong thing once, and then learn. No one (including our parents when we were young) would need to chastise us for something more than once. We would grow up simply *learning* and not having a complex. This would be optimal. But that's never how it goes, is it? For some reason, as I said in the opening chapters, no one comes out of his childhood unscathed. No one comes out without some degree of pain, and the greatest emotional source of that pain is *shame*. Shame is what happens when a simple guilt message, such as, "This is wrong or bad," turns inward to damage the self: "I am wrong or bad."

Shame is the most toxic of all emotions. When you experience too much of it, it reinforces your belief that you are worthless, weak or flawed. This is the Leviathan we fear the most, that ugly monster that dwells under our trap door, lurking there for anyone to discover at any time. Buried deep within, we are utterly, utterly ashamed of ourselves. Shame is the root of most problems in our human relationships.

Shame begins when we are mere infants. Take a look at any eight-month-old baby. They're just learning to pull themselves up on the coffee table and have a little looky-loo and walk around. One baby spies a lovely crystal bowl filled with brightly coloured candies in foil wrappers. The baby's hand reaches out with great enthusiasm, and she grabs the edge of the bowl with a look of sheer glee. Suddenly Mommy says a firm "No! Don't touch that!" The baby's whole world has now changed. Incapable of speech patterns in her brain, she nevertheless "thinks" something like the following:

- Mommy is displeased with me.
- I may be shunned by Mommy.
- I need Mommy to stay safe in this world.
- This is no good! ('cause I really *wanted* that bowl of candy)
- I am disappointed and sad now.
- I will try to convince Mommy to change her mind about the candy *and* accept me and care for me. I will smile at her and go for the bowl.
- Okay, that didn't work; now Mommy is really angry.
- I am afraid if she's angry, she'll leave me, and I'll die.
- I can't believe there's something wrong with Mommy; if she is flawed, she may not be able to care for me, and I'll die.
- There must be something wrong with me.

If the baby's emotional process ends here, with this helpless feeling, she will grow up with shame. If it continues in ways such as the following, then the child may experience an adaptive feeling of guilt, resulting in learning.

- I can fix what's wrong with me (in this case, not touch the bowl).
- If I fix what's wrong with me, Mommy will be 100 per cent available to me again.
- I will not touch the bowl.

But shame will lurk there somehow no matter how good Mommy is at teaching and relating.

Anyone with a baby knows that this process doesn't always work in their little pea-brains right away; it often takes a few tries. And some babies seem to be more willing to have Mommy happy than go for the candy. Nevertheless, the process in their brains is the same, and it is a process of shame. It is inevitable that we come out of childhood feeling some degree of shame because as human beings with a highly developed neocortex, we are *learning* organisms. The only way we can possibly learn anything is if we make mistakes, or at least *are mistaken*, and then we acquire knowledge and move on (to the next mistake). It's a ridiculous notion that you can go through this life and expect not to make any mistakes or get anything wrong, or not know something, or not do things perfectly. Perfection is utterly impossible. To believe that it is possible is the height of foolishness.

The baby in the above scenario will turn out all right in life, if the only thing Mommy does is tell her not to touch a bowl on the coffee table, and similarly guides her into other socially acceptable behaviours. The trouble comes when Mommy has her own issues and starts getting angry at the child for things the child has no control over, because he's still going to think he needs to fix *himself* in order to solve his problem. But he cannot possibly fix himself enough if it's Mommy's issue. Even worse, of course, as we can all well imagine, is the mother who yells at baby or, God-forbid, hits him across the head for something that he didn't do at all, or for some transgression that plainly did not call for that drastic a response. This is how a kid's head gets messed with. This is how stuff gets crammed under the trap door.

Sometimes it doesn't come out until in the therapist's office 40 years later. "Oh my childhood was great," they'll say at the beginning. Then you find out that they were smacked across the face for such silly things as "talking back" (exerting their personhood, a completely natural behaviour for a child). I'm not saying that parents should just put up with a child speaking rudely to them. But *inappropriate* scolding or punishing—punishments that don't fit the crime—lead to an inordinate amount of shame.

There's a lot of controversy out there about spanking children. Needless to say, I am completely and totally against it. Very few parents who spank children do so calmly and rationally after having thoughtfully decided upon this course of action and then carried it out. It is usually done out of anger and nothing else. It is a measure not of the child's crime but of the parent's impatience and the parent not knowing what else to do to stop the child's behaviour. I wish there weren't a separate word for hitting children ("spanking"). If we used the word "hitting" more and "spanking" less there would be less hitting of children. Hitting a child does only one thing to her: it sets up her parents—the people who are put on this earth to keep her from harm—as dangerous individuals.

It's possible that you mean well if you hit your kids; you may believe you are teaching them good behaviour. The problem is, your children may not talk rudely, and they won't grab bowls of candy off tables, but what you are also teaching them is that you are a dangerous person and cannot be trusted. The only way your child can "trust" you if you're someone who hits him is if he comes to believe that *there is something wrong with him*, not you. And the something wrong is not just that he touches crystal bowls or speaks rudely or throws baseballs through windows. The something wrong, that he believes about himself, will be a deep sense of being flawed, helpless or worthless.

The same is true of yelling at children, being angry, unnecessarily scolding them, ignoring them, punishing them or forcing them to do things or see things "your way." All this instils shame: the idea that they are useless, stupid, foolish, flawed, frightened, weak or worthless individuals. This is far more damaging to a child than whatever it was they did that deserved your anger, abandonment, punishment or hitting.

It may be obvious to you by now that all this talk of children is written because *you* were once a child, and this is what happened to you. It happened to you to a degree, which falls along the Scale. The amount of shame you carried into adulthood is directly related to where your parents fell along the Scale.

Shame and Anger

Since shame is such a terrible feeling, and you will do anything you can to avoid it, it is intricately linked to your fear and anger systems. Whenever you feel ashamed or there is a possibility you *might* feel ashamed, anger flares up to "fight off" whatever the thing is that will or might shame you. Unfortunately, this is often another human being.

When Olivia felt shame, she became instantly angry. She wanted to lash out at her children, but feared being like her mother, so instead she became overly permissive, didn't know what to do, and failed to give her children any guidance at all. She would lash out at other people, however: people at work, at the mosque, in the grocery store. She was known as "a bitch" in all of these settings because she seemed chronically angry, and anything would set her off. People formed superficial friendships with her and smiled at her through gritted teeth, further reinforcing her feelings of shame and inadequacy and her belief that others are not genuine and cannot be trusted. Most folks avoided Olivia if they possibly could. Her husband left her, fed up, after 10 years. She was angry about the divorce for the next 20 and regularly spouted off with some other angry friends about how useless men were in general.

Shame in the Body

The feeling of shame is unmistakable in the body once you become accustomed to identifying it. It is perhaps the most horrible of all the feelings, and thus the reason why we go to such lengths to avoid it. For many people, so much anger has been used over the years to avoid shame, that they can't even identify shame itself. Even saying the word "shame" or suggesting they might be ashamed reinforces the feeling and sends it back into hiding. Fear also may cover up the feeling of shame. This makes emotional intelligence very difficult.

When shame is felt purely, it can often be identified as embarrassment, and you may experience a flushing of the face (blushing). It is then associated with feeling "hot." If one scans the upper body and detects this slightly "hot" feeling, shame is probably at play. Shame can be an almost morbid, sickly feeling: a sinking of the stomach and a recoiling feeling in the body. While anger has the body language of moving "forward," shame retreats and makes you feel like you want to curl up in a ball and have the whole world go away. In a sense, it is as if you are naked or violated, your vulnerable underbelly exposed for all to see. You feel as if you want to run away, sink down or assume a foetal position.

Shame, as well as guilt, paralyzes a person. Rather than motivating or having you move forward to solve your problem, it makes you feel as if there is no solution and thus no point in trying. That's if you're not frozen in fear or puffed up in anger to cover/avoid the feeling of shame at all costs. Shame is Leviathan's name and the number one reason for wanting to shut the trap door forever. The feeling of shame can easily be overwhelming, as if you cannot possibly tolerate even a fleeting smidgen of it.

Shame in Leadership
Olivia will have a great deal of trouble in leadership, for everyone she attempts to lead will somehow trigger her shame—it's inevitable. Unless she works to heal it. Shame comes up in leadership again and again. As a leader, you must be prepared to be criticized and even hated. If your shame is triggered easily or if your feelings of shame are particularly acute, this may be impossible for you to manage.

It is important to be able to take responsibility for one's mistakes as a leader, another thing that easily triggers shame. Leaders, being human, always make mistakes, don't know everything, can't please everyone and sometimes move in the wrong direction and have to change course. If you cannot take responsibility for your actions because you are afraid to feel ashamed, you will inevitably fail. This is true whether your fear of shame is manifested in avoidance (retreating) or anger (aggression).

Good leaders must also be able to apologize well. Saying you're sorry for what you did or said or decided is extremely difficult because shame is triggered whenever you admit you were wrong or apologize for something. It is a good exercise in leadership to apologize and take responsibility in something small, kind of like working your way up to the big stuff. I will discuss a more practical approach to taking responsibility and apologizing in chapters 19 and 20. The difficult truth is that the more people you lead and the more significant the organization you lead is, the more likely you are to be wrong, to make mistakes or not to know exactly what you're doing, and therefore the more likely it is for your shame to be triggered. Learn to "sit in" the shame and understand what it feels like and realize it isn't *dangerous*. It won't kill you or drive you to insanity. Sitting in shame is something that should be repeatedly rehearsed. Luckily, leadership will give you lots of practice.[64]

Shame Awareness Worksheet

Down deep, I'm most ashamed of:

_____

The place(s) I feel shame in my body is/are:

_____

The triggers for my shame are:

_____

My earliest memory associated with this shame is:

_____

---

[64] If the exercise of "sitting in shame" brings about physical reactions in your body, unusually high or intolerable anxiety or depression, you should seek professional help immediately and work through your shame issues under the guidance of a trusted and compassionate therapist.

Chapter 15:
Emotional Awareness: Sorrow and Joy

The deeper that sorrow carves into your being, the more joy you can contain.
—*Kahlil Gibran*

Sorrow

The emotion of sorrow could also be called sadness or grief. Whatever its name, it is always the body's response to *loss*. When you lose someone that you have formed an attachment to, your sorrow system is triggered, and you will suffer intense emotional pain. I do not use the term "pain" lightly, or even as a metaphor. The brain system for sorrow evolved, partly, from pre-existing pain circuits.[65] It is also true that these systems are physically very close in the brain to where physical pain responses are generated. To lose someone we love, then, truly is a painful experience.[66]

The sorrow system is quite primal, and we share it with other mammals who in various ways "mourn" the loss of their young or their mothers. At the lowest level, sorrow is experienced as loneliness or sadness; at the highest level, it is sheer panic. This brain system is therefore hooked into the amygdala, which "stands on guard" whenever we become attached.

The idea of losing your primary caregiver at a young age means death to a mammal, instinctively. If those feelings were stimulated only briefly in childhood (such as Mummy going shopping and leaving you with Grandma), the brain circuits eventually rewire themselves, and you are okay. However, if they were stimulated strongly in childhood (such as you suffered the loss of a significant person, abandonment or abuse—physical or verbal) then the emotion is still

---

[65] Jaak Panksepp, *Affective Neuroscience*, 261.
[66] Jaak Panksepp, *Affective Neuroscience*, 267.

"raw," and can get triggered quite easily. If your earliest experience of loss/sorrow was significant enough, you may have panic attacks or another form of anxiety disorder or you may become so fearful of the intense sorrow that you shut yourself down from all emotions and become clinically depressed.

Although there are other chemical factors involved, depression and anxiety disorders are signs that you have not adequately processed your earliest experiences of loss or fear of loss. If this is so, as time goes on, you may begin to avoid any and all painful feelings. Avoidance of pain is always a factor in mental illnesses such as anxiety and depression.

Even if you do not physically lose your attachment figures, but they merely disappoint you or frighten you (no matter how mildly), these brain circuits will be activated and are at risk of being triggered and reactivated throughout your adult life. That is, unless you intentionally seek to experience and process these important emotions.

Unfortunately, we become attached to *things* as well as people. "Things" can be as concrete as a favourite sweater or as abstract as an idea. When we experience the loss of anything at all that matters to us, sorrow is triggered. If you have experienced a significant loss, and any of it resides below the trap door (which it inevitably does), then a "minor" loss in the future will trigger the whole kit and caboodle. You really need to watch out for those caboodles. Since sorrow is so painful, you will naturally seek to avoid it, rather than experience it, even though experiencing it is the only way out of it.

Emotionally intelligent leaders can learn to become aware of even mild feelings of sorrow in the body. Once you have this awareness, you can respond by *grieving the loss*, which is usually a simple process of crying, and/or allowing yourself to feel sad. This processing of sadness will not be overwhelming even though you may think it will be at first. If you really reach deep into your sadness it will, in an odd way, feel "good," and you will most certainly not get worse by feeling it, nor will it last forever. If, on the other hand, you feel sad all the time or cry all the time, or if you cannot feel sad or cry even when you try, this may be a sign of a more serious mood disorder, and you should seek professional help.

The only way out of sorrow is into it. Unfortunately, society gives us the exact opposite advice. So incredible is the human tendency to avoid pain at all costs that we have made a veritable institution of it. Well-meaning others will foolishly advise you to "cheer up," "get your mind off it" or "think positively"—anything but feel your feelings. This kind of advice is such stupidity, I cannot emphasize it enough. Covering up or avoiding pain has become a North American pastime, complete with an entire retail and pharmaceutical industry. Then we wonder why depression and anxiety are running rampant in our culture!

Identifying Sorrow in the Body

You may detect sorrow in your body in any of the following:

- Crying, or tearing up
- Stabbing pain, often in the chest ("a broken heart")
- Tightness or a "lump" in the throat (if tears are held back, the tightness often extends to pain in the chest)
- Weakness
- Apathy, lethargy (a sort of physical "slowing down")
- A feeling of "welling up" from within, rather than rising up like fire (as with anger) or hitting you with a "bang" (as with fear)
- Sinking feeling, as though you are being made smaller

The feeling of sorrow is very painful, and in some social circles (particularly for males), it is unacceptable to express sorrow, so you may go to great lengths to cover it up or avoid it. You may be so successful at this endeavour that other emotions take over and replace the sorrow. The most common one is anger.

An angry person often may be someone who is afraid to experience her sorrow. Anger is an emotion that protects us like a "street fighter" against our pain. Unfortunately, such protection is temporary and most unhelpful in long-term healing. Often, when the anger is fully expressed (such as a "fight" with your partner), you may dissolve into tears. If you think about yourself as an "animal" for a moment, this doesn't make any sense. Why would an animal cry when it needs to fight against something dangerous? Body responses of sorrow mixed in with anger are a sure signal that the anger is secondary. If possible, it should be "set on a shelf" while you experience the sorrow.

Sorrow and Leadership

In business, you can become attached to your visions, creations, ideas, even your office space. If any of these are "lost," you may go to great lengths to avoid feelings of sorrow. The problems come when you find some other emotion to replace sorrow that you think is more socially acceptable. Often this is anger, disguised as "assertiveness" or "strong leadership." Sometimes it is fear or panic, which you may hide. Be aware that both emotions of anger and fear are amygdala-centred emotions ("fight or flight"), and therefore your cognitive thinking process shuts down or becomes severely impaired. If you can take "time out" in leadership, either alone or with a trusted other, to feel your pain and express your sorrow, you will be a much more clear-headed leader.

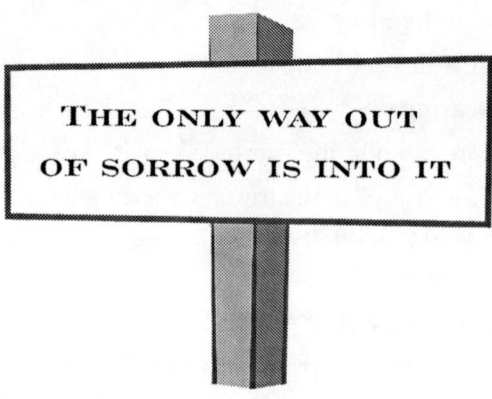

Sorrow Awareness Worksheet

The biggest reason(s) I feel sorrow is:
_____

The place(s) I feel sorrow in my body is/are:
_____

The triggers for my sorrow are:
_____

My earliest memory associated with sorrow is:
_____

I believe that I may currently express my sorrow as:
- Denial
- Guilt
- Anger
- Bargaining
- Other:

_____

Joy

Much like myself, my sister, Sheila, is an intelligent, educated woman. She produces and manages large theatre productions. Nevertheless, when the two of us were going through menopause at the same time, we were subject to brain farts. (Did I not mention these in the chapter on the brain?)

One morning, we were carpooling some folks downtown during a local bus strike. Sheila was driving, and I was on the passenger side. We stopped at a corner to pick up the first woman, and she couldn't get the back door of the car open. Since it normally sticks, Sheila reached back with her hand and fiddled with the lock. "I can't get this door," she said, frustrated. "Oh geez...I can't get this door!" Finally, she managed to open it. The woman got in the back, and we were set to go. Before putting the car back into drive, Sheila paused, frozen, looked at me with a blank expression and said, "Did someone just say they have to get to the store?" It sounded familiar, so our eyes were locked in a mutual vacant stare. The woman in the back chimed in as though speaking to complete imbeciles or visitors from Neptune, "No, *you* said, 'I can't get this door.'"

We completely lost it laughing. Sheila laughed so hard the tears ran down her legs. We stopped at a restroom. Back in the car, only seconds would pass in silence, then one or the other of us would lose it again in fits of hysterics. We laughed the rest of the way to town, dropping off the two women we barely knew who sat in an awed silence the whole trip. That was funny, too. We laughed so much at the mall, we couldn't shop. Then we drove home, and told every person in the family the story and lost it all over again. When I was retelling the story to Charlie, Sheila *literally* fell off her chair laughing. That was exceptionally hysterical. We told the story to my daughter, Alex, who was recovering from an appendectomy she'd had the week before. She had dissolving stitches but laughed so hard some of them ripped open, lending authenticity to the phrase, "I busted a gut laughing."[67]

It is now five years later. Whenever we get together as a family, all someone has to say is, "Did someone say they had to go to the store?" or "Remember the time Alex busted a gut laughing?" and all of our brains automatically "remember" to activate the joy system.

This story is an example of joy at work in an adult who might otherwise be described as "no fun." My husband accuses me of this on a regular basis,

---

[67] I heard the line "She laughed so hard the tears ran down her legs" from author and humorist, my good friend Gordon Kirkland. Gordon's joy system works overtime, and he has the ability to stimulate yours! He is three-time winner of the Stephen Leacock award for humour in Canada. Check him and all his writings out at www.gordonkirkland.com

because I don't like amusement park rides, wrestling on the living room floor or being ambushed and squirted with water. Nevertheless, I do seem to enjoy a good brain fart. Apart from that, my idea of fun is sitting in a coffee shop for hours talking with one of my geeky PhD friends in existential or theological discourse. (What a hoot, eh?)

The part of our brains responsible for fun we share with other mammals: it's often referred to as rough and tumble play or "RAT play." Even rats enjoy RAT play. All infant and adolescent mammals kick it up with their friends. So long as their fear centres aren't activated, you can put two teenage rats together for the first time, and they'll have a heyday. Throw a little cat hair into the cage, however, and they'll spend the whole time freaked out and sniffing around, even if they've never seen a cat in their whole three-month-long lives.[68] This just goes to show you that if we could manage our stress and anxiety, we'd have a lot more fun in general. Show me someone who's *truly* no fun, and I'll show you someone who's probably terrified all of the time: terrified of pain, terrified of Leviathan.

Other mammals' joy systems are most active when they are young, or even adolescent. Young calves skip across the field, kicking their hind legs up just for fun, but you won't see this behaviour in a cow over a year old. Luckily, for us humans, the activation of our brain systems for joy remains throughout our lifetime. I swear I'll still be losing it in the nursing home over that "bust a gut" story. Perhaps the stimulus for fun at this age shifts to cribbage, bingo and shuffleboard, but who cares?

You'll know if your joy system is activated because you'll be smiling. Preferably laughing, but definitely smiling. Smiling is a wonderful human response that starts at a few weeks of age. Smiling originally, in ancient times, showed others that although you possess a number of scary-looking sharp teeth, you do not intend to use them, so you are not a threat. Very early on, smiling became a way to attract our mothers to us. If babies want to be picked up by their mothers, they can do two things, *either* cry or smile. Smiling makes Mother smile, gets Mother's attention and keeps Mother close. Similarly, when adults smile, laugh and are generally fun people, it attracts others to them. People who are negative, whining or frowning all the time are just not all that attractive to other human beings. This unfortunately gives them more cause to whine and be negative. Similarly, people who "fake smile," as if through gritted teeth, unknowingly alienate others. At some level, other people do not trust them.

---

[68] Jaak Panksepp, *Affective Neuroscience*, 18.

Humans can tell the difference between a genuine smile and a fake one. People who fake smiles don't realize that it isn't only our mouths that show a smile on our faces. There are hundreds of little muscles in the face, and most of them are involved in the smile response. If you fake a smile, you are still "frowning" with a lot of your face, therefore, and this is how someone else seems to be able to intuitively "sense" that although you are smiling, you're not actually happy. The moral of this story is that it's best only to smile when it comes naturally. If you're not happy about something, be honest and let the other person know. Then the two of you can work it out, and you can both smile for real.

Joy in Leadership

It would be optimal if a leader were joyful most of the time. This is only possible, however, if the leader is free of fear, anger and sorrow, as once any of these systems is engaged, joy systems are overridden. The best way to experience joy is to feel fully all of your emotions. Believe it or not, once you get good enough at it, you can "schedule" times to process your anger or sorrow. This will serve to lower your level of overall anxiety and stress, so you are less likely to be hijacked by fear. You can then be more successful at "scheduling" joy, and your joy system will be more accessible to you at all times. "Joyful" people are remarkably calm and can even remain playful when others are anxious and serious. Conversely, people who "fake" joy (perhaps laughing nervously, or constantly smiling when there doesn't seem to be anything to smile about) become anxious and serious when others are anxious and serious. The leader who is playful when others are serious will calm the system down. The leader who tries to be playful while experiencing anxiety will come across as sarcastic and disrespectful. In other words, if the playfulness is not genuine, but rather "put on" as a nervous response to the situation, it will be infinitely transparent.

Identifying Joy in the Body

The feeling of fun in the body is pretty easy to spot when it is highly activated; it feels *good*. Unlike being centred in the heart space, the feelings of joy are spread all over the body. Toes tingle, facial muscles lift, tummies jiggle like bowls full of jelly. Joy is a high, like being in love. It's a release of those yummy chemicals along with adrenalin (needed for laughing and rolling on the floor). Unfortunately, because joy and the natural chemicals that come with it feel so good, some people seek after it all the time in an artificial way. They are not willing to go to the hard work of opening the trap door and healing what's under it so that joy just comes naturally.

I once killed a woman laughing. My author-friend, Gordon Kirkland, who won the Stephen Leacock award for humour three times, is envious of me for this particular accomplishment. The woman was 96 and living out her final few weeks in this world in bed in her nursing home with severe chronic obstructive pulmonary disease. In her case, this disease was incurable and would soon be fatal. I was volunteering as a chaplain in the home and dropped by her room for a visit. When I got there, she was propped up in bed leaning over her hospital table, the best position to keep airways open. Her breaths were slow and laboured. "How are you doing?" I asked first.

It took her three breaths to say the one word: "weak." I looked at the information on her chart and was confused by her admission dates. I didn't know why I hadn't seen her before. "How long have you been here?" I asked next. Two more long, slow, difficult breaths, and she replied "a week." It came out as single, breathy word, "week." I smirked at her in my winkish way and said, "That's easy, eh? The same answer to every question." She laughed, then kept laughing. This was not a good idea. Only a few seconds of laughter, and she aspirated fluid, her pupils dilated, and she died. She was DNR (do not resuscitate). Before I told my therapist this story, I let him know that when he heard it, he could laugh first as long as he liked, then he'd need to settle down and help me, for after all, I had killed a woman with laughter. Eventually, I felt reassured that this was probably the best way for her to go.

If only we could smile, laugh and frolic in water, win every game we played, and open presents at a perpetual birthday party until the day we die. And if only we could all die laughing.

Joy Awareness Worksheet

I feel the greatest joy when:

___

Joy, in my body, feels like:

___

The triggers for my joy are:

___

My earliest joyful memories are:

_____

I could activate my feelings of joy more often by:

_____

Chapter 16:
Emotional Awareness: Nurture

Love is a many-splendored thing.
—Sammy Fain

Sarah and Kyle are 17 years old and in their final year of high school. They sit on the couch in front of the TV, entangled in each other's arms, gazing into each other's eyes. She softly reaches out and touches his mouth. "I love how your bottom lip curls over just a bit when you're happy." He responds, "And I am happy," then kisses her. Sarah and Kyle are "in love."

A small child looks up into the face of his father as they walk through the park holding hands. "Are we going to get ice cream, Daddy?" the boy asks. Dad glances down adoringly at his son. "Of course, we are, sport!" He picks up the little boy and swings him around, the pair of them giggling.

"Ah!" remarks a passerby. "See how much he loves that boy!"

Down the street from the park and Sarah and Kyle's place, young Adam, age 10, is playing with his new puppy. Puppy and youngster tire out and flop down on the floor by the fire. The puppy snuggles in under Adam's arm, and the two of them fall asleep. Adam loves that puppy more than life itself. The feeling he gets from just holding him is a deep tenderness he can't remember ever feeling before. He would do anything for that pup.

Elderly Mrs. Parker answers the door on a bleary night. It's young Mary from church, sobbing her eyes out. "What's happened, dear?"

"He broke up with me!"

"Oh dear, dear, dear. Come on in, luv. I'll put on a pot of tea and make you some nice cinnamon toast." Mrs. Parker's compassion for Mary comforts her and makes her feel better. But this act of "love" also makes Mrs. Parker feel better.

Love, or nurturing someone, or being nurtured by them, *feels good*. Enough love and we literally get high on our own brain chemicals, which mimic such drugs as morphine, cocaine or heroin.[69] These feel-good chemicals in our brains are based on the warmth and security of our mother's arms when we're infants or young children. "When we nurture our children...their brain chemicals evoke the comfortable feeling that 'everything is all right.' When children are neglected, other chemical patterns prevail in their brains."[70] The good feelings of the nurture system ensure that we will care for and protect our young. This system is therefore associated with systems for joy as well as for sorrow and panic.

Another Name for Love

In chapters 2 and 7, I discussed the meaning of the word *Love* and the difference between Love and love. Love (capital L) is an action: a way of behaving and making choices or decisions that ultimately help another to grow. As opposed to the active Love, love is a feeling and reflects an emotional process happening in the brain. The stories described above show this emotional brain process in action.

I am more comfortable with the term "nurture" for this brain process than "love." It comes from the same root as "nourishment" or "feeding," which appeals to me because we nourish or feed our own selves as much as others in the nurturing process. Mothers or primary caregivers provide much more than food to their offspring; they also "feed them" at a soul level, by providing them with protection from harm, touching, holding and other forms of soothing. Although I will often use the term "nurture" in this section, you may substitute the word "love" at any time.

The emotional systems in the brain responsible for nurture are intricately linked to attachment. To oversimplify a complicated brain process, nature makes certain that humans experience the emotion of nurturing so that they will care for their offspring, thus ensuring the continuation of the species. It makes sense, therefore, that women are more nurturing than men are, since if left to nature alone, mothers are more important than fathers are to the care, feeding and protection of young. However, men certainly have the capacity for nurture. There is some evidence that males of other mammal species have brain

---

[69] M. Bekkedal et al (1997). "Brain Systems for the Mediation of Social Separation-Distress and Social Reward: Evolutionary Antecedents and Neuropeptide Intermediaries. *Ann. N.Y. Acad. Sci.* 807: 78–100.

[70] Panksepp, *Affective Neuroscience*, 250.

systems for nurture, even though caring for young is not common for male mammals. My friend Doug once saw a father cat "herding" his kittens over a bridge and home after their mother was killed by a car, a far greater anomaly than penguins sitting on eggs or dads pushing strollers.

The nurture system in humans is linked not only to joy, sorrow and panic but also to sexual attraction or lust. It is interesting to note that in our society, nurture and sex do not necessarily go together. Although it has probably been true since the beginning of orgasmic time, now more than ever, people are engaging in sexual activity purely for the sake of the sex, without a long-term commitment to nurturing one another. Nurturing someone *feels good*, and so does sex. Although it is obviously not the same sort of feeling as the intense feeling of sexual arousal or orgasm, nevertheless, when we care for someone else, even if it's making them tea and cinnamon toast, we get a warm fuzzy feeling inside ourselves. Endorphins in the brain do the Watusi. If they get worked up enough, we feel "in love." Contrary to popular myth, and much to the dismay of concerned parents, there's no such thing as puppy love. Teenage pups and octogenarian old dogs have exactly the same chemical process going on in their brains (and yes, I'm talking about humans).

Not only do we love others, but others love us, and in doing so, they feel good themselves. It's important to let someone help you when you need help. Far from "putting them out," you're doing someone a favour if you let her help you or give you a gift. Saying things like "You shouldn't have" to a well-meaning auntie or good friend hurts her feelings and destroys her production of the brain chemical Wf (warm fuzzy). If you want to be equally nice to her, then take the gift and say, "Thank you so much. It really means a lot to me that you would do this." The exception to this rule would be accepting a gift that was inappropriate or ridiculously extravagant.

The nurture system is linked into the systems for sorrow (loss) and fear. Mothers are "programmed" to panic if something happens to their offspring, and offspring are "programmed" to panic if something happens to mother. This is the attachment process at its best. The panic feeling ensures the protection of the young from predators. *If* for some reason something happens to the youngster, or to mother, then both will suffer tremendous grief, a concept that needs no explanation. The mere thought of this grief is overwhelming (Leviathan), and therefore any hint that we could one day lose the one we nurture or are nurtured by invokes fear. A great deal of unexplained anxiety in adulthood is the body's memory of this panic experience (being separated from your mother or your mother harming or neglecting you) at an early age. Often a person was too young to remember these feelings, but his body remembers it with crystal clarity.

Being tuned into your body (emotional intelligence) is imperative, therefore, for healing.

People with anxiety disorders merely experience this same fear to an outlandish degree. But everyone else on the planet knows they don't even want to think about losing someone that they love. This is why when you get dumped, it hurts a lot more than if you dump someone else. The "dumper" has probably ceased to feel feelings of attachment or nurture. The "dumpee" often has not.

The possibility of the pain associated with this kind of loss raises our anxiety and keeps us close to the people who are important to us, especially our families. Healthy, mature couples who are long into their relationships understand that these Watusi-love feelings diminish over time. They are replaced by real Love, and a genuine affection and warmth of companionship. But for some couples, the endorphins were all that they believed they had, and once gone, there seems to be nothing left. They describe this as "falling out of love" or "not loving him/her anymore." If one partner experiences this and not the other, great difficulties and emotional pain may ensue.

We often demand that our children love others when children are not capable of offering nurture to much of a degree, only of receiving it. "Don't you love your brother?" we ask. This is a ridiculous question of a child, because the child does not feel what we feel in relation to her brother. It would be abnormal for her to say so. You sometimes catch a kid hugging or kissing a sibling and talking about how much they love them. This is either a mild foretaste of an adult nurture system (not normally activated until child-bearing years), or else the child is seeking nurture from the sibling, or from his parents as a reward for his good behaviour. Generally speaking, our kids just feel guilty when we ask if they love us or if they love their siblings. My sister and I (neither of whom felt much closeness with our mother, compared to our father) both discovered that we have often mistaken the body feeling of guilt (duty, obligation) for the feeling of love toward our mother.

Many people who are described as loving (also helpful, caring, generous or nice) are in reality anxious individuals. This is not to say that there aren't genuinely loving or nice people. But it is difficult sometimes to discern what is true compassion (nurture) emanating from an individual and what is anxious "niceness." To be sure, whenever the nurture system and the panic system (amygdala) hook together, there is going to be a problem. This is true whether it is you who suffers from "chronic niceness" or any of the people you lead.

An important question to ask oneself is, "How much of this nurturing feeling that I am experiencing is anxiety?" It is good to know how your body behaves, especially subtly, when fear is operative. Once you gain this emotional intelligence you can then examine yourself whenever you feel you want to "help" someone else. How much of what you want to do will help them *grow* and how much will only help you feel good? There is nothing wrong with feeling good, unless you are so concerned about feeling good that you are anxious. If your best friend loses his job and *you* feel anxious and want to help, this is more than likely about your need to feel better yourself. So if you experience fear feelings in your body when you want to help someone, then you need to pull out your "not self" list and turn on that automatic butt-kicking machine.

Identifying Nurture Feelings in the Body

Nurture feelings are delightful in small quantities. The body feels warm, perhaps glowing, usually at the centre of the chest, which is why these feelings have been historically linked to the heart. In large doses, nurture brings about elation, euphoria, pure joy, even giddiness. Generosity will flow out of your pores. (Take note that this will be precedent setting. Once you start ironing her blouses or washing his car, you'll be expected to keep doing that long after the feel-good nurture system has become inactive!) If you haven't been in love lately, watch a good romantic comedy. My favourite at this writing is *Love Actually*, a brilliant film for its genre. It is pretty easy to identify the nurturing feeling in the body when we're in love. There is not even a hint of anxiety associated with it.

The first sign of a bit too much love juice is when you want to say, "My heart went out to him." This is undeniably a feeling "in the heart," reflecting the nurture system at work. However, this sort of sympathy or empathy can go beyond compassion and right into co-dependence or feeling the feelings of another.[71] It is important to examine whether pain (the grief/loss system at work) is associated with it. Painful feelings mean your heart seems to genuinely *hurt*. Pity is nurture mixed with pain. You are entitled to feel pity, just as you are entitled to all your feelings, but the pain associated with it slows down your thinking, and so you are less helpful to the person needing your help. It's best to identify pity and grieve the real loss, which is your own. Doing this will be more fruitful in the long run than fussing about someone else's feelings.

The sign of *way* too much love juice is when the feeling of anxiety kicks in. You feel you *must* help someone because he cannot help himself. You panic *for* someone else. This is not good. Unless you are protecting a (young) child or a truly helpless adult (elderly or mentally challenged, perhaps). Anxiety means

---

[71] A simple definition of codependence is the dependence upon someone depending on you.

the amygdala is activated, and your cognitive functioning is impaired. You will not be much help to others. You will anxiously assume they are not grown-ups and cannot help themselves, so whatever you do for them will only appease your anxiety rather than encourage their spiritual growth. You may be praised, congratulated or even given awards for your generosity or caring, when in fact what you are doing is calming yourself down in the name of compassion for others.

Nurture in Leadership

A good leader will not only love people, he will also love (nurture) them. As a Christian minister, it is easy for me to encourage other ministers to love their parishioners because Christ calls us all to love one another as he loved us. As a parent and a spouse, it is easy for me to encourage others to love their spouses and their children, for this is what society expects us to do. But it is another thing to say to a CEO of a large business, "You should love your employees."

Whatever your level of comfort with the language, the imperative question is this: do you care? Good leaders care about *people:* not their own agenda, not the bottom line, not solely the mission or purpose of the organization. They care about everyone in the system. If it is an anxious caring, it is a problem of yours. But if it is a sincere compassion, a genuine love for your people, it will be a problem for your competitors.

You may be reading this and thinking, "Geez, I really don't give a rat's ass about these people." Don't despair. You do not need to quit your job, and you do not need to learn how to pretend that you care. That would be utterly transparent and worthless. If you don't care about people, then perhaps something is not quite right with the way the nurture system is working in your brain, and it can be fixed—without surgery. What is happening in your brain is anxiety, whether you are aware of it or not. People who come across as cold, uncaring "asses" are anxious people. Anxiety shuts down not only clear thinking but playfulness (joy) and one's capacity to love. Anxiety is present to "protect" what is under the trap door. Leaders who care too little *and* leaders who care too much have the same project to work on: self.

Nurture Awareness Worksheet

I am aware of nurturing feelings when:

_____

The place(s) I feel nurture in my body is/are:

_____

The triggers for my *anxious* nurture feelings are:

_____

The triggers for my *non-anxious* (genuine) nurture feelings are:

_____

My earliest memory associated with nurture ("love") is:

_____

I could activate my own nurture system by:

_____

Chapter 17:

Lesser-Known Emotions

Let's not forget that the little emotions are the great captains of our lives, and we obey them without realizing it.
—Vincent Van Gogh

Motivation

Whenever I wander into a store to look for something, the last thing I want is a sales clerk helping me. For the longest time, I thought that was because I was intimidated and fearful of looking foolish, but as time went on, I came to discover that I was not a shy person. I don't mind asking for things. If something is sold behind the counter, I'm happy to go ask for it. The thing is, it's just no fun if someone else finds it on the shelves. *I want* to search the shelves, excitedly scanning row by row, section by section. Then when I see what I want, I feel a tremendous sense of satisfaction, not only that the thing has been found but that *I was the one* who found it. I guess, as humans go, I have a rather extraordinarily stimulated brain system for "seeking." This system has also been labelled curiosity or *motivation*.[72] Neuroscientist Jaak Panksepp writes, "I would suggest that 'intense interest,' 'engaged curiosity,' and 'eager anticipation' are the types of feelings that reflect arousal of this system in humans."[73]

The motivation system is dependent mainly upon the natural chemical dopamine (affectionately referred to as "dope"). Good dope, man! Dopamine mimics cocaine in the brain. Now I don't have any experience with cocaine, but I've heard that apart from the three small drawbacks of : a) being so addictive that after one hit you have to have more or you go crazy, b) ruining your entire life and c) eventually killing you, cocaine is apparently a lot of fun. I personally

---

[72] Panksepp originally called it the foraging/expectancy system while Jeffrey Gray called it the behavioral activation system....Richard Depue chose to call it the behavioral facilitation system and most investigators now working in the field are beginning to agree that it is a general 'incentive or appetitive motivational system' that mediates 'wanting' as opposed to 'liking'. (Panksepp, *Affective Neuroscience*, 145.)

[73] Panksepp, *Affective Neuroscience*, 149.

have a lot of fun just going into a store and looking for something. I suppose as a vegetarian, it's the closest thing to hunting I'm ever going to do.

I have a brain that produces at least a normal amount of dopamine. The ever-growing number of people who suffer from depression do not. Mild depression is often interpreted as "laziness" or "procrastination" or "lack of motivation." If you have been like this your whole life, you may well suffer from a mild or moderate form of undiagnosed depression. Therapy, or in some cases medication, could make a huge difference in your lifestyle and the way you approach the world.

My 20-something daughter, Katie, is a professional ballet dancer, but she eats up books by the thousands. When she was barely old enough to read and had gone through all the Dr. Seuss and Beatrix Potter collections in the house, we took her to a library for the first time. She was about five years old. The look in her eyes was priceless. She stood in the doorway of the library frozen, beholding with awe the insurmountable number of written pages, sitting there free for the devouring. Katie has a highly developed motivation system. Much like her mother, she has boundless energy for new projects, new ideas, problems, challenges, new ways of seeing something or helping someone else see something. My son is pretty much the same, his drug of choice being electronics rather than books. My husband and my other daughter (both with post-graduate university degrees) learned whatever they had to in as little time with as little effort as possible.

Many people enjoy solving problems, so long as the solution is not so difficult that it overwhelms them or takes up an inordinate amount of time. The solution to problems and discovery of new knowledge is as exciting to the mathematician or academic researcher as it is to the construction worker, homemaker or short-order cook.

If the chemicals and wiring in my brain were just a little bit more activated, I would probably be in big trouble. For, like a tad too much cocaine, too much stimulation of the motivation system and you can end up with a narcissistic or grandiosity disorder. Too much dopamine might explain manic behaviour in people with bipolar disorder; it gives you the feeling that you can do anything.[74] Those with schizophrenia may also have far too much activation of this system in their brains. They believe in the endless possibilities of life to the point where they can no longer distinguish what is real and factual from what is fantasy. The ability to see possibilities for solutions to problems, new goals or what can

---

[74] Panksepp, *Affective Neuroscience*, 144.

be accomplished is said to be *visionary*. Vision is a magnificent gift. Too much "vision" can be anything from a little bit weird to downright psychotic.

Brain systems for motivation probably developed throughout evolution to help us get excited about the prospect of seeking for food and other things we needed for our survival. It would explain why my uncle is far more thrilled about his annual hunting trip than is his buddy. Buddy is independently wealthy and goes for fun. My uncle's family survives the winter on that moose.

According to Panksepp, seeking systems and pleasure/joy systems "must be intimately intertwined in the brain."[75] People who like to solve problems, see new visions and hunt for things get a charge out of it. Otherwise, they wouldn't do it. Lazy people are lazy because they get no charge out of getting up and doing something, whereas the rest of us, at least at some level, find it *fun*. It is therefore not appropriate to judge people who are "lazy," because if we didn't have the dopamine production we do have, we'd be lazy, too. Rats whose seeking systems are electrically stimulated will induce "the most energized exploratory and search behaviours an animal is capable of exhibiting. Stimulated rats move about excitedly, sniffing vigorously, pausing at times to investigate various nooks and crannies of their environment."[76] So apparently, if you just stimulate the right part of the rat's brain, he'll finish the drywall in the basement in record time.

Motivation in the Body

Like joy, motivation is felt throughout the body: a brilliance, a rush of adrenalin, a lightening of all the limbs and almost a tingle. (Ooh baby, look at all those mathematical formulas!) The feeling is very similar to joy/laughter/pleasure, except that rather than feeling like being stationary (as in, in the car with my sister, laughing), I have an overwhelming desire to *move forward*. It's so intrinsic that I can't explain it. Devoid of this feeling in my body, I am most unmotivated. Perhaps that's why I get such a thrill out of those intellectual conversations in coffee shops; I *lean forward*, eager to learn something new. Sports, various forms of exercise or carnival rides just don't do it for me. The tough part is that once I've had my fun researching a book and outlining how I'm going to write it, this system is no longer stimulated, and the grinding out of page after page is utterly excruciating. I know first-hand that seeking has nothing to do with the reward system because I set up rewards for myself for finishing a given number of pages or words, and I don't give a flying fig. It is still boring torture.

---

[75] Panksepp, *Affective Neuroscience*, 149.
[76] Panksepp, *Affective Neuroscience*, 145.

Motivation in Leadership

It is more or less "normal" to be sufficiently motivated to do your job well as a leader. You don't need to get as excited as I do about looking for a particular brand of Roma tomatoes in order to be sufficiently motivated to do well. If, however, you have no zest for your job, don't want to get up in the morning, couldn't care less what happens at work and don't look forward to learning anything new, then you might want to think about doing some work on opening up that trap door. If you're so unmotivated that you cannot do the basic amount of work it takes to do your job, or any job, then it is very likely you suffer from depression and should seek professional help.

It may be that you have sufficient motivation to do your job well, but you would still not describe yourself as visionary. You have little interest in picturing the future and being willing to risk in order to go after it. Well-integrated, mature leaders who are also visionaries make truly extraordinary leaders. However, it is not necessary to be a visionary in order to lead well, because other people in your organization will be visionary. They may not possess much wisdom. They might even border on psychotic. But if *you* are working on self, toward greater maturity and integration, then you can allow other people to be visionary. Listen to them with interest. Trust that they have something to offer. Try not to create or enforce too much bureaucracy that will hold them back.

Motivation Awareness Worksheet

On a scale of 1–10, my experience of feelings of motivation is:[77] _____

The place(s) I feel motivation in my body is/are:

_____

My motivation system is most activated by the thought of:

_____

My earliest memory associated with energetic motivation is:

_____

---

[77] If you answer less than 5, you may wish to consider seeking professional help from a psychotherapist. The lower you score, the more imperative this will be.

When I do not feel motivated, I could stimulate this emotional system by:

Competition/Dominance
Competitive behaviour, and the thrill of competition, is another emotional *system* in the brain. It is a common part of our human experience that winning feels so good and losing completely sucks. We try to convince our children that "it's not whether you win or lose; it's how you play the game" and the equally foolish adage "winning isn't everything." The first time my six-year-old daughter came in second place at a dance competition, she said to me back at the car, "Mom, winning isn't everything, but losing sure is *nothing*." The insight of such a little girl!

Trying to convince our children that winning doesn't matter may change their behaviour (which isn't a bad thing—best to teach kids to be good sports), but it is probably fruitless. Although we want to hold up the principles of inclusiveness and fair play, still, even very mature adults know that winning is the most fun.

Pride
Pride has traditionally been held up as sinful, but in its purest form, there is nothing sinful about it. The problems come in when feelings of pride mix with other emotions. Pure pride is linked to the systems for joy and motivation. A small child may smile when Mom comes in the room or when a clown does a cartwheel in front of him, but just watch what happens when he tries to pile 10 blocks, one upon the other. The tower is teetering slightly with the ninth block. Then…ever so carefully…he places the 10th one on the top and removes his hand. The tower stands! A smile will break out across that child's face. The joy he feels at his own accomplishment is *pride*. If he doesn't know anyone is watching and doesn't tell anyone about the tower, he is feeling purely pride and nothing else. This is not sinful. Pride is the "reward" feeling that will keep him motivated later in life to work hard and find satisfaction in his work.

The problems may arrive when systems for anxiety, and/or competition and dominance come into play. Depending on how much stuff there is under the trap door, the pride system can pair up with insecurities or excessive need for nurture. Pride above the trap door and below it look quite different. Pride (a valid, healthy emotion) should never be mistaken for vainglory.

Anxiety and pride can lead to perfectionism or arrogance. Arrogance will be immediately rejected by others in the system, but perfectionism may be embraced, more so in some cultures than others. We should remember that perfectionism is a neurotic *disorder*, and not the least bit admirable. Some candidates in job interviews have tried to respond cleverly to my question about their weaknesses by claiming to be perfectionists. Imagine the look of surprise on their faces when I stand up and shake their hands uttering the proverbial, "Thanks for coming out."

Shock

Researchers almost all agree that there is a system in the brain for shock; it is evident in the facial coding of every race and culture. Shock registers immediately on the face and is usually linked into the amygdala-based "startle reflex." People with anxiety disorders have overactive startle reflexes and will shock more quickly and easily. When I suffered from anxiety, I used to stand in front of the toaster every morning and watch my toast. Without fail, when it popped up, I would jump. After about 10 years of this, my husband said, "Anna, why don't you just eat cereal in the morning?" Interestingly, since I've been successfully treated for the anxiety disorder, I no longer jump when the toast pops.

In leadership, you can prepare yourself for shock so that the impact of it is less intense. When the sweetest, kindest, grandmotherly school teacher comes into my office to confess to me her deepest, darkest secret, I think to myself: she's going to tell me that she murdered someone and buried them in the church basement. Then when she says something like, "I'm an alcoholic," I don't even register any shock.

If you are ever caught off-guard and hit broadside with something extremely shocking, remember to *think*. Airline pilots are trained over and over to *follow procedures* when alarms go off in the cockpit. The first thing they're told is: don't touch anything right away. Momentarily freezing enables the cerebral cortex more time to respond as it is slower than the amygdala. Almost every time a pilot or a doctor accidentally kills someone, it is because she acts out of her shock and anxiety, rather than with careful thought.[78]

---

[78] I am indebted to Air Canada pilot, Karl Sorensen, and aviation safety instructor, Ross Bailey, for this information.

Disgust

The human animal has a brain system for disgust that is amygdala linked. Disgust serves to keep us away from something that could make us sick or kill us or otherwise expose us to danger. We all agree on the standard disgusting things: filth, vomit, feces, pus, blood, guts and the thought of our parents having sex. If your disgust level goes up high enough, anxiety will kick in, and you will want to "flee or fight" to avoid what disgusts you. This fear response can be so mild, you don't notice it, or it can become completely out of control.

A large part of my therapy practice is treating people with very serious anxiety disorders related to the fear of disgusting things: vomit, germs, blood, medical procedures. These disorders can be completely debilitating in one's life. The cure is to very, *very* gradually expose yourself to what you fear in a safe environment with an extremely caring therapist. Treatment should also include opening up the trap door and having Leviathan sit in the therapy session for a while.

If you do not have an anxiety disorder, but you find yourself disgusted easily (perhaps you even faint at the sight of blood), this can be "treated" or overcome quite easily. When doctors and nurses first begin to train, they have quite high levels of disgust and some even experience anxiety, but as time goes on, they all become accustomed to it and experience very little, if any, disgust.

Although people I treat for anxiety disorders linked to these things adamantly protest, I am happy that our society is less easily disgusted than it once was and that we're very likely to see something disgusting in every movie currently produced. I'm happy because in our civilization we are no longer in any danger when we see something disgusting. We all know about good hygiene, we have access to excellent medical care, and we want men to be changing diapers.

Chapter 18:

Growing into Leadership

We are not born all at once, but by bits. The body first, and the spirit later. Our mothers are racked with the pains of our physical birth; we ourselves suffer the longer pains of our spiritual growth.
—Mary Antin

In order not to be hijacked by your emotions, you must experience the ones you most fear or avoid, and in doing so, "process them out." This is the only way to heal your pain. It is a lifelong process, but you can certainly make a significant dent in it and become a leader who is capable of evoking lasting change, whether as a prime minister, parent or partner. There is only one way to heal your pain, and that is to open the trap door and let it rise up and swirl around you like a cistern full of shit. Then sit in it a while until you get used to it and realize that it's not that bad. There is no way to eliminate Leviathan. And it will not just go away on its own. Unless you are willing to encounter Leviathan, you will never reach that point in your life where you fully and completely and deeply comprehend that Leviathan does not exist.

Self-definition is not possible purely by acquiring knowledge, skill or expertise in one's field. In order to define yourself clearly, you must be emotionally aware so that you know if you are basing your beliefs on logical, rational fact and on ideas or visions that have been well thought through and centred in your principles and core values. The emotional systems operating in your brain have the ability to fool you into thinking you are clear on what you believe or will do when you are not.

The emotions you especially need to be aware of are any that trigger the amygdala. Once that fear centre is triggered, there is a danger you'll turn into a reptile. Your neocortex is so hijacked it is as if it shuts down or, at very best, slows down, and you will not know what you think. Unfortunately, you will not realize that you do not know what you think, and you will assume that you are acting out of well thought-through values when you are really acting out of your anxiety.

If your emotional response is subtle, you may not be emotionally intelligent enough to identify what emotion is at work in your body and will have no clue what is going on. You may make quite foolish decisions out of your anxiety without even knowing it. By "decisions" I mean anything that involves opening your mouth and saying something. By "foolish" I mean that you may alienate or "infect" others and therefore raise the anxiety in the whole system. This will most certainly lead to chaos, moving the system you are trying to change backward rather than forward.

Becoming emotionally aware of your feelings and how each is manifested in your body, especially subtly, is the goal: expertise best learned with the help of an emotion coach of some sort. But as I've said in earlier chapters, it is possible to do with any therapist, coach, spiritual companion or occasionally on your own through the spiritual disciplines of any world religion. This book will not make you emotionally intelligent, no matter how many times you read it. It will hopefully, however, get you started, and inspire you to do further work.

The first step is to develop an "internal eye" for your emotions. Next time you are really angry, for instance, instead of focusing on what it is that you are angry about, try to focus inwardly on your own body. It will be helpful to have a journal or notebook handy to write down what each emotion feels like to you. Notice how you're breathing. Is it quick? Shallow? Do you hold your breath? What about your muscles, specifically in your face, neck, shoulders and legs. Are you holding them tight? What temperature would you describe this emotion as? Sometimes a colour is a helpful thing to think of. Most people think of anger as red, for instance. But what is shame? How does the colour of shame differ from the colour of guilt?

It may be more helpful for you to think of how *old* you feel. I know as soon as I ask myself this question, the answer inside my head is most certainly never 48. I'm in the principal's office when I was 10. I'm fuming in my bedroom at 14 after my mother has scolded me. I'm pining after my sister, who left home when I was four.

Most important is to learn *where* in your body you feel this emotion. Is it primarily in your chest, your "heart" (heart space or solar plexus) or your stomach? These are the three primary sites for feeling our emotional responses. Sometimes, in the case of intense fear or intense joy, we feel a tingling or a wracking throughout our entire body from head to toe. But in milder forms, most emotions can be felt in the chest, centre or stomach. Is it a brimming up sort of feeling or is it a sinking down? Perhaps it is a quick drop in the stomach or a crushing feeling in the chest.

Ask yourself if this emotion urges you to move forward or back. Although extreme anxiety will cause you to retreat, recoil or otherwise withdraw bodily, mild anxiety may cause you to subtly move your body forward as in the desire to fix someone or something. You'll notice people lean forward when they are intensely involved in a conversation, particularly if they want someone else to see something their way. Moving forward may also resemble a loving embrace, when the feelings of nurture are activated, but this is easy to distinguish from anxiety. Pride and the thrill of winning in competition are an upward motion (literally "jumping up and down") whereas shame and guilt lead us to sink, crouch, curl up or cover up. Anger may move you forward as well, but in a more "fighting" motion, or it may cause your body to stiffen. Mild fear may move you slightly backward as in "stay away from me" or "get off me."

Although there are some similarities, people differ in the way they experience or *feel* their emotions in their own bodies. This is why it is necessary to sit up and start taking notice. Once you become emotionally intelligent, you will be able to separate what you think, believe or are willing to do from making decisions or taking actions that merely help you to avoid the feelings of a particular emotion.

Once you have identified the emotional responses in your body—the nature of them as well as their location—you will begin to notice each one more *at low levels*. This is key. What you want to do when you experience painful or fearful emotions at low levels is to *lean into them*, rather than do what is typical and natural—avoid them. Leaning into undesirable emotions unfastens the trap door just a crack. Soon, you'll begin to realize that you can lean in a little more, and a little more. This leaning in opens the gate of healing to the path of spiritual growth.

Mind-Body-Spirit Connection

Few people know how to heal, nurture or foster a mind-body-spirit connection in themselves, despite the plethora of literature and media attention the concept receives. "Mind" means the neocortex where you have decided on the right thing to do in any given situation. In your *mind*, you know how you will parent your children or behave with your beloved spouse or partner. You know that children spill milk and spouses cannot be 100 per cent there for you and your needs because they have needs of their own. You also know what you think about the company's purpose and how that relates to sales and service. You know how employees should conduct themselves and be treated by management. You know what the mission and vision of your church or community service group is, and you know that it cannot be compromised for one or two or even a handful of neurotic people who think differently. This is what is happening in the *mind* of a good leader.

In your body, something else is going on. You are an emotional being, and your emotions are having a hoo-ha in your body. Your body is responding to the hoo-ha by producing adrenalin (which can be thrilling, but in leadership scenarios, it generally feels awful). It also produces other chemicals, good and bad. Your body uses up energy and responds to the stress by mounting a full stress response, which can compromise your immune system and leave you vulnerable to everything from the sniffles to incurable forms of cancer.

In the Christian Bible, the apostle Paul says that our bodies are a "temple for the soul"[79] Every religion understands this connection. Your body can be your best friend or worst enemy. The point is that you can't possibly live your life spiritually, the way you want to, doing the things you want to accomplish—a spiritual journey—if your body gives out on you. It is imperative to look after it. Good leaders will eat properly, get sufficient exercise and as much as possible avoid toxins in the form of junk foods, drugs or excessive alcohol. They will also do their best to manage their bodies' stress response. The way to achieve this is not by taking more days off or longer vacations. It is to inhibit the body from mounting a stress response in the first place. This means healing what is under the trap door so that the amygdala no longer needs to alert you to **DANGER!** when you are in no danger.

It may be a ridiculously obvious statement, but your brain is a part of your body. A healthy brain is a brain that is not continually mounting a stress response. In a healthy brain, the neocortex is in charge of (aware of) the various emotional systems and their triggers. A leader who is healthy in body (brain) will also be clear in mind, knowing not only what she thinks but what she feels as well. Only then will she be able to move from the bourn of self toward others.

---

[79] 1Corinthians 6:19 and 1Corinthians 3:16 (author's own translation and paraphrase from the original Greek text)

Meaningfully Connected

Chapter 19:
Bourn Leaders

The ability to relate and to connect, sometimes in odd and yet striking fashion, lies at the very heart of any creative use of the mind, no matter in what field or discipline.
—George J. Seidel

The bourn of self (which is you, of course) can only evoke change within itself/you by growing spiritually. Growing means becoming more emotionally intelligent, opening up the trap door and healing your pain. This step is unconditionally essential before it is possible for you to make any other change in the only other bourn within which you have influence: that of your closest relationship systems.

The Five Bourns

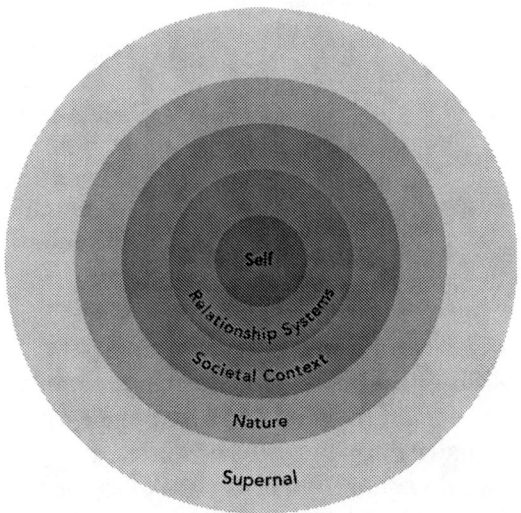

You alone may be the *vehicle* for change in the societal context (the "world"), but not without the help of others in the next bourn to you. This may seem obvious, yet many object to this concept asking the classic question, "Cannot one person make a difference in the world?" A simple answer is yes: Martin Luther King Jr. made a difference. David Suzuki and Princess Diana have made a difference. But their relationship systems were large, or at least became large over time. Each of their societal-changing groups of people began and ended with those who were closest to them, and these eventually numbered in the thousands.

You may help to change laws by writing letters. But if the only letter the world leader receives is a letter from you, it will not change a darn thing unless you are perhaps another world leader. So if you are important enough to the system, and your closest relationship system is large enough, then it may be possible for the societal context to change because of what you do or say. But the change will not be brought by you alone; it will be brought because your relationship system numbers so large that these sheer numbers of people thinking a different way bring change to the rest of the world. For example:

Bourn of Self	Bourn of His Closest Relationship Systems	Bourn of Societal Context
Martin Luther King Jr.	➤ At first, his family, friends and colleagues ➤ Eventually, his church congregation ➤ Later, a small, but ever-growing crowd of people at demonstrations ➤ Ultimately, large crowds who came to hear him speak	Human rights legislation and attitudes about segregation and racism were eventually changed, *indirectly* by King, *directly* by the sheer numbers of people who came to hear him speak, quoted him and marched with him. *Because of these numbers*, King was given the influential position of consulting with lawmakers and powerful leaders.

It does not matter if your closest relationship system is your immediate family, the people within your office, your church or community group, a large corporation or a nation. You must be *important enough to the system itself* in order to evoke the change. You must have sufficient influence or authority within the system. You do *not* need to be the leader in the traditional sense.

In some families, for instance, Uncle Fred is described as a grumpy old man whom the rest of the family virtually ignores or tolerates once a year at Christmas dinner. Fred could change himself by growing personally a great deal, but this growth may not have much of an influence on the extended family because he is not in contact with the family very much. His relationship with the rest of them is just not "close" enough that he can evoke much change to the entire family system. However, a favourite uncle who is visited by and visits with all the cousins and grandchildren regularly may be able to embark upon a journey of spiritual growth, and become a much more wise and integrated individual, thus inducing a great deal of influence upon his family. Even Uncle Fred may work at *becoming* more important to the family system.

You are able to evoke change in relationship systems that hold you to be important because the change that happens when you grow will naturally force those closest to you to grow also. The way this growth and change occurs will be discussed further in Part Three, but here's just a tip: *it is impossible to grow without talking to people*. Especially people whom you don't want to talk to! There is talking to people (connecting) and there is talking to people (meaningfully connecting). The conversations cannot just be about the weather or the hockey game. There is both a science and an art to meaningful connection: the methods must be learned, practiced and perfected. The next two chapters will discuss more fully how this can be done through effective listening and the giving and receiving of feedback or criticism.

Starting Conversations

There is no better method to practice processing your emotions in a healthy way than to connect with others who trigger these emotions. Murray Bowen described the family of origin as the best "laboratory" to experiment with defining yourself, then observing others' emotional reactivity as well as your own. I will expand upon this concept more in subsequent chapters when I discuss how the bourn of relationship systems works and how to "think systems."

Although knowledge of systems is very valuable, even if you don't know anything about them, the formula for change is the same: the leadership trinity. While connecting with others, then, a good leader will have two goals: defining self and becoming more emotionally intelligent.

This translates into two important questions that you must keep in your head. All the previous chapters should have given you adequate preparation and tools to answer them:

1. What do *I think*?
2. What is going on with me (emotionally)?

The third component of the leadership trinity, meaningful connection with others, provides the vehicle for the work of spiritual growth. It's pretty easy to stay calm, keep your amygdala from being activated and keep the trap door nailed shut if you never talk to anyone or anticipate talking to anyone. If you want to grow, you have to be able to risk your anxiety being triggered and experiencing your pain.

A meaningful connection may look like any of the following:

➢ Setting up a meeting with the person who you've heard is angry with you or displeased about something in your group or organization

➢ Going over to your brother's place when you know there has been tension between you for some time

- Calmly responding to someone who keeps saying, "I don't want to talk about it" by insisting that a conversation take place and that ignoring the situation is unacceptable
- Being strong enough to tolerate what gets triggered in you when any of the above examples risks triggering the other person's rage or sadness
- Actually inviting others to get together for a meeting to "air grievances"
- Striving to have all conversations that may become emotional in a face-to-face manner, rather than on the phone or by e-mail
- Immediately picking up the phone whenever you sense that there is an emotional response in someone's e-mail (and preferably setting up a face-to-face meeting)

A *Note about E-mails*
E-mail communication *does not count* as meaningful connection. It is not "meaningful." Nothing could be more meaning*less* these days than hiding behind a computer screen like a coward. E-mails are one step worse than a writing a letter. If the e-mail triggers an emotional response in the person on the receiving end, there is a possibility she can click "send" when her amygdala is still firing **DANGER!**, rather than when her neocortex has thoughtfully processed through all the information. For that matter, you may have clicked "send" under the same circumstances.

If the anxiety triggered in you is too high for you to be able to consider coping with a face-to-face meeting at this time, it is acceptable to *begin the connection* with an e-mail or a letter. The process you go through before sending the e-mail or the letter should look something like this:

- Compose the e-mail in a word-processing document first, so there is no risk you'll click "send" too soon.
- Write in the letter what you'd really like to say if you didn't care about the consequences. Print this letter out, burn it in your fireplace and delete the file from your computer. (I usually fill the time waiting for the letter to burn by stomping around the house screaming, but that's just me.)
- Compose a wise, thoughtful, carefully worded letter to the other. Take as much time as is necessary for this. Don't rush the process.

- ➤ Ensure that the letter *defines self*. It should not contain you statements, accusations, scolding, blame, insistence that the other change or imposing of your will upon the other.
- ➤ Ensure that the e-mail states the *goal you wish to achieve* through this communication and that it is proactive in suggesting a face-to-face meeting at a later time.
- ➤ *Leave it for at least 24 hours.*
- ➤ Read the letter again, being mindful of anything that could be misinterpreted by the other.
- ➤ Run this test: *could I publish this e-mail in the Globe and Mail?* If not, go back and reword it in such a way that you could.
- ➤ Have the most mature, integrated person that you know read the e-mail and point out any parts that sound angry, accusatory, or that could be misinterpreted.
- ➤ Rewrite it and leave it for another 24 hours.
- ➤ Reread it the next day, make any final adjustments and copy it to your e-mail software. Then say a prayer and click "send."

The best way to meaningfully connect is in a face-to-face meeting. I know I've said it before, but it bears repeating: *in order to be a good leader, you have to talk to people.* Folks in different forms of leadership often come to me for advice or share stories in my workshops about some problem or other that they have within their organization. I am continually blown away by the fact that very seldom have they even attempted to speak to the person or people involved in any kind of meaningful way. Here is one example.

The Case of Kayla and Grandma

Twelve-year-old Kayla's parents, Sanwari and Mark, have been divorced for nearly 10 years. Although they shared joint custody, about two years ago Mark ran off to another suburb of the city with a new girlfriend and did not contact his daughter, Kayla, for several weeks. This was a "last straw" for Kayla, and so when Mark finally called her, she refused to speak to him. She vowed never to contact her dad again.

Mark's mother, Kayla's grandmother, maintained a good relationship with Kayla as well as kept in good contact with her son. Grandma blamed Sanwari, whom she never liked, for Kayla's reluctance to see her father. She was under the assumption that Sanwari was putting pressure on Kayla never to connect with her dad again. Grandma remarked to me, "Sanwari doesn't want Kayla running into Mark at my place. I had to promise to keep them separate."

Grandma was becoming increasingly stressed that when Kayla came over to visit, Mark might show up and not only would this be an awkward situation, but it would make Sanwari furious. Grandma went to a great deal of trouble to arrange different visiting times for Kayla and Mark. Even so, she was terrified that during one of Kayla's visits, Mark might just drop in, as he often did. Our conversation about the matter went something like this:

Grandma: I just have to make sure that Kayla and Mark never run into each other. I feel sick every time the doorbell rings when she's over here.
Anna: What are you afraid of?
Grandma: Sanwari! She's such a bitch. She threatened me that Kayla must under no circumstances run into Mark. I can't chance that no matter what.
Anna: What exactly did Sanwari say to you?
Grandma: She said that I had to make sure Kayla never saw him again.
Anna: Were those her exact words, or is that just your assumption about what you think she meant?
Grandma: [looks puzzled]
Anna: Try to recount to me, as best you can, the exact conversation
Grandma: Well, I don't really remember. It was just something in the doorway when I went to pick up Kayla. Sanwari told me, "Make sure Mark's not over at your place when Kayla's there."
Anna: What are you really afraid of?
Grandma: [tearing up] I'm afraid of losing her. That Sanwari will say I can never see her again, either. But Mark's my son, and I can't never see him again either.
Anna: Have you talked to Sanwari about your feelings?
Grandma: No. I never talk to Sanwari about anything.
Anna: Do you think you could? What if you called her up and asked her to go out for a cup of coffee?
Grandma: I guess I could do that. What would I say?
Anna: Well if I were you, I'd just tell her the truth [define self]. Use your I-statements. Try something like this: "Sometimes my son drops in unannounced. I'm afraid he'll do that when Kayla is there, and then you'll get upset. I'm terrified that you'll stop me from seeing

her. I love her, but I love my son, too, and I don't know what to do." Then I'd ask her, "What's your thinking on this?"

Once Grandma was able to tolerate her anxious feelings, she connected with Sanwari, something she had never done in the 14 years she'd known her. It turned out that Sanwari was quite open to the conversation and had no intention of cutting off Kayla from Grandma. She was only concerned that Grandma didn't plan some sort of "ambush" of Kayla and attempt to throw her and her dad together before Kayla was ready.

I wonder how much stress Grandma would still be under if she had not come to the workshop that day and asked this question. Sometimes we have no idea of our ability to evoke a small change like this within our closest relationship systems simply by *talking to someone* rather than assuming we know what they think or want. The next two chapters will discuss two ways to meaningfully connect with others by listening effectively and by giving and receiving feedback or criticism.

Chapter 20:

Listening

To listen is an effort, and just to hear is no merit. A duck also hears.
—*Igor Stravinsky*

Good leaders are not only self-defined and emotionally intelligent. They are also able to remain meaningfully connected with others no matter what their relationship is to them. To be meaningfully connected with people, especially people with whom you disagree, means being able to sincerely and deeply *listen to them*. For most people, this is a skill they have never developed, although they may think they have. To listen to someone properly means two things:

1. You are not waiting for your turn to speak. You have nothing to say; you only want to deeply understand what they think.
2. You believe you have something to learn from them that will potentially change the way you think about a problem or issue or perhaps change your core values or operating principles.

Our learning about how to communicate with others begins when we are mere infants. We hear our parents' voices and may be interested, soothed or perhaps shamed. Whatever we hear, we learn from it. At a very young age, we learn how to speak in order to get what we want or need from others. We learn what they expect of us, so we can please them (especially our parents). This is why we hear what they say to us and respond accordingly. We want to please them, ultimately, so they will not abandon us alone in the woods to die, or more mildly, so we can get what we want or need. By the time we are six years old, we learn to communicate through reading and writing. But by this time, the skill of speaking and hearing what others say is deeply ingrained. At no time yet have we learned how to listen. In fact, if we don't take special training in listening skills as an adult, we may never learn it.

At nine o'clock on a Tuesday night, I make the foolish decision to tell my husband, Charlie, something important. He's watching "Law & Order." I unload a long sob story of what happened at work that day, and he doesn't even look up from the TV.

"Are you listening to me?" I whine.

"Yes, of course, I'm listening. You said that Bill and Marty resigned from the Finance Team, and now you have no idea how the treasurer is going to cope with it."

The thing is, that's exactly what I said. He could always repeat it word for word. And I could never understand what on earth was wrong with me when I felt so horrible, so uncared for, when obviously he was listening because he just repeated back precisely what I had said. As the years went by, unfortunately for Charlie, I learned a lot more about listening. I learned that *listening* and *hearing* are two different things.

People can hear one another quite well when they're not listening, as Charlie demonstrated. They can even repeat what you have said word for word. They have obviously heard, but have not listened. Listening involves more than hearing words. It means being fully *present* for the other person. You must also be ready to learn something yourself, and perhaps share that new insight with them. Sometimes, as in the case of listening to a life partner who's had a bad day, you may need to be available to clarify with her what she has said and what she is feeling so that she can get more perspective on the problem. This kind of active listening is not the same as giving advice.

Good listening skills involve the following:

➢ *Undivided attention* (no TV on!). Charlie knows now that even if it's nine o'clock on Tuesday night, if I start to talk about something important, he will immediately switch off the TV, God bless him. I have also learned to save my stories now for after "Law & Order."

➢ *Body language that shows being interested or engaged.* You will note if you've ever talked with your clergyperson or a professional listener such as a therapist or spiritual director that his chair will already be set up in a way that is directly across from you. This means that his body will be facing in your direction, something that demonstrates he is fully there for you.

➢ *Eye contact.* When people talk, they occasionally glance at the listener, but generally do not keep eye contact with her. An engaged listener, however, will maintain eye contact always. The listener is watching the speaker for facial expressions and body language that accompany the words. This shows how the speaker is feeling emotionally about the subject matter.

> *A genuine interest in what the other person has to say.* (This may be harder to achieve if you aren't the least bit interested in her opinion.) You may not value this person at all. Nevertheless, you value yourself as a leader and want to be a better leader. In order to do that, you need to be genuinely interested in what the other person has to say.

> *A true desire to understand something you do not understand now.* You may think you understand why she feels what she feels or believes what she believes, but if you've never listened to her, then you do not. If you had, you probably wouldn't have a problem. If you really want to understand her, then you have to make up your mind *not* to find fault in what she is saying or come up with something more valid, sensible, logical, interesting, creative or holy.

> *Willingness to leave silence.* When given enough opportunity to think clearly, while another is genuinely listening, people can often sort out and solve their own problems. This is the premise of crisis counselling. Crisis counselling is the easiest kind of counselling to learn because you seldom need to say anything when someone is in crisis. You can essentially sit there and listen in silence. There is no need for "reflective" listening skills, which I personally find annoying and not genuine. Some therapists and counsellors and other professional listeners swear by this method, but I think if I'm in need of this, I'll buy a parrot. Silence is golden, however. If you honestly care about the other, you can sit there fully engaged no matter how much silence there is.

> *No sense that you need to say something.* Listening is *not* waiting for your turn to speak. Go get your highlighter pen. When listening, you are not simply waiting for her to say something so that you can argue with it, find fault with it or challenge it.

> *Setting aside your assumptions.* This is a tough one. Before someone begins to speak, we already have an idea of what we think she thinks, believes and values. And we often don't like what we assume! So truly listening means that you have to set aside *everything* you assume and start by giving the person the benefit of a blank slate.

> *Care and compassion.* You need to care about the person you're listening to. If this is a family member, then it should be an easy concept to integrate. Surprisingly few spouses or parents think of it immediately.

When you're angry or frustrated with a family member, you still care at the deepest level. But perhaps it is a co-worker you hate or who hates you. The best leaders love even their enemies. They care about the people they lead because there is no other way to have integrity in leadership. If you're angry or frustrated with the person, then all the while you're listening to her, try to remind yourself that you love her, that you care. Perhaps when she says the thing that most irks you, visualize holding her in a warm embrace. Embrace her with the love that great religious leaders express clearly. Embrace her with the love of your organization, its vision and its mission in the world. If you only care about making money, then think of it this way: the best way for you to make money is if you are a good leader. And good leadership means caring about the people you work with and really listening to them.

Once you have fully listened to the other person, you may wish to ask what she needs from you. Perhaps it is something that you can deliver. Maybe she only needed you to listen as you've just done. Maybe she needs to know you still care, or love her, or respect her as a co-worker, or value her work and won't fire her. Although she may not express it, one of her needs is what all humans need: to know that she is *not* worthless, weak or flawed.

People don't always see their need for worth and express it that way. Instead, they say things like, "I need you to assure me that the choir will *not* get those gold and purple robes." Well, if you're the choir director and one of your choir's values is democracy, and everyone in the choir but the person you're listening to voted for the gold and purple, then you can't deliver on that. You'd have to say something like, "I'm sorry, I can't do that, because I have to respect the wishes of the majority. What do you *really need* from me—that I'm able to deliver?" You might be surprised that while this is no magic formula, every once in a while, a person responds to it! One time a woman who originally demanded from me that we never change the traditional music in the worship service, responded ultimately, "I need to know that I'm not useless in my old age, and that the church still cares about me." Wow, that was an amazing revelation!

Asking Questions

The only reason you should ask a question while listening is for honest clarification. Sometimes when hearing (not listening) someone will say, "I don't understand," but he doesn't mean it. "I don't understand how you could think that way" means "I think it's ridiculous to think that way." He doesn't want to *understand.*

> Try to avoid "why" questions such as "Why do you care?" "Why do you let him have so much power over you?" "Why do you value that?" "Why do you think that way?" and so on. It's more helpful to frame "why" questions another way, if you are genuinely seeking clarification. For example, "Help me understand your deepest feelings about this issue," "This is really important to you," "So you put a lot of value on responsibility in the workplace" and "Can you say more about your thinking on this one?"

> Be aware that sometimes the same question asked genuinely or not genuinely can have two meanings. For instance, saying, "Why do you care how many other pitchers the team has besides your daughter?" often means "You should not care that the team has several other pitchers besides your daughter." But it can also genuinely mean "Why *do you* care how many other pitchers the team has?" You may assume that he just wants his own daughter to be the star pitcher. You may assume that he only cares about his own kid and not the team at all. But that is an *assumption*, not a fact. It is something in your own mind, and more often than not the way *you* would act in a similar situation!

Just the Facts

There are three things to listen for:

> Facts

> Assumptions

> Feelings

Most people have a difficult time distinguishing the three. They make assumptions when they speak, and talk as though some things are fact when they are not. An active listener will gently ask the person what happened, who actually said what to whom or how he knows something to be true. This is not because the listener will make a value judgment about the answers but because this is *good* listening. Helping the speaker to distinguish between facts, assumptions and feelings will be immensely helpful to him. Here is an example of a client who is experiencing trouble in his marriage. I've added some "commentary" to the dialogue in square brackets:

Client:	She doesn't trust me.
Therapist:	[not knowing if this is fact or assumption] Did she say that?
Client:	Not in so many words.
Therapist:	How do you know she doesn't trust you? [an honest question]
Client:	She's always asking me if I love her.
Therapist:	[genuinely seeking understanding] And for you, that's about trust.
Client:	Well, of course. If she trusted me, she wouldn't ask me that all the time.
Therapist:	So your assumption is that her questions about love are indicative of trust.
Client:	I guess so.
Therapist:	Can you think of any other reason why someone would ask her partner all the time if he loves her?
Client:	I dunno. Maybe she's just insecure.
Therapist:	It could be saying something about her then.
Client:	I suppose.
Therapist:	How does it make you feel when she asks you if you love her?
Client:	It makes me feel like I'm not trusted.
Therapist:	[at this point, the client attempted to go on, but I backed him up a bit for further clarification] Sorry to interrupt you, but that wasn't exactly a feeling, was it? "Not being trusted," I mean. I wonder what emotion is really activated for you in this scenario?
Client:	[who has had a fair bit of emotion coaching already] Well, I suppose it's anger. I do get pissed off when she asks me that. But I guess that's secondary. Down deep I feel…ashamed, I guess. Like maybe I don't love her enough. Or I'm not good enough for her.

At this point, the client now has a clearer insight about himself and can go on to process some of the emotions such as his sense of shame and the anger that it triggers. If the client can feel less ashamed, he will be able to be less reactive to his wife when she asks if he loves her. He will either be able to be playful with her, lessening the serious tone of the interchange, or else clearly define himself by saying something like, "I do love you, as I've told you many times. However, I find it very frustrating that you continually ask me. In the future, I won't respond to this question, but I will only tell you I love you of my own free will." His goal would then be to stay calm and connected to *her* through her inevitable emotional reactivity to this statement. I will outline strategies for how to do this in a later chapter.

There is a good reason that therapists get the reputation of being people who only ask, "How do you feel about that?" and the joke made that it's all you have to know how to do to be a therapist. But like any good stereotype, it's often based on something true. "How does that make you feel?" is an excellent question, as this is what leads to emotional awareness and intelligence. It is a clear question that asks the listener to identify the particular emotion he is experiencing at the time. You should not have to be a therapist to ask it. Good leaders, including spouses and parents, will ask this question often. In listening, this question helps the listener know what is happening for the speaker emotionally as well as what facts or assumptions are coming out of his mouth. Equally valid, yet less made fun of, is the question "What do you think about that?" Knowing what someone thinks is equally valuable information to knowing what emotions she is experiencing. It is a simple rule of thumb to follow that if someone is overly emotional, it's best to ask what she thinks, and if she is overly rational, it's best to ask what she feels. These questions will both engage the neocortex of her brain.

In Stephen Covey's, *The 7 Habits of Highly Effective People*, habit #5 is "Seek first to understand, then to be understood." It reminds me of some words in the prayer of St. Francis: "Grant that I may not so much seek…to be understood as to understand." Covey's "habit" is most helpful in business negotiations or any other time when both parties have something they need to say. In the therapist's office or when speaking to employees or when your wife interrupts *Law and Order*, there is probably nothing you need to say; you only need to listen. But at other times you may have a point you need to get across. If this is the case, you must first listen to the other person(s) as fully and completely as you possibly can. If at all possible, there should be no rushed meeting or time limit. I find it takes at least an hour to fully listen to someone if you are quite skilled and can gently keep them on track and lead them to be more fully disclosing. If you are not a trained listener, it could well take up to two hours. That's before you get to speak. And that's if there's only one of them. If you're dealing with a committee or panel or group of partners, they do *not* all think alike, despite what you may believe or what you have been led to believe.

Covey claims that if you have something to offer the people (as in a business or service or proposal), and you take the time to fully and completely listen to them first, more often than not, they don't even need to hear what you have to say, they will immediately agree with it.[80] This has certainly been my experience as well.

---

[80] Stephen Covey, *The 7 Habits of Highly Effective People*, 254–255.

If you do have something to contribute, such as in a business negotiation, it is sometimes difficult to know when you have fully listened and when you should begin speaking. An easy way to tell if you've listened sufficiently is to watch for how emotionally reactive the other person becomes when you try to say something yourself. If you've never listened to your spouse or your child or your employees, they will at first not trust that you're going to do that. It might be helpful if you announced that you've been reading up about listening and *from now on* (one of my favourite expressions), you're going to be listening more honestly. They still won't trust you completely right away, so try not to get too frustrated with that. Here is an example of a wife who is seeking to really listen to her husband for the first time.

Wife: You seem upset. Why don't you tell me about it? I've been reading this book on how to listen better, and I really want to give it a try.

Husband: Well that would be a first.

Wife: [ignores the sarcasm and waits in silence with a body language that says she's really listening]

Husband: I can't believe those people at work. They're such idiots. Especially my boss. He calls me in on the carpet this afternoon.

Wife: [genuinely seeking clarification] What do you mean by "called you in on the carpet"?

Husband: [expecting perhaps that she doubts his word] What do you think I mean by it? He called me in on the carpet! Demanding answers about the McMillan account.

Wife: [ignores his emotional outburst, doesn't take it personally, and stays the course in trying to listen] What did he say, exactly?

Husband: He *said*, "So tell me what's happening with the McMillan account."

Wife: How did that make you feel?

Husband: What are you, a therapist now?

Wife: I really want to understand how you felt when your boss asked you that question, because in some contexts that might just be a simple question. But it seemed really meaningful to you.

Husband: Well I felt like shit, that's how I felt.

Wife: [has a genuine, puzzled look on her face, but keeps silent and attentive]

Husband: I don't even know what I'm doing with the McMillan account.

Wife: Oh.

Husband:	It freaked me out, that's how I *feel* about it. I don't know how the hell I'm going to get any of it finished by the deadline. Maybe I should just quit right now and get it over with before I'm fired.
Wife:	Wow. [She notes with interest, but doesn't respond out of her rising anxiety that he may be serious about quitting his job.]
Husband:	If I just had more time, I could probably get it done, but everyone keeps bugging me with a thousand other things.
Wife:	[sits in silence as the husband processes through the problem]
Husband:	Maybe if I just called a meeting tomorrow morning of all the staff and let them know not to bother me for two days. Cancel all my useless appointments and delegate some of the piddly stuff to the rest of them. Then I could e-mail the boss and tell him I'll have something final on the McMillan account by Thursday.
Wife:	[affirming] Sounds like a plan.
Husband:	Ya. I guess it's not so bad. Hey, thanks for listening. That was really helpful.
Wife:	What do you need from me the most?
Husband:	Nothing really. It was good just to know you care.
Wife:	Might you have to work late the next two days?
Husband:	Ya, probably. Especially if I get on a roll tomorrow. I won't want to stop.
Wife:	Well, I'll make something for dinner that keeps then. And we'll make plans for the weekend with the family!
Husband:	Great. Thanks, hon. [gives her a hug]

How this interchange could have gone if the wife were not listening:

Wife:	What's bugging you tonight?
Husband:	I can't believe those people at work; they're such idiots.
Wife:	What are you talking about? Who's an idiot? I thought you liked your job.
Husband:	It's got nothing to do with liking my job. It doesn't matter whether you like your job or not, when you get called in on the carpet by your boss then nobody likes their job.
Wife:	What did he call you in on the carpet about?
Husband:	Oh, he's all uptight about the McMillan account. He must think I've got nothing but time on my hands, when I have to deal day in and day out with a bunch of idiots in my department that can't even figure out something simple without knocking on my door and asking me stupid questions.

Wife:	Why don't you just shut your door?
Husband:	What good would that do? They're still idiots! It's still my problem to make the boss happy.
Wife:	I don't think you should put up with that. You're doing a good job on that account. Why don't you give him a piece of your mind?
Husband:	What, and get fired?
Wife:	You could always find another job. People like you are in high demand.
Husband:	I don't want another job. I like this job!
Wife:	I thought you said you worked with a bunch of idiots!

At this point both partners are angry—at the boss and at each other. Nothing has been solved. The husband has not been listened to and thus not been enabled to look at the problem differently and think clearly through it. Furthermore, the relationship between this man and his wife is now compromised.

The Language of Emotion
One of the challenges people have in communication is that they take hearsay or second-hand information and treat it as fact. Another problem is that despite what words come out of someone's mouth, people can *sense* when something is wrong in a relationship. This is true even when nothing is being said. It is imperative for leaders to understand the four essential elements of communication:

- ➢ Words spoken
- ➢ Tone of voice
- ➢ Body language and facial expression
- ➢ Emotion felt (non-verbalized)

Experts in communication vary as to the degree each of these contributes in human relationships, but all agree that *the highest percentage of communication is non-verbal.* I believe communication happens something like this:

- ➢ Words spoken—20 per cent
- ➢ Tone of voice—10 per cent
- ➢ Body language and facial expression—30 per cent
- ➢ Emotion felt—40 per cent

You may choose your words very carefully. You may pay close attention to the tone you are using (speaking calmly and pleasantly, for instance). You may assume body language that looks relaxed and open. You may even smile while speaking. But if you are anxious (including angry) to any degree, no matter how subtly, this *will be* communicated. I believe this phenomenon is the primary source of frustration in most human relationships.

All people have some sort of emotion "radar," so we *know* what's going on despite the other's attempts to hide the truth. Those who are particularly tuned in to their radar are said to be more "intuitive." Intuitive people are perpetually frustrated by people who hide behind spoken words as their only evidence of what has been communicated.

Efforts to keep "family secrets" such as alcoholism, abuse, a lost job or a terminal illness are futile. Every family member knows something is wrong in the family. If the details are kept secret, they will make the details up in their own minds. Sometimes what they make up is worse than the actual secret. Even small children know something is up; their anxiety is raised *higher*, and they are therefore under more stress if they don't know what the secret is. Children are born more capable of coping with bad news than with confusion and secrecy. Businesses about to fire someone or go bankrupt have an "ethos" about them, and if the board is plotting something behind the priest's back, trust me, he'll know.

Effective listening skills are imperative for any leader who wants to meaningfully connect with others. If the leader cannot listen, she will come across as cold and uncaring. Furthermore, people who do not "feel heard" quickly become anxious. In an anxious system, if the leader is devoid of the ability to meaningfully connect, the system is eventually doomed to failure.

Chapter 21:
Giving and Receiving Feedback

Criticism is something we can avoid easily by saying nothing,
doing nothing, being nothing.
—Aristotle

No matter how much you hate to think about it, a vital part of meaningful connection in leadership involves both the giving of helpful feedback or constructive criticism to others and the ability to receive it. In order to really love someone, you must be able to give her feedback that will help her to grow. In order to be a good leader who can evoke meaningful change, you must be able to receive feedback and integrate it into your life without it destroying you. Good leaders know and understand which emotions are getting triggered when receiving feedback, where these feelings come from and how to work toward healing them. Poor leaders project blame when criticized, or else try to do everything perfectly so that they are never criticized. Both kinds of leaders may waste their time and energy obtaining more knowledge, skill or expertise, assuming that the more they know, the better they are able to lead.

The more emotionally mature and integrated you are, the easier it is to take criticism. Here's a well-kept secret: *no one* likes criticism. Anyone may become emotionally hijacked when receiving it. At the deepest level, we believe that we are somehow flawed, weak or worthless. And so at some point, criticism will inevitably trigger these feelings. If there is a lot under your trap door, criticism will trigger you easily and often, and you will not be able to hear it without feeling extremely wounded. You will avoid conflict, violating the imperative of meaningful connection and you will not define yourself clearly to others out of fear of being criticized.

Receiving Criticism

Here's a little card I give to everyone in my classes. It's a simple four-step formula to use whenever you receive criticism (or feedback).

1. Do not defend yourself.
2. Ask yourself how much of this is true. Own up and apologize.
3. What emotions are being triggered? What do you feel?
4. Decide how much of this is their issue and respond with compassion.

STEP 1: *Do not defend yourself.*

When you are criticized, to some degree or another, your amygdala will become immediately engaged. People are afraid of criticism for a number of reasons. If you are far enough down the Scale, you will fear criticism because it triggers your trap door, which may be covering a whole mess of pain. Even those near the top of the Scale fear the door opening at some point.

Human beings also naturally fear rejection. As part of the animal kingdom, we live in groups. We cannot live apart from the group; we need other human beings, not just for companionship, but to learn life skills, to work or to shop. We also need friends and a pleasant environment in which to work, preferably where we are not hated. So being rejected from the group is something to fear. Hence, when you are criticized, before you can possibly *think*, your amygdala signals you: Oh, no! He's going to say something about me that I can't possibly fix! I'll be fired/divorced/punished/hated. **DANGER!**

Once the amygdala is activated, you cannot think about how best to respond unless you are fortunate enough to have either been in this situation before or to have previously thought through what you would do or say if a situation like this ever arose. When the amygdala is engaged, the *first* thing you are likely to automatically respond with is a defensive statement such as:

- I didn't do it.
- It wasn't me.
- I have no idea what you're talking about.
- I'm sorry; I didn't mean it.
- I'll change back/fix it/change my mind.
- Yes, I did it, and it was right, and who are you to say otherwise?

None of these may be the best response. In fact, there is nothing thoughtful about any of those responses if they automatically come out of your mouth in the first few seconds after you hear the critique. The only way to engage the neocortex is to memorize this important response to criticism: *do not defend yourself.* If you cannot defend yourself, then your brain is forced to engage other parts than the fear response. It is forced to think. Now this doesn't mean that you will never *eventually* defend yourself; in the end, you may refuse to take responsibility for the thing being said about you. But you should never do this without thinking it through.

Some people's amygdala immediately engages whenever there's any hint of blame. One member of my family, who shall remain nameless, defends himself before anyone even includes him in the conversation. "All the cookies are gone," I say to someone else in a perfectly calm, blame-free tone of voice. "I didn't eat them," he quickly chimes in, although no one was talking to him. Now, did anyone say that he ate them? Or that anyone did for that matter? What we have here is an overactive amygdala!

Not defending yourself right away will be uncomfortable. It will force you to sit in the feeling of shame for a time. Since shame is the most toxic and uncomfortable of all feelings, many people avoid conflict and hate criticism. It is the avoidance of that horrible feeling of shame. Shame is triggered in almost all people with the mere implication that they have done something wrong or have not understood something properly. Since we hate shame more than anything, we want to dispose of it quickly. Nevertheless you will discover that if you can sit in the shame for even a short time, you can tolerate more of it than you thought. After all, you have not admitted to any sort of blame or even responsibility by not defending yourself. You're just standing there listening.

STEP 2: *How much of this is true that I can own up to right now?*

Often when you are accused of doing something, you genuinely have done it. You just don't want to admit it. If you are chronically late, then it might indeed be true that you don't care about the feelings of the people who are constantly waiting for you. Perhaps you hate waiting around, so you would rather that others do it. If such is the case, and someone sits you down Lovingly and respectfully and tells you that your lateness is a problem, then shame or no shame, it's best if you admit to it and try to do better from now on. This is good leadership; this is growth.

Admitting that you were foolish or thoughtless or careless or uncaring or disrespectful or unthinking or selfish in any given situation does not make you a foolish, thoughtless, careless, uncaring, disrespectful, unthinking, or selfish *person*. It means that you, as a normal *good* person, slipped up and didn't engage your brain fully before you spoke or acted in that one instance or period of time. *Everyone does this.* Slipping up, making a mistake or using poor judgment at any given time in your life makes you a member of the human race and nothing more. Anyone who would judge you for this all the time has a problem himself, and such judgment says more about him than you any day.

It's okay to admit when you are wrong, or even when you didn't think about others before you acted. If Mother Theresa were never seen to have acted poorly, it is because she was able to accept criticism about herself at some point in her early life, took responsibility for what part of the problem was hers, learned and grew from it. She was not *born* a better person than you. Besides, everyone knows it takes an exceptionally great person to admit he is wrong and take responsibility for his actions. So why wouldn't you want to be thought of as an exceptionally great person? To defend yourself, especially when you and everyone else know darn well you made the mistake, does not make you a great leader; it just makes you an ass.

Effective Apologizing

People do not know how to apologize properly in this world. This may seem like a grossly general statement, but I'm sticking to it. When you force a child to muster a resentful, "I'm *sorry,*" it's more about you winning a power struggle with the child than it is about the child actually learning something. Merely *saying* "I'm sorry" does not necessarily make anyone else feel better. The truth is, you are often still not *thinking* but merely reacting emotionally in defence when you apologize. You are still trying to defend your own actions, words, honour or your *self* in the process. Then you wonder why people don't think you're very sincere.

What We Say	What We Really Mean
I'm sorry you feel that way.	But I'm not sorry for anything I did or said.
I'm sorry *if* I've done anything to offend you.	But I really don't think I have.
I'm sorry I'm late; there was a lot of traffic (or any other excuse).	I wouldn't have been late except for the traffic, so I'm really not to blame. Never mind that I didn't leave early enough to allow for traffic. I'd rather you wait than me.

I'm sorry you were hurt by what I said.	Although there was no need to be; this is entirely your problem.
I'm sorry I let you down. I'm going through a really hard time right now.	I'm not really sorry, because it wasn't my fault. I'm a victim. Sob, sob, poor me.
I'm sorry I said what I said but *you* were being really demanding.	I'm not really sorry. It's all your fault. *or* Although I'm taking some responsibility, I'm still as good a person as you, because you make mistakes, too.
I'm sorry, but….	I'm not really sorry; there was some other, outside cause or person or situation that made me do what I did. I am not responsible for my own actions.

There is only one way to apologize, and that is to take full and complete responsibility for what you did or said, with absolutely no excuses whatsoever. Along with that (oh yes, it gets better) you must find some quality of your *character* that was compromised in this particular situation, admit to it, and seek to improve, learn from the experience, and do your best not to compromise it again. Rather than saying, "I'm sorry I kept you waiting so long" you should make a more genuine apology by saying, "I'm sorry I kept you waiting so long. That was really *selfish* of me." Or "that was really *thoughtless*" or "that was really *disrespectful* of me."

The reason you don't normally say things like this in an apology is that a) it triggers your shame, and shame feels horrible, and b) it leaves you vulnerable to another potential "attack." You assume (unconsciously, usually) that the other person now has ammo and will use it at every turn. You fear they'll respond, "Aha! So you admit you're selfish! About time. Let me fill you in on all the other times in the past year when I've seen this selfishness." This situation is your worst nightmare, because you imagine you will be sitting in shame for an eternity while they dredge up every darn thing you've ever said or done in your lifetime. The opposite is almost always the case, in my experience. Once you make yourself vulnerable to someone else and admit that you're wrong, and have growing to do in terms of your character, they're usually completely gob-smacked. A true apology will often bring the biggest, meanest bully to his knees in admiration of you.

It is also helpful to end every apology with a sincere promise to do better. And then follow that through, of course! I find that once people are willing to make themselves vulnerable enough and tolerate the shame enough to apologize deeply and properly, the whole exercise leads to their spiritual growth, and they are far less likely to commit the same or similar "offences" again. In other words, seldom will anyone memorize the words above and prattle them out when caught in some indiscretion, without any intention of changing anyway.

STEP 3: *What emotions are being triggered? What am I feeling?*

There may be no need to apologize because you may not be responsible for anything. Perhaps it's everything you can do to keep your mouth from flying open and a steady stream of defensiveness to come pouring out. Now is the time for emotional intelligence! While it is obvious that shame is triggered in most of us whenever we are criticized, there may be other emotions at work, as well. Although fear and shame are linked together, for some people the fear can be crippling. If it is, your ability to think through the problem and refrain from defending yourself will be even more compromised.

It may be that anger immediately comes up, probably as secondary to your fear. You can easily confuse a sort of "righteous anger" about the issue itself with your own emotional reactivity in defence of yourself. I routinely hear from the graduate students in my seminary classes that anger is a legitimate response in some situations. While I cannot argue that fact in general, in particular I am always skeptical. It takes a tremendously wise, integrated person to be able to differentiate between anger as a *chosen* response, deemed the only appropriate one for this occasion, and anger as merely being hijacked by your amygdala, and seeking to defend yourself.

I don't consider myself to be tremendously mature, although I think I have some understanding of what that would look like at least. But I promise you that whenever I have assumed that my anger is justified and I'm choosing it, I've been wrong. After some time to think about the matter, I have always come to realize that my anger has been a reaction of mine that is "covering up" fear. Once I work through whatever it is I'm afraid of, lo and behold, the anger goes away. When it does, I am able to argue the facts of the issue much more effectively. Again, emotional intelligence is the key. Anger is primary if you or a helpless person or child is being violated. Even when this is so, secondary or "unresolved" anger may lead you to places you don't want to go. Having said that, it is still important to emphasize that anger is always legitimate or justified *as an emotion of yours*. You have a right to feel any and all of your feelings. The issue is only one of responsibility: "I am angry," not "You make me angry."

It is possible for criticism from another to trigger your grief or sadness. If it does, you will do everything in your power to stop it because no one likes the feeling of grief. If grief is triggered, you need to sit in your grief and mourn whatever it is that's your primary loss: a parent, a childhood or an innocence gone at too early an age. If you can sit in your grief instead of running away from it, then it is far less likely to come up and bite you in the backside when someone at work criticizes you.

You might well be asking, "When exactly am I supposed to be analyzing my emotions while someone is reaming me out for being late or not listening or boobing up something at the office?" You can definitely do it while you're being yelled at. The more you work at emotional intelligence, the more quickly you'll be able to know what's going on for you. During the reaming out, you can be scanning your body for recognizable signs of certain emotions, especially the ones that tie into the amygdala (grief, shame, anger, fear).

Once you start thinking about your emotions, you will begin to engage other brain systems such as:

> The neocortex, or cognitive *thinking*

> The seeking system (being curious about what is happening to you, what is up with the other person, how you might learn/grow/look differently at the problem)

> The pride system

To engage the pride system when one is criticized is not about covering up your mistakes or trying to pretend you're perfect. Be proud of the fact that you are able to experience this shame. Be proud that you are learning and growing. Be proud that you can hear this criticism and integrate it into your life without blaming others. Be proud of *who you are*, knowing full well that who you are and what you do are two different things. You are not your mistakes. You are not your selfish or uncaring slip-ups. You are so much more than that. Believe this! Engage the pride system in your brain. It will absorb the criticism and make it feel less painful.

STEP 4: *How much of this is their issue?*

Only after you have fully and completely explored Steps 1—3 can you move on to Step 4. While it is important to take responsibility for your actions and words so that you will learn and grow, it is equally important not to make yourself available for blame when you are not to blame. Conflict expert, David Augsberger, in his book, *Caring Enough to Confront*, draws a clear difference: "I am willing to take responsibility. I am not available for blame."[81] It may even

---

[81] David Augsberger, *Caring Enough to Confront*, 75.

be that you are not even responsible for what has happened or what the other person is upset about.

Sometimes it is just not about you or what you've done. In which case, the other person's feedback is not feedback at all, but projection of his emotions or emotional issues onto you. Do not make yourself the target of someone else's emotional reactivity. And do *not* react back. This will get you into a feedback loop or "hot potato" of reactivity, and you will get nowhere.

The more emotionally reactive the other person is (angry, blaming, rude, unreasonable), the more likely it is that the issue is not about you, but a projection of hers. People give helpful feedback or constructive feedback in a calm, rational, respectful manner. They project blame in an angry, accusatory manner. (It may be that there is some element of both in either that you will need to discern.)

If you decide that this is not something you've done at all or have any part in, then it's good to pull out that "INAM" card from chapter 6. Remember, it stands for "It's not about me." It is about *her* emotions, *his* issues, *her* reactivity, and *not* about you, what you've said or what you've done.

I believe I heard Marianne Williamson once say that if someone else is upsetting you, and it's really about them, then the only appropriate response is compassion. Once you are free from the fear of sitting in shame and can exercise more mature control over your own emotional reactivity, you will be capable of caring deeply for those who have not yet made this journey. Compassion vibrates in our cells and is transmitted mysteriously to others. True compassion (felt, not spoken) is also the music that soothes the savage beast.[82]

---

[82] I know that's a misquote. William Congreve's line from *Mourning Bride* reads, "Music hath charms to soothe the savage *breast*." I just got tired of my readers "correcting" it from right to wrong!

Part Three

The Bourn of Relationships

Chapter 22:
Thinking Systems

You cannot understand a cell, a rat, a brain structure, a family, a culture if you isolate it from its context. Relationship is everything.
—Marilyn Ferguson

To become a good leader who may begin to evoke meaningful change, you must define yourself, discern what you think and value and the principles out of which you will operate. You will learn listening skills and covenant to stay meaningfully connected with others. You will also develop a good understanding of your own brain and work on yourself to become more emotionally intelligent and mature. Good leadership definitely begins in the bourn of self. However, to be effective as an agent of change, it is also necessary to understand the bourn of relationship systems, for human beings exist and function in relationship with one another. *While it is impossible to be a good leader without focusing primarily on self, it is equally impossible to be a good leader without understanding the emotional systems in which you are operating.* You must learn to "think systems."[83]

Human beings do not live independently of others. This is a simple fact. You require other people for your own survival. Even a hermit living in a cabin in the woods is dependent on the knowledge of other human beings in order to survive. (How else would he know how to farm or build anything?) Not only

---

[83] This section on "thinking systems" is credited to James Grier Miller, *Living Systems*. New York: McGraw-Hill, 1978, and James Grier Miller and Jessie L. Miller, *The Earth as a System*, Center for the Study of Democratic Institutions, University of California at Santa Barbara, in "The First International Electronic Seminar on Wholeness," www.newciv.org/ISSS_Primer/seminar.html, (2000).

do you need others to live, you have less control over your individual life than you think. As much as you may balk against it, you are part of a living system, intricately linked to other human beings.

Since you do not live independently in this world, it is impossible for you to take leadership in the bourn of self without reference to the living systems (closest relationship systems) in which you exist. These two bourns have a symbiotic relationship; each exerts influence over the other. In order to evoke a change, *even in your own life*, you need some knowledge of systems and the way they work. Whether you are aware of it or not, the system is changing and influencing you all the time.

The fundamental nature of all life is *process*. If life forms stop processing energy or information, life will end. The process that happens in an amoeba is fairly simple to perceive and understand. Over the years, scientists have also made great advances in figuring out how the various processes in the human body work. However, even mapping out our entire DNA has not brought every answer to why bodies sometimes work well and at other times break down. As systems become larger (such as groups of humans existing together), the number of variables that may or may not contribute to how well either our own bodies work, or how we work together in relationship, become increasingly larger and more complex. It is the premise of this book that not only our emotional health but even our physical health and well-being is highly influenced by the relationship systems in which we exist.

A system is any set of components with common properties that interact with one another in relationship. A system behaves a particular way because of the interaction of its components. *Living systems* have organic molecules such as DNA. Non-living systems (like computers) do not. A living system can be as small as an amoeba or as large as a multi-national assembly. Each of these has similar characteristics, believe it or not, which "systems scientists" have identified. A living system interacts with its environment as it exchanges information and energy with it.

James Grier Miller has identified seven levels of existence within living systems:

1. Cells—made up of molecules.
2. Organs—as particular groups of cells, organs carry out the processes of the system.
3. Organisms—multiple cells and organs together (an example of an organism would be a plant, animal or human).

4. Groups—any two organisms that interact form a group. A family is an example of a group. Most animals do not form living systems any higher than groups.
5. Organizations—this is a group that has two or more levels ("ranks" or "echelons") in its structure. An example would be a religious denomination, a university or a province.
6. Societies—a society has all the components necessary to survive without anything else. It is made up of many different kinds of organizations.
7. Supranational systems—these are two or more societies that decide things together, such as the United Nations.

Figure 21 shows the various components of living systems from the perspective of the five bourns:

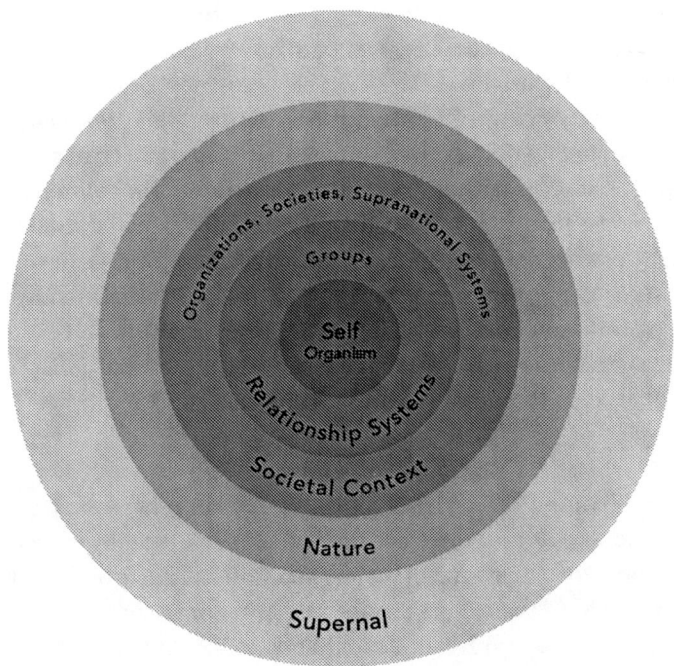

No Escape

Most people understand that cells, organs and organisms are "living systems" in that they are biological or "alive." But what about systems beyond this level, particularly the *group*, as Miller calls it, such as the family unit? Although there is no physical link between organisms, systems theory tells us that there is some sort of energy that links us to the other organisms (other humans) within our group or relationship system, and insofar as there is, these systems are "alive" *and function as a whole.*

What your family does, says and experiences affects *you*—as an organism; it affects your very *organs and cells*. We don't like to think about this too much. Part of what makes us human is our ability to think for ourselves and figure out our own problems. We like to be in control of our lives, and when others threaten, anger or upset us in some way, we often wish that we could just not be around them any more. Systems theory, supported by quantum theory and the "new biology," tells us this is scientifically *impossible*. You cannot move to Siberia to get away from your toxic family members. You will carry the toxicity in your very *cells*. Talk about baggage! In psychopathology, we also see the opposite—grown-up people who are excessively dependent upon others, cannot live their lives independently or cannot figure out how to get their own needs met.

A number of years ago, I was in a university library and read a study done on African wildebeests. Unfortunately, I didn't note down the reference, and I have never been able to find it since. So this is most unscientific, but I have never forgotten it. A researcher equipped various members of a herd of wildebeests with heart-monitoring devices. When the animals on the outside of the herd saw a pride of lions approaching, their heart rates shot up. But the wildebeests on the other side of the herd, which could not see the lions, *also* had elevated heart rates. It is as if the anxiety was "contagious" and it rippled through the herd.

You may like to think that human beings are above the level of wildebeests. But in my professional experience both as a leader in an institution and a family therapist, I have found we are more like them than most people believe. Although we can work on becoming *more* separate and distinct, at some level we are still "hooked in" to the others around us. And contrary to popular belief, we cannot become more separate and distinct as an organism by ignoring others in our relationship systems or by moving away from them and never speaking to them again. If anything, this has the opposite effect, making us vulnerable to replicating the (unhealthy/stressful) relationship with everyone else we meet.

Consider this extreme example: even if you have never spoken to any member of your family for years, and don't intend to, if every single one of them were killed tomorrow *you would be affected* and on a physical level. Most people would experience a profound grief response in their bodies (including physical symptoms). Even those who despise their families experience the "if only" kind of grief ("if only he had loved me"; "if only I had tried harder to reconnect with/understand him"; "if only she had been a real mother to me.")

The higher up the levels of systems, the more complex the process is among the components. This means that families are more complicated than the human body. Nations are trickier to lead than the PTA. Yet the same principles apply. A factory worker will have a family and perhaps a small group of co-workers in his relationship system. Someone whose job it is to lead a nation must consider every citizen as part of her relationship systems bourn.

Homeostasis

Homeostasis is one of my favourite five-syllable, big words. (The other two in my top three are "theologically" and "delicatessen.") Try memorizing *ho-me-o-sta-sis* and throwing it into the conversation at your next cocktail party. It means the state of being held steady, balanced and calm. The nature of systems is such that when one part of the system is affected by something (change), *all* parts are affected. Everything works together to respond somehow in order to *restore homeostasis,* to return the system to the balanced, stable state in which it normally exists.

Living systems maintain homeostasis by the input, processing and output of energy and information. If any of these get upset somehow, the whole system is called into action to restore homeostasis. If the previous homeostasis cannot be restored, each component of the system has to *adapt*. The ability of systems to adapt to new information or energy flow allows them to *evolve* into something new. Human beings are highly evolved and adaptable. We've learned how to fly in the air, walk on the moon, breathe underwater and survive in Antarctica. As a species, we will figure out how to survive a flu pandemic and global climate change.

Subsystems

Each part or component of a living system that performs some process is called a *subsystem*. Miller's theory identifies 20 of these subsystems critical to the process of any living system: reproducer, boundary, ingestor, distributor, converter, producer, matter-energy storer, motor, supporter, input transducer, internal transducer, channel and net, decoder, associator, memory, decider, encoder, output transducer, timer. For the purposes of this book, we need only concern ourselves with two of these subsystems: *decider* and *boundary*.

The decider (leader) is an information-processing subsystem that controls how the process in any system operates. In many systems, there is more than one decider, but if so, each one will be in charge of one "level." Sometimes there is a decider at the "top" level with control over the others, but not always. So it is possible for a seemingly leaderless group to still be considered a living system because there are deciders within the system, just not one at any top level. Conclusion? You don't have to be the official leader in order to lead, to *decide* to evoke change in the whole system.

In the human organism, the brain is pretty much in charge. In a family, it can be anybody's guess, so while there may be no ultimate decider in a family, there are still deciders in the whole system, that is, everyone's individual brains. Once a system has no decider at all, it ceases to be a system. It can be taken over by another system at this point, such as one society conquering another in war and disbanding its government or a hospital caring for a group of brain-dead people.

Boundaries

Back in chapter 6, "Self/Not Self," I gave a simple definition of boundaries and fusion. To further expand on this concept, a boundary is a subsystem at the edge of the system that holds all the components together, protects it from outside harm and permits or excludes energy or information. A boundary "knows" what part of the system is itself and what is not itself. This is the only way it can choose what can be permitted in and what cannot. A human organism knows what is human and what is not. It knows what is its own liver, for instance, and what is a liver transplanted from someone else. Without a lifetime of drugs to fool it, the body will reject the liver that is not *itself*. The same can be said of viruses that infiltrate the human body. Immediately, the various components of the body forge an attack on the virus to kill it because it does not belong. It is not "self."

As human beings, we have two kinds of boundaries—physical and non-physical—for we are more than merely our physical bodies. We are made up of thoughts, ideas, qualities of character, personalities and emotions. Some of these emotions we share, to some degree, with other mammals, but our emotional complexity is far greater than even our closest siblings in the animal kingdom: the great apes.

As far as our physical boundaries are concerned, we seem to know where we stop and another person begins. We know if it's our knee on the chair, our finger in the pie. When it comes to emotions, however, our boundaries are quite unclear. Perhaps we were created this way for a purpose, which seems to keep us close together in groups—something we need for our survival. But the fact that it isn't crystal clear where you emotionally "end" and another "begins" can spell trouble. Nothing ruins your day more than your partner coming home in a rotten mood after you've gone to a lot of trouble to prepare a celebration dinner. It is as though your emotions are hooked into hers. Anyone in close proximity to his or her family knows what I'm talking about. It's as if you have an invisible umbilical cord with another; when her blood pressure goes up, so does yours, instantly.

Here's the good news: you don't have to wait another four billion years for evolution to give humans better control over our emotional boundaries. With some knowledge and practice, and a life-long commitment to the process, you can become quite emotionally intelligent. At least you can get closer to it than most. And as you do, you will be able to better identify the boundary between what is *self* and what is not. Then you will be able to observe another's emotional state and remain in relationship with her without succumbing to that emotion yourself. The optimal state of being in a human system is to experience healthy togetherness without *fusion*.

Emotional Fusion

Fusion literally means "stuck together." When you become stuck together in a system, it is as if you borrow self from one another, rather than work to develop a better sense of self as an individual by becoming more emotionally intelligent and integrated. For example, you will try to get your self-esteem from your partner in the form of compliments from him, rather than to develop your own sense of self-esteem. Another example of "borrowing self" might be someone who projects her anger onto another by blaming him and trying to get him to change, rather than working on changing herself and her own emotional reactions to that person.

The farther down the Scale a person is, the more self he will need to borrow from others. The problem is that if you're in the market for self, the only people selling it are those at the same level of maturity as you. In other words, the immature borrow self from the equally immature. If you have a high level of emotional intelligence and integrated wisdom, you will not "lend" self to another; you will work instead to stand on your own with your individual ideas, visions and values (self-definition) while remaining meaningfully connected to others (interested in, caring about, learning from). Figure 22 represents two very highly integrated, wise individuals.

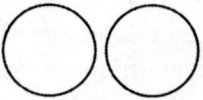

Notice that the circles enjoy closeness with one another, but there is still a clear space between them. People who are extremely far down the Scale will be more dramatically fused with one another. They can be diagrammed thus:

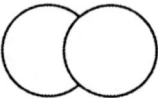

Since no one is at 100 on the Scale, it is impossible to have two individuals within any system who are not somewhat fused. This means that when one gets angry, grievous or afraid, the other one will be somehow affected emotionally. This "umbilical cord" of emotional reaction between the two of them is known as the *degree of fusion*.

It only takes one (important) person in a system to take leadership in terms of the leadership trinity in order for the system to be prevented or cured of its fusion. Figure 24 shows an emotional system where the members, including the leader, have poor boundaries–represented by the dotted lines.

Figure 25 shows the same system with a self-defined, emotionally intelligent and meaningfully connected leader. Members are prevented from being fused together in this system.

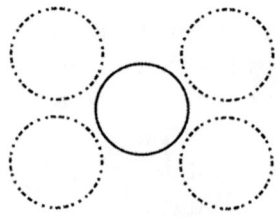

People who are lower on the Scale experience more fusion, and borrow self back and forth from one another often. This is due to a powerful force of togetherness that pulls all living organisms together. It takes a great deal of maturity and integrated wisdom to "stand strong" against this force of togetherness. As human beings, we are drawn into personal relationships with others as well as forming ourselves into groups or communities. Togetherness is not a *bad thing*, therefore. In fact, it is quite normal. It's just that succumbing to it completely can lead to a great deal of fusion, which results in people becoming unable to think for themselves.

The danger in extreme fusion is that a "group-think" mentality pulls people toward immaturity rather than building them up into more mature, integrated and wise individuals. The road to emotional maturity is always one's own road and must be traveled alone. As soon as you solicit help or "support" from someone else, unless he is a completely neutral person (such as a professional coach or therapist), then you are adding to your immaturity rather than helping yourself become more mature. The path to our own healing is only within. Since this personal journey must be done in the context of *relationships* with others, fusion will become an occupational hazard.

Because seeking togetherness is so natural for humans, we often are not aware of how fused we truly are with others. As soon as a group of people within an organization begins to herd together and criticize the leader, it is natural for him to seek out allies as well. He will want to sit down at coffee with someone, anyone, and preferably a group of people, who will tell him how great they think he is and what idiots the others are. This *feels good*. It has the effect of calming our amygdalan response to the situation. It fools us into thinking that we are indeed loved and valued and/or that a large group will protect us from attack. But this kind of seeking of togetherness, while mildly pleasant for a short time, is not good leadership. I'm not saying you should never do it; one of my favourite pastimes when I'm criticized at work is to get together with my best friend on a Tuesday night at the pub and fuse like crazy. My daughter coined the term "fusion fest" for some of our family discussions. Fusion fests relieve a great deal of anxiety—they can even be fun—but when morning comes, there is work to be done, and the work to be done is on oneself, one's emotional reaction to the criticism, one's own thinking about the problem at hand.

What About Community?

These concepts of boundaries and fusion are often met with disdain by those who hold up the value of community and community decision making. Boundaries and community are not mutually exclusive notions. There is nothing wrong with finding value in community, with discerning directions together, brainstorming solutions to problems or making decisions together as a group. In fact, community is a value that I personally hold up as a member of the Christian faith. For centuries, we have lived in democratic societies that value group decisions—the opinion held by the majority of people. For a much longer time, our Aboriginal brothers and sisters have embraced and espoused the value of consensual community decision making. Lately, consensus-making methodologies, learning circles and the World Café[84] philosophy are gaining popularity in our culture. None of these valuable contributions to group process is fusion. Nor do any of them exclude clear individual thinking. As the leader of a Christian community, *I believe* that the whole community must discern together which direction their ministry should go. This is how I define myself: one of my core values is community decision making.

"What do *you* think, Mr. President/Reverend/Chief/Rabbi?"

"I think the community must make this decision together without my influence." You can't get any more of a self-defined "I-position" than that.

It may be true that others in the community, even *everyone* in the community, hold the same value. This is not wrong; it's just a reality. It would be impossible for each of us to hold separate and distinct values; there just aren't enough values to go around!

Communal decision making holds up the importance of meaningful connection and thus *not* getting caught up in emotional reactivity. Such processes value respect of others and deep, intentional listening to one another. *The key to the success of such processes is that the anxiety, thus emotional reactivity, is kept low.* An anxious system will fall into fusion, we-thinking, and herding around immature individuals to resist change or sabotage good leadership. There is a clear and unmistakable difference between these two systemic conditions.

Rebellion

To make this concept more complicated, fusion is sometimes displayed in rebellion as well as closeness or friendship. A family in conflict is a family that is fused. If you have enough self-definition and emotional maturity, you will

---

[84] Brown, Juanita, *The World Café: Shaping Our Futures Through Conversations That Matter*, Berrett-Koehler, San Francisco, 2005.

not get yourself into a feedback loop of emotional reactivity with others in the family, and so you would not be a family in conflict. People who rebel against another are still thinking *in terms of* the other, rather than in terms of themselves. This includes everything from worrying about another's problem, to diagnosing or trying to fix another, to outright blame of another for one's own problems or the system's problems.

A teenager who smokes in order to rebel against her parents' strict forbidding is not a teenager who is "self-defined." She is smoking because Mom and Dad don't want her to, not because she has carefully and logically thought this through and come to the most mature choice for her. It could be said that the child is not seeking "negative attention," but rather "negative togetherness." This is not to say that all smokers are highly fused individuals, but they probably were when they started!

The best way to prevent your child from taking up smoking or doing anything else you disapprove of is to clearly define *yourself only* around the issue. Family systems therapist and researcher Michael Kerr writes in his book, *Family Evaluation*, "When it comes to parenting '*I will not*' is much more powerful than '*you will not.*'"[85]

Here is an example of an approach you might try with your teenager. I share it a bit tongue-in-cheek, but you'll get the idea:

> ➢ I choose not to smoke because it's highly addictive and unhealthy. But you're free to smoke if you wish. I encourage you to look into it and do some research. Weigh out the possibilities and options. Whatever you decide about smoking is fine with me. Of course, I'm not willing to tolerate anyone smoking in my house.

You would also calmly point out any other rules or consequences you might have such as these:

> ➢ If you choose to smoke, you won't be given allowance anymore because it's against my (core operating) principles to give you money for something that will harm you physically.

> ➢ If you choose to smoke, you won't be allowed to come into the house with any of your clothes on because Mom is allergic, but if you can figure out a way to leave the clothes outside and launder them elsewhere, then smoking is fine with me.

---

[85] Michael Kerr and Murray Bowen, *Family Evaluation*, 213.

A parent who could say these things to a teenager in a completely non-anxious and *genuine* way would not have to worry about his child smoking. If there's nothing to rebel against, the child will not rebel. Rebellion will no longer provide the desired fusion. Besides, it's just no fun.

Being a self-defined parent is not the same as being a "permissive" parent. Permissive parents are excessively fused with their children. They anxiously fear that if they define themselves, or set down rules, their children "won't love them anymore." Defining self and permissiveness for the sake of receiving love from a child are not at all the same thing.

The cure for fusion in any living system is the same as the cure for everything else: someone must take leadership in the form of the leadership trinity. The leader must define self, rather than be tempted to give in to the force of togetherness and go along with what others think for the sake of "keeping the peace." When someone within the system defines herself, the system will rebel, one way or another, against the leader's self-defining effort, but if she can stay the course without getting wrapped up in other people's emotional reactivity (fusion), the system will eventually calm down and adapt itself to the new situation and the leader's self-definition. Others in the system will then be forced to work on themselves, since changing the mind of the leader will finally appear to them to be a "lost cause." And once people start to look within themselves for what they can do about the problem, they start to grow up. When they grow up, the whole system calms down and "grows up" as well. The entire system will now be less fused.

Often what is referred to as "love" as well as what is referred to as "hate" is actually fusion at its worst. Fused couples either finish each other's sentences, make everyone sick with their entangled gooeyness or are constantly at each other's throats. When the two are a parent-child relationship, the child is usually somehow impaired, either with a physical or emotional illness, extreme rebellion, addiction, criminal behaviour, clinginess, or "acting out." That is not to say that it is the parent's *fault* that her child has an impairment. Furthermore, it is not known whether the emotional fusion in the family led to the impairment or whether the impairment led to the fusion. Murray Bowen and other family systems theorists would claim the former, most support groups are adamant about the latter.

I believe it is a bit of both. If so, then the parent has some influence over the health of the child. If the parent can work on herself, she will become less fused with the child, as opposed to devoting her whole life to the "problems" of the child, which only further underscores the fusion. At the very least, it is harder on a child who has to deal with a health or emotional or behavioural problem to also have to deal with his mother's anxiety (often seen as "fussing" or "worry"). Don't get me wrong; there is nothing bad about a parent being concerned over impairment in their child. After all, who wouldn't be? What I am talking about is the *degree of anxiety* in the parent. The parent can be concerned (*thoughtfully*) and "do what's right by the child" (getting him any help he needs) *without* being overly anxious and fussing. The more the parent can think through what is best for the child, then calmly act on it *and* not spend 100 per cent of her life energy on the problem, the better the child will do even *with* impairment. I will return to this theme in chapter 26 when I discuss emotional process in a family system.

Living systems have maturity levels of their own. In other words, they also fall along the Scale. Systems also tend to be at about the same level as their leaders. So the litmus test for spiritual growth in leadership is the growth of the whole system. There is therefore no such thing as a mature leader who is just unlucky enough to be leading an immature system, unless he has been leading it for a very short time. Similarly, there are no remarkably mature people married to immature people or who have immature adult children (especially just one). A family is only as mature, systemically, as its least mature member. Systems theory excludes the possibility of one person, department or group being "just troublemakers" or "the black sheep." This may be profoundly disheartening news! Fear not. The more you can learn to "think systems," the more easily you will be able to take leadership within the system and evoke change. Let us now turn our attention to the one factor, other than the maturity level of any individual, which can influence a system's capacity for change: it is systemic anxiety.

Chapter 23:
Systemic Anxiety

Neither comprehension nor learning can take place in an atmosphere of anxiety.
—Rose F. Kennedy

Just as individuals experience differing levels of anxiety, so too do herds of wildebeests, families, synagogues and chartered banks. Any group of organisms capable of displaying anxiety will have a collective anxiety level. Apart from the exceptionally trained eye, this anxiety is virtually invisible.

The anxiety level in any living system is the variable in our leadership struggle toward greater maturity and integrated wisdom. Systems experiencing little change and with little at stake will be relatively calm, making leadership simpler. Systems on the brink of extinction or demise will be so anxious that exerting good leadership is nearly impossible. A leader who has not done the difficult work required in the leadership trinity can easily be fired in a highly anxious system. A poor leader can also survive a long time, appearing to "succeed" in a system with low anxiety.

As you know by now, the captain of the anxiety ship is the amygdala, and wherever the amygdala is in charge, havoc may ensue. Imagine what can happen when a whole group of people get together, each of their amygdala triggered by something else and to different degrees. Then imagine what happens when those people begin to react automatically and emotionally, lashing out in anger, clamming up with fear or weeping with hurt. This behaviour will *raise* the anxiety level in others, slowing down or even shutting down their thinking, triggering them to react emotionally *back*. Even between two people, the anxiety can quickly escalate and emotional reactivity may get into a "feedback loop" where each person is not reacting to facts or even actual problems anymore, but only to the other's emotional reaction to the facts or the problem. Add a few more people into the system (family, business, church, art gallery), and you will see everything from paralysis of the organization to absolute chaos.

A living system may be pictured in terms of a big vat filled with people swimming around, as in Figure 26. The more mature the system is, the bigger the vat.

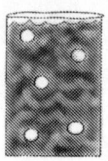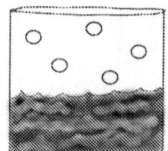

Into the mix may be added situations or events that increase the anxiety in the vat. Bigger vats can contain a lot of this anxiety without flowing over. Smaller (less mature) vats cannot contain much at all. Some families seem to cope with acute anxiety such as a tragic death, hurricane or layoffs at the plant. Others completely self-destruct. This ability to cope with a one-time ("acute") anxiety is related to how mature the system is as a whole and how much *chronic* anxiety is present at all times. Highly anxious systems are by definition less mature than calm ones.

Change

It is inevitable that anxiety will rise in any organization or group where there is any sort of change. *All change is loss.* Even if the change is a "good change," and people are celebrating in an organized way, it will still contribute to rising anxiety. A baby is born, a new rabbi arrives, there's a record year for profit, Mom got a great new job, the house finally sold. They are all significant changes and can be seen through another lens as losses. The anxiety may rise similarly to that of a system where grandmother dies, the organist is fired or the company is restructured.

Change	Loss Experienced
A new baby	The couple's time together, intimacy, freedom, choices about the future
A new rabbi arrives that everyone likes better than the last rabbi	The old rabbi's way of doing things. The "comfort" of knowing exactly what to do: complaining about the rabbi, not having to engage the issues of faith or the future of the congregation

Change	Loss Experienced
A new house	The memories attached to the old house, the old neighbourhood, the comfort of a smaller mortgage
New music in Sunday worship	The old music, the joy of singing what you know; the refusal to see that you're getting older; the safety of church in a changing world
New technology	The comfort of understanding how the world works; being able to move at a slow pace when integrating new knowledge; being "older therefore wiser"

When living systems experience change, the homeostasis of the system is upset, whether that change is seen as "good" or not. People now have to relate to one another in a new way and carry out new activities. It may be that the anxiety rises higher when the change is "bad," because people will consciously be afraid of what might or has happened and how it will affect them. But far too many naïve leaders have been caught off-guard by a "good" change in the system. Everything is going along great, and suddenly they find themselves out on their bottoms. I remember a story from one minister whose 75-member congregation was delighted to welcome 50 new members all at once from another church down the street after it approved of the ordination of homosexuals. The influx of members covered the deficit budget and tripled the Sunday school. Suddenly there were new people to run programs and help mow the grass. But before long, the congregation was torn apart (over another issue) and the minister was fired.

When the homeostasis of any system is disrupted, the system (whether amoeba, algae, schools of fish or partners in a law firm) will do everything in its power to *change the system back*. This cannot be emphasized enough. It is something that every leader must know and fully understand, or she will be broadsided by it. Often the people in the system are not aware that they are trying to change the system back. They may seem as though they welcome the change. It may be that, at the surface level, they don't want the system to return to what it was, but this is *logical*, the process happening in the neocortex of their brains. Meanwhile, at the back of their brains, their amygdalae are firing off **DANGER!** signals and creating a tremendous force in an attempt to restore homeostasis. This is as scientific and biologically true as light traveling in a straight line or water flowing downhill.

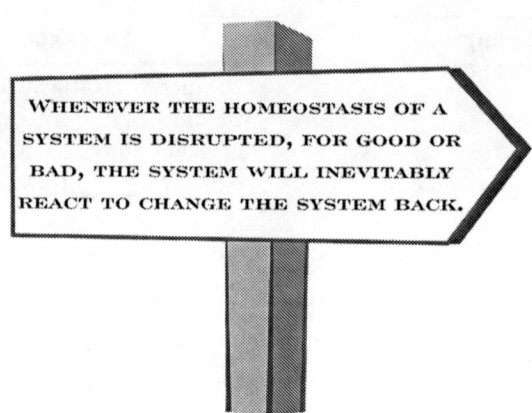

WHENEVER THE HOMEOSTASIS OF A SYSTEM IS DISRUPTED, FOR GOOD OR BAD, THE SYSTEM WILL INEVITABLY REACT TO CHANGE THE SYSTEM BACK.

The response of any system to good leadership will be absolutely predictable: it will be met with resistance and sabotage. According to Family Systems theorist Murray Bowen,[86] this resistance will always take the form of a predictable, three-fold formula:

1. You are wrong.
2. Change back.
3. If you don't, there will be consequences.

Here are some examples of what this would look like for a leader who defines self in an anxious system:

You Are Wrong	Change/Change Back	If You Don't, There Will Be Consequences
➤ You are uncaring, unfeeling, cold, inconsiderate. ➤ You only think of yourself. ➤ You're taking this company entirely in the wrong direction. ➤ This is a big mistake. ➤ This is all your fault.	➤ You need to start thinking about someone besides yourself. ➤ You're going to have to rethink this. ➤ You're not allowed to make that decision.	➤ We're going to lose a lot of business. ➤ People will leave the church. ➤ I'll hate you if you do this. ➤ I will get worse if you do that. ➤ I will make a bad decision.

---

[86] Murray Bowen, *Family Therapy in Clinical Practice*, 495.

You Are Wrong	Change/Change Back	If You Don't, There Will Be Consequences
➢ People in this family don't act like that. ➢ You're not thinking about the good of the whole (organization). ➢ Your father would be so disappointed with you. ➢ This is not the "Acme-way." ➢ This is not how we do things in our culture. ➢ You've been brainwashed. ➢ It's all those books you've been reading (or courses you've been taking). ➢ I feel like you're patronizing me, talking that way.	➢ I think you need to start doing *x*. ➢ That makes me more mad (so stop doing it). ➢ There's still time to change your mind. ➢ You're going to have to make some changes pretty quickly. ➢ Go back to your office and bring us a proposal that makes more sense. ➢ You're going to have to *follow our rules* if you want to be part of this family (company, church, community group).	➢ The whole team will fall apart. ➢ We'll never make our budget. ➢ You can just get out. ➢ I'll trade you in for a new mother. ➢ Nobody will want to work for you. ➢ I will withdraw my financial support. ➢ I'll go live with my dad. ➢ I will never speak to you again.

If you hear this three-fold formula of reactivity directed toward you, *and you are leading faithfully via the leadership trinity,* then you can immediately exhale a sigh of relief, pat yourself on the back and say to yourself, "I must be showing some excellent leadership."

One major difference between being a good leader and a poor one is your ability to manage yourself emotionally through the predictable backlash to your self-definition; you must be able to "stay the course" and weather the storm. If you can do that, the anxiety will be calmed, even though it will necessarily get worse before it gets better. Most "leaders" simply go back to the way they were, adapting to the most reactive person or people in the system, instead of staying the course and forcing the immature person to do the adapting. In order to have the emotional fortitude to stay the course, a highly developed emotional intelligence and meaningful connection with your dissenters is imperative.

Signs of Rising Anxiety

There are several clear signs that anxiety is rising or has risen in an emotional system. Leaders can take note of these signs and proactively respond in terms of the leadership trinity. The individuals who partake of these behaviours are seldom bad people. There is no room for judgment in systemic thinking. Emotional systems, whatever they are, behave in predictable ways when the anxiety gets up too high. The more people in the system mature enough to take leadership, the less likely the anxiety is to go up in the whole system.

Those who contribute to group anxiety by engaging in highly anxious group behaviour typically:

- Are anxious about the issue and invested in the outcome
- Are not mature enough, in terms of the leadership trinity, to manage their anxiety with good leadership
- Project their anxiety onto others, often the leader
- Believe, even subconsciously, that changing the system back will calm their own personal anxiety
- Seek the "togetherness" of others in their thoughts or plans, which makes them feel calmer
- Need "support" from others because they are not mature enough to stand up straight on their own (define self and connect meaningfully with those with whom they disagree)

Because of this very human response, any or all of the following will be observable:

1. We-thinking
2. Resistance and sabotage
3. Overfunctioning
4. Diagnoses and blame
5. Herding
6. Secrecy
7. Cutoff

Let's take a look at each of these in more detail.

We-Thinking
People cease to speak for themselves or state clearly what they believe, want or are upset by. Instead, they say things like, "I speak on behalf of the entire accounting department," "A lot of other people think the same way I do," or "I have heard that some people don't believe you should have…" Usually the least mature person will speak for the whole group as in "We don't do things like that around here," or "That's not our idea of observing the Sunnah." I have worked with many families who are stuck in we-thinking. One person in a couple may say something like, "We feel that our daughter's behaviour is out of control." I am astounded at the number of times I can turn to the other spouse and say, "And what do you think?" only to have him or her continue to express things as "we." The higher the anxiety in the system, the more likely you are to hear evidence of we-thinking.

Resistance and Sabotage
You're probably thinking that something like sabotage would be reserved for people in business, and certainly never for the church, your family or the local chapter of Greenpeace. Think again. Anxiety rising in a system brings out the worst in people, and in every organization, including churches, monasteries, synagogues and mosques, there are people lurking in the shadows that you might never expect would behave badly.

Resistance and sabotage can take a number of forms. Sometimes it is so subtle that you don't see it for what it really is. At other times, it is malicious and intentional. A favourite form of sabotage is for someone to demand his own way or he will withdraw his funding or quit his job. This needs to be seen for what it is: intentional sabotage. Any organization that lets itself be held up for ransom this way will not last long, and if it does, it will have little impact on the world or make little profit anyway. It may hobble along for another 50 years, but it will be wracked with problems forever. There is no member, employee nor amount of donations worth that.

What is important to remember is that the "cure" for resistance and sabotage is the same as the cure for everything else: the leadership trinity. If the leader emotionally reacts to the sabotage, it can be just as damaging as the sabotage itself. The leader must instead focus on his own self-definition, his own emotional reactions, and connect meaningfully with the saboteurs and others who become involved in this process. The thing to focus on systemically is the anxiety itself, *not* the sabotage or the saboteurs.

Overfunctioning
Someone starts to work long hours, volunteers to fill positions that no one else wants, even though he already functions in another position. He claims, "If I want this done properly, I have to do it myself." If you as a leader, or someone else in the system, begins overfunctioning, especially if you have not done so before, this is a good indicator of rising anxiety in both yourself (if you're the overfunctioner) and/or the whole system (if it is someone else).

Diagnoses and Blame
Blame is seldom about the person being blamed or the thing for which she is being blamed. In fact, it is very common in a system for the leader to be blamed whenever the anxiety rises, regardless of her personality, skill or leadership ability. Anxious leaders may also diagnose others within the organization rather than diagnosing systemic anxiety itself. In an anxious family, there is often one child who is diagnosed as the "problem" child. These problems may be behavioural, but oftentimes they are even health related. Anxious focus on a child will be explained more fully in chapter 26.

As soon as the anxiety in the whole group goes up, it is often seen first in the "problem person." Rather than looking around at the whole system, members begin to focus on the problem one, because this is the most normal and comfortable thing for them to do. When I say comfortable, I mean from the point of view of homeostasis. It might *appear* most uncomfortable to have this person be a problem, but in reality, it is only when he is a problem that the system's homeostasis is maintained and everyone else seems "normal."

In a business or other organization, the "problem" can be the Parts Department or the choir director, secretary, or vice president of finance. The personnel may change or be replaced, but the diagnosing often remains: "We can never find anyone good to manage the Calgary office anymore. The entire town must be clueless." (I actually heard that once, verbatim!) In both my roles as a family therapist and an organizational consultant, whenever I hear an organization or a family "diagnose" someone or blame someone, I immediately begin to look for the systemic problem. Mature families and mature organizations look around at the whole system, and everyone takes responsibility for their own part of the problem. Couples who have healthy marriages take equal responsibility for challenges that arise. Problem couples blame one another for their problems. Occasionally, both partners agree that it's one of them who should be blamed or diagnosed. This is equally unhealthy.

When you as a leader encounter diagnosing and blame, the first thing to do is to ensure you're not the one doing it. There is no need for blame, nor diagnosing someone as the "problem child" in your organization or, as Edwin Friedman calls them, the "identified patient."[87] Such blame means that you have ceased to become an emotionally intelligent leader, ceased to examine yourself for ways you could be more mature. It also means you have stopped thinking in terms of your own self-definition: what you will or will not do, what you think about the problem. You will not be meaningfully connected with others if you're diagnosing them or blaming them. You will not be willing to listen effectively to them, remaining open to new learning.

Leaders also err in a system of blame when they are the one being blamed. They do this in two equally destructive ways:

1. Assuming they are the problem when they are not, or
2. Assuming they are not the problem (but rather the system is only anxiously blaming them) when they are.

Herding

Much like we-thinking, an anxious system will develop "camps," often touted as being two "sides" of an argument, issue or discussion. The soccer association executive has decided to replace the treasurer. Those who want to support the treasurer get together at Jim's house on a Wednesday night to plan how they might work together to keep him. This is, of course, a secret meeting, made through a few whispered conversations in the parking lot and carefully placed telephone calls.

If anxiety is high enough, there will be more than two camps. Sometimes the camps result in splits in an organization, and it is worth noting that organizations which ensue from such splits seldom if ever prosper no matter how well-intentioned, gifted and "together" the people in that particular camp seem to be. *The camp itself is the problem, not the content of the issue that the people encamp themselves around.*

When anxiety is high, camps *always* form around the most emotionally immature person in the system. This can be deceiving, because the leader of the camp may *appear to be* mature; she might look perfectly calm and seem to be talking rationally. But just the fact that she's heading up a camp and herding other folks into it suggests anxiety and the force of togetherness at work, fusing her with others and rendering them unable to think or speak for themselves. What the leader must do when camps form is to address the issue of the camps themselves and not focus on the issue that the camp wants to discuss. In other words, it is not the firing of the treasurer that is the issue; it is the forming of

---

[87] Edwin Friedman, *Generation to Generation*.

camps that is the issue. A good leader will connect meaningfully with *individuals* to discern what each one thinks (or he will facilitate a process that does so). He will be curious about the problem and the system. Practical ways to address systemic anxiety will be outlined further in Part Four of this book.

A simple way to remember that the problem—whatever it is—is anxiety in the system, is to paste a sign up above your desk that states:

THE ISSUE IS NOT THE ISSUE

Secrecy

Secrecy, often disguised as "confidentiality," may involve secret meetings, whispering, people "in the know" or on the inside, and others on the outside, or gatherings in the parking lot after a meeting. If secrets are being kept, or worse, passed around by means of one person at a time, then it is a given that anxiety is rising. One step toward reducing the anxiety is for the leader to announce the secret to the group, in a non-anxious way.

Many people in my classes and workshops express concern when I talk about secrecy being anxious. "What about confidentiality?" they ask. These concepts warrant a more in-depth discussion.

Secrecy versus Confidentiality

Secrecy and confidentiality are not black-and-white issues. *They fall along a continuum.* At the one end, if someone tells you she murdered the postal carrier and buried him in her backyard, then it is obvious you should not keep this a secret. If she is thinking of committing suicide, and swears you to secrecy, it is perfectly acceptable to say, "That's not a secret I'm willing to keep," and call the mental health authorities. Yes, she'll be very mad at you. That's okay.

Apart from murder and suicide, it is often difficult to assess what is appropriate to be kept confidential and what is a secret that is unhealthy and should not be kept. This can be a difficult decision for a leader to make. Secrecy and confidentiality fall along a continuum that may look something like this:

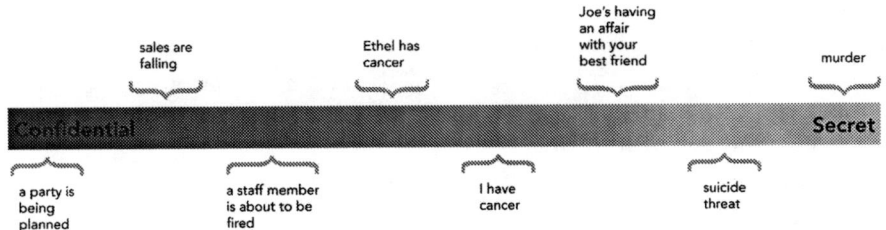

Let's start at the far left side of the continuum shown in Figure 28. If a surprise party is being planned, it's obvious you will want to keep that confidential! The other extreme, a murder, is also obvious: it is a secret that should not be kept. The other examples may fall anywhere along the continuum. You will have to judge for yourself in each situation. It has been a great relief to many a leader to discover that sometimes it's perfectly acceptable to define yourself by saying, "That is not a secret I'm willing to keep." In every case, the leader must make her decision based on the welfare of the system as a whole rather than out of fear of the emotional reactivity of individuals.

Secrecy and confidentially may present any of the following issues in a system:

> Normally, something is confidential if it is information that someone shares with you about *herself*, except where harm is being done or may be done to herself or someone else. For example, she says, "I have cancer."

> Information shared about someone else is up for grabs. ("Ethel has cancer, but told me in confidence.") It may be appropriate to go to Ethel and say, "So-and-so told me you have cancer." After all, maybe Ethel should know that the people she's confiding in are blabbing it around, one person at a time.

> People often use secrecy, feigned as confidentiality, for power. It creates an "in" and an "out" group.

> Power works to calm peoples' anxiety. But so does good leadership. Go for the latter.

> Entire systems often use secrecy as the primary way they calm or at least address their anxiety and keep it at bay. These systems are crying out for good leadership.

Cutoff
The final indicator of anxiety rising in a system is people cutting off from it: family members who no longer "speak to" the rest of the family, or one family member in particular. It is also people quitting their jobs, quitting the team, resigning their position as coach, artistic director or volunteer chairperson, and people leaving the organization. When cutoff occurs, inexperienced or immature leaders focus too much on the person or group who has cutoff, or the "reason" they cutoff, perhaps even blaming someone for the cutoff and trying to convince them to change their ways or shape up so the cutoff person will return. Leaders need to think instead about the anxiety in the whole system that led to the cutoff and concentrate on themselves and their own functioning as good leaders within the system.

Cutoff is the one place where families differ from other human systems. Blood really is thicker than water. (That's an expression. If you're adopted into a family, you will be just as much a part of them forever as if you are born into the family.) Cutoff in a family is devastating, and the family should work as best it can to heal the cutoff. In an organization, it is doubtful that the cutoff person or persons will ever return, no matter what. Before they left, they would have most certainly made demands that the organization "change back," but even if it does meet those demands (the height of foolishness), they will likely not return anyway. If they do return, they will be in such a position of power and control that they will be the *de facto* leader(s). This will be devastating to the actual leader and the organization itself, because only immature people cutoff in the first place. Mature people stay, define themselves, and remain connected to the rest who may think differently than they. Who wants the most immature ("If you don't play my way, I'm taking my marbles and going home") person or people in the system to be running it?

This is not to say that only immature people leave an organization. Mature people may leave, but they will do so because their core values do not line up with those of the system, and they calmly and rationally make a choice to go elsewhere. They will meaningfully connect with the leader and others about their decision in an open, transparent and non-anxious manner. Those who leave in this way often remain friendly and connected to the others.

The Cure for Systemic Anxiety

Many an institution, family or group has been desecrated by anxiety, but all is not lost. The only thing necessary for a system to calm down is for one person who is important to the system to take leadership. The system will calm down and begin to move forward. To "take leadership" always means this:

Therefore, when anxiety rises, it is imperative that the leader:

- ➢ Is self-defined and is willing to clearly state what she *thinks* about the situation,
- ➢ Is emotionally intelligent enough to know what is going on with *her*, where her own anxiety lies and what other emotions are at play and
- ➢ Can stay meaningfully connected with others who are anxious, who disagree with her self-definition or who are acting in an immature or destructive manner.

The leadership trinity is not a "snappy comeback" in the heat of the moment. Nor is it a tricky little technique to apply in the face of a problem situation at home or at work. It is an ongoing *process* to be working at all the time. When anxiety rises, and the leader applies the imperatives of the leadership trinity, it may take weeks or months before the positive effects are evident throughout the system.

> All it takes for a system to calm down is for one person, who is important to the system, to take leadership.

Chapter 24:
Triangles

The biggest liar in the world is They Say.
—Douglas Malloch

In the vat of a living system, people *relate* to one another in quite predictable ways. At first, they will enjoy the togetherness of a two-person relationship. This works well when anxiety is low, but when it heats up, the relationship becomes unstable and a third person will be "triangled in." Murray Bowen discovered after years of observing family members interact with one another that emotional triangles are the basic building blocks of all human relationships.

Figure 31 shows a relationship between A and B.

```
                    C



    A ─────────────────────────────── B
```

When B says or does something that raises A's anxiety, it will be difficult for A to talk directly to B about it. B's words or actions may bring feelings of anger, shame or fear for A. A will thus feel too vulnerable to discuss it directly with B, and will naturally triangle in C. Let's call these three Allan, Bill and Carlotta.

When Allan goes to Carlotta, he will give some altered version of the story about Bill. By "altered" I do not mean that Allan will intentionally lie or exaggerate, but he will relate to Carlotta all three of the following:

- ➢ Facts
- ➢ Feelings
- ➢ Assumptions

241

and he will do so in a way that appears to portray facts only (i.e., "what happened").

If Carlotta is not an astute leader and gets "sucked into" the energy of the triangle, rather than remaining neutral, she will take as fact what Allan tells her about Bill. Allan and Carlotta will then occupy an "inside position" in the triangle, and Bill will occupy the outside position. Allan's relationship with Carlotta will probably be a secret to Bill. Bill may perceive that there is a problem in his relationship with Allan, but Allan is not talking. This further raises the anxiety and may force Bill to triangle in someone else.

Andrew and Bob serve on the finance committee of Sunnytown Church and get along well together. One day Bob states his opinion that "all finance committee members should be tithing to set an example for the rest of the church." Andrew does not tithe; in fact he gives very little to the church. But he is too ashamed to admit this and feels offended and angry at Bob. Instead of talking to Bob about his feelings, he goes to Clarence and says, "You'll never guess what Bob suggested at the finance meeting. He basically said that people who don't tithe are not even Christian."

"He's one to talk!" exclaims Clarence. "He never shows up for the charity auctions or work bees. What a hypocrite!"

Bob, sensing a problem, may come back to Andrew and say, "What's up with Clarence? He seems standoffish lately."

Andrew replies, "Oh, he's just full of himself sometimes." A classic emotional triangle is born.

Triangles are not *wrong*, they just *are*. If I'm frustrated or fed up with Buddy, I will go home and tell Charlie about it. If Charlie can remain neutral in the triangle and not try to fix the relationship between me and Buddy, or take my side, then the triangle will remain healthy. If I tell Charlie about Buddy to relieve my own anxiety and get the matter off my chest, then I won't expect him to do anything about it and the triangle will remain healthy *so long as Charlie's opinion of Buddy and his own relationship with him do not change.*

It takes a huge amount of courage and therefore a high level of maturity to relate to someone directly. Even those very high up on the Scale cannot do so for very long without triangling. It's the reality of how we interact with one another in human systems. When the going gets tough in relationships, what's the first thing you're going to do? Call a friend, get on the phone to mother or say to your wife, "You'll never guess what so-and-so…" In a tense relationship moment, you probably can't wait to get out of the room and go talk to someone *else* about it all!

See how long you can talk to a member of your family without triangling in another person or discussing an issue (news or weather). Talk to him or her about the two of you and your relationship, not about anybody or anything else. How long do you think you can do it? A minute? Two? The mere thought of this exercise with most families sends people screaming from the room. The more immature the family system, the less of this talk there will be.

If triangles are the building block of all relationships, then the "wild card" or variable in all relationships is anxiety. When A can't handle her relationship with B, and triangles in C, if C does not remain neutral, she will end up with A's anxiety, almost as if she's been passed a hot potato. Since no one wants a hot potato, she will pass it on by triangling in D. D would be well advised to go back to A and say, "Do you know C is really upset with you? Why don't you work it out with B, because I'd like to talk to C about something else!"

Stephen Covey writes, "One of the most important ways to manifest integrity is to *be loyal to those who are not present.*"[88] Sometimes triangling is a breach of trust and not reflective of people of integrity. Everyone has heard a conversation like this one at the office water cooler:

Angie:	I heard that Beth is getting a promotion.
Carol:	Yeah, I can't believe it. She doesn't deserve it. She just sucks up to Darlene all the time.
Angie:	Darlene's too dumb to see it. I don't know how much longer I can even work for her. You totally should have gotten that job.
Carol:	Thanks, Angie. It's good to know you support me.
(Later that day)	
Angie:	So, Beth's going to be our new manager of marketing I hear?
Darlene:	Yes, she's certainly earned it. But I think Carol may be a little disappointed.
Angie:	Oh well, that's her problem. She's always whining about something. You did the right thing, Darlene. It was a good management decision.

The important thing to understand about conversations like this is that while Angie may think that she is endearing herself to both Carol and Darlene, she is showing them both that she speaks about others behind their backs, and therefore cannot be trusted. So deep down (and not too deep), they both know that when they are not present, she is talking about them as well.

---

[88] Stephen Covey, *The 7 Habits of Highly Effective People*, 196.

Behaving this way in a triangle shows a lack of personal integrity. But triangles are inevitable in human relationships. Unhealthy triangling is not black and white but more a matter of degree. To never speak of someone who is not present would be nearly impossible. Gossips, on the other hand, are notoriously bad leaders who may rise to the top but will enjoy very short "terms of office." The greater the leader, the less she will speak to others of anything other than her core values and principles. For this reason, she will not cultivate close friendships *within* the organization.

If you find yourself caught in an unhealthy triangle, the only way out is through the leadership trinity. Cutting off ("I'll just stay out of it.") is not a solution. Cutting off means that you are so anxious, you cannot relate meaningfully to both sides. Since you will be working on emotional intelligence at all times, when you become triangled into an uncomfortable situation, you will need to define self and stay meaningfully connected with both sides. Emotional intelligence work will help you understand why you don't want to define yourself or stay connected with certain people. Leadership trinity imperatives will be evident by the use of "I-statements", especially statements that let the other know how you feel. That is not to say that you expect them to be responsible for your feelings, but merely that you are communicating with them so that they get to know you better. Your statements will also relate only to the person you're speaking to at that moment. Unhealthy "triangling talk" does not contain I-statements.

Unhealthy Triangle Talk	*Good Leadership Response*
People are saying…	What people? What are their names?
There are some of us here who think…	Since the others aren't here right now, why don't we talk about what you think?
A lot of people feel the same way I do.	I'll be speaking to a lot of people about this issue myself, but right now I'm most interested in what you think.
I just want to give you a "heads up" about something…	While I appreciate your being concerned about me, I find it more helpful to encounter problems as they come. However, if there's something you'd like to talk to me about that concerns *you and me*, I'd be happy to listen.
I have heard that there's a problem with *x*.	(seeking after facts) What have you heard, exactly?

Unhealthy Triangle Talk	Good Leadership Response
You and I feel the same way about x.	I've noticed whenever we focus on x, we avoid discussing our own differences.
If only we could get the personnel department to see it our way.	I wonder why we've been so ineffective in dealing with the personnel department?
You'll never believe what Dave just did to me.	How are you going to manage yourself with Dave?

When someone presents you with a problem, concern or even "news" about a third party, ask yourself, "Whose problem is this?" You may occasionally have to honestly ask this of the one presenting the problem to you.

Your wife comes to you and says, "I can't stand it when Junior keeps his room filthy. I know I can shut the door, but there are chicken bones in there and pizza boxes and God knows what! We've got to do something with Junior." Whose problem is this? It may seem as though it is Junior's problem, but it isn't. It's your wife's problem. She has a problem dealing with her anxiety around a messy room in her house. Or the fact that she's raised a son who's a slob.

Family Systems therapist and rabbi Edwin Friedman expressed seven laws of emotional triangles.[89] I have reproduced them below (in italics), with some commentary of my own on the first four. Much more in-depth information about triangles, how they operate and how to define a self within them can be discovered by reading more about Bowen Family Systems Theory. There is a suggested reading list at the back of this book.

Friedman's Seven Laws of Triangles

1. *The relationship of any two members is kept in balance by the way a third party relates to them. If a relationship is stuck, there is probably a third person that is part of that homeostasis.*

Removing yourself from a triangle is not easy, particularly if you've been stuck in it for years. It's even more difficult if it's a family triangle. Many novice leaders believe that "just staying out of it for a change" will do the trick. While sometimes this can be an important first step, it usually indicates that your anxiety is so high that you cannot remain in it and stay neutral. This violates the leadership trinity imperative of *staying meaningfully connected* to both sides.

---

[89] Friedman, *Generation to Generation*, 36–39.

2. *If one is the third party in a triangle, it is not possible to bring change to the relationship of the other two.*

If your husband and daughter are fighting, you cannot fix that. You can't do anything that will make one bit of difference; you can turn pirouettes, have a nervous breakdown, win a lottery, bring out a gun or die, but there is absolutely nothing that you can do to change the relationship of two people, one of whom is not you. This insight should save you hours of time.

You can, however, change *yourself* in relation to the other two. When you change yourself, becoming more mature, this action in itself will upset the homeostasis of a triangle that has become "stuck" (meaning the energy moves around it in the same old familiar patterns). The other two will automatically try to compel you to change back. If you can refuse to do so and stay the course, the two will be forced to adapt by dealing differently with one another. So in an indirect way, you may evoke change to the relationship of the other two. But if you try to *tell* the other two how they should interact, (an imposing of the will), your efforts will most certainly fail.

3. *Attempts to change the relationship of the other two parties often backfire to the opposite intent, that is, trying to bring two people closer will generally bring more distance between them.*

This is the time to take a hard look at yourself and what you're doing. Repeat slowly to yourself one of Dr. Phil's famous lines, "How's that workin' for ya?"

4. *To the extent that the third party tries to bring change to the other two (unsuccessfully), the third party will end up with the stress.*

This is especially true in the child-focused family or in a work system where everyone is focused on the weakest link. The whole system revolves around the weaknesses or problems of the "child." As a result, the child will not be supported but rather he will take on a huge amount of stress. Almost always in families where there is a "problem child," once the family *stops* fussing about him and his problems, the child gets better. It's scary to see the consistency with which this happens.

5. *The various triangles in an emotional system interlock. Usually one triangle is primary. Change in this one will induce change in the others.*

6. *One side of a triangle tends to have more problems/challenges than the others. In a healthy system, the problems/challenges swing around the compass. In unhealthy systems, the problems tend to be located in one particular side (focused on one symptom bearer).*

7. *We can only change a relationship to which we belong. Therefore, the only way to bring change is to maintain a well-defined relationship with each and to avoid the responsibility for their relationship with each other.*

Healthy Triangles—A Summary

Triangles are not wrong; they are the building blocks of all our human relationships. They are the way that humans relate to one another in living systems and relieve some of their anxiety. In some systems, there is one "primary triangle." For example, Mother and one child maintain a close relationship, and Father is left on the outside. Mother always takes the child's side against Father. When the primary triangle is "stuck" like this, the system will be quite unhealthy. In healthier systems, the triangles "swing around" from person to person. It behoves you as the leader to become aware of the various triangles in the system and your own role in them. There will be very little positive result if you just stay out of a triangle that you've normally been stuck in. The emotional cutoff violates the leadership principle of meaningful connection. The best way to relate in a triangle is to stay connected to both sides wherever possible and *remain neutral.*

Chapter 25:
Emotional Process I

The family is the nucleus of civilization.
—Ariel and Will Durant

Every living system finds a process in order to manage its anxiety and maintain its homeostasis. In human systems, at least at this point in our evolution, these processes often become unhealthy. Insight into emotional process will help the leader "think systems" when problems occur or progress toward change is slow in the group. It is more important for the leader to be curious about the emotional process that is present, as well as the triangles, than it is for her to focus on the content of issues.

The easiest system in which to observe emotional process is the family—one's nuclear family or one's family of origin. The way that anxiety is managed and homeostasis is maintained in your nuclear families is either an imitation of, or a rejection of, the process in your family of origin. You may either admire your parents and try to parent like them, or despise your parents and resolve not to parent anything like them. At lower levels on the Scale, people do not even give parenting any thought at all and are doomed to repeat (unhealthy) patterns in their family of origin—especially abuse or neglect. Bowenian psychiatrist Dr. Roberta Gilbert, in her book *Extraordinary Relationships*, identifies five patterns of emotional process in a family, and I am indebted to her for the clarity with which she outlines them.[90] My list is a slight adaptation of Gilbert's, and I have added one more ("togetherness") that I have observed in my work with families. The six emotional processes or patterns that I will discuss over the next two chapters are:

1. Conflict
2. Distancing

---

[90] Roberta Gilbert, *Extraordinary Relationships*, 41.

3. Emotional cutoff
4. Togetherness
5. Over- and underfunctioning
6. Projection onto a child

It is important to say that there are very few families who manifest these emotional processes clearly. In other words, this is more theory than direct observation. You tend to see these patterns only in the extreme, particularly in families low on the Scale. If a family is low enough down, there will also be a number of these patterns occurring at the same time.

Conflict

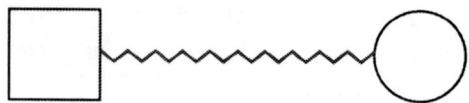

Entire books are written, courses are designed and diplomas are offered in the area of conflict. We live in anxious times, particularly in the Western world, when everyone is trying to get ahead, achieve more, earn more, have more. Not everyone can succeed at this. Some people have to fail or lose in order for others to win. It doesn't take a genius in economics to realize that for there to be "haves" there must be "have-nots." Since the wannabe-haves will be clamouring over the have-nots to become haves, there will be conflict. And in a postmodern world where nothing is certain but change itself, there will inevitably be conflict.

Conflict is not something to be feared, but unfortunately because of what lies under our trap door, we do fear it. Conflict expert and author David Augsberger writes, "Conflict is normal, natural and neutral."[91] Stephen Covey once said, "If two people think the same way, one is superfluous."[92]

I have actually had some leaders in my workshops almost proudly refer to themselves as conflict avoiders. "I avoid conflict at all costs," one man told me.

---

[91] David Augsberger. *Caring Enough to Confront*, 11.
[92] Stephen Covey said this to me personally at one of his seminars, in answer to a question.

"I hate it." It makes me wonder how on earth this fellow's organization could continue to exist.

Conflict may occur when someone is mad at you, doesn't accept you or doesn't think the way you do. This brings out your feelings of shame, imperfection, rejection, loss, weakness or worthlessness. Depending on your own emotional reactivity, you may become angry instantly in a conflict situation, or you may behave in such a way that conflict will never occur. Many leaders of organizations fear conflict because for them, conflict is Leviathan. On a more practical note, they fear losing their jobs. But since most people who work for a living continue to work for a living, loss of a job is not the end-of-the-world-Leviathan that many make it out to be. There are other jobs. Enough time, energy and effort, and we could all probably find a more fulfilling or better-paying job anyway. Most of the time, we just don't want to put in the effort. But more than that, we fear that being fired will trigger our shame, open up the trap door, and allow Leviathan to leap out and devour us forever.

Conflict can be the result of anxiety in the system rising due to *change*. This also runs along a Scale. In systems that manage their anxiety through conflict, the higher the anxiety goes, the more conflict there is. I had one astute student in my seminary class describe to me once how his home congregation had become enmeshed in conflict when there was no change at all. The priest had been there 15 years; everything was exactly the same. Upon further investigation, my student revealed that the congregation became anxious about the lack of "change" (meaning, new things happening that might attract new people). Since the *world* was rapidly changing and people were getting less interested in church, the congregation feared for its own survival. Whenever any organism fears its own survival, the anxiety will go sky-high. So although the priest had not changed, and the programs, worship services and governance structure had not changed, nor had there been anyone new come to church, the attitude and perspective of the congregational members changed over time, and this change inevitably bumped up against the priest, leading to the anxiety rising. Conflict ensued.

Families who manage their anxiety through conflict are either constantly bickering, arguing or bitching at one another, or else there is quiet and calm for a time when family members "steam," or distance, then blow up. Yelling, fighting and even throwing things may begin. In extremely emotionally immature families, conflict is manifested as violence or child abuse. Moderately immature couples just treat one another like crap. Sometimes I sit in my office listening to them, and I can't believe my ears. They virtually despise one another; they are sarcastic, critical, offensive and rude to the one they love. I have also witnessed people act this way toward their own children, believe it or not.

The usual pattern in conflictual families is that so long as the homeostasis is maintained through togetherness (fusion), everything is calm. However, if one person defines herself in the family, the other member(s) of the family react to it with anger and the imposing of their will upon her. She immediately reacts back through anger (yelling, fighting). Somehow the conflict is resolved: either someone "gives in" to her and sees it her way or else she concedes and sees it their way. Seldom is a third option or healthy synergy achieved. Then, once everyone is resolved to think the same way again, togetherness returns and the fighting is over. Conflictual couples often seek counselling in order to have a third party take one side or the other when their conflicts become more and more irresolvable. When they realize that couple's counsellors do not take sides, and that each partner is encouraged to work on him or herself rather than the other, they often quit counselling and file for divorce.

In a conflictual couple, each partner believes that there is something wrong with the other. Each is highly invested in changing the other or giving the other advice. Of course, you cannot change anyone but yourself. If you do change yourself (meaning, your emotional reaction to him), eventually he will change anyway because, if you grow up, it naturally forces him to grow up. But it's sort of a Catch-22. If you *set out* to change someone else, it won't happen. But if you set out to change yourself in relation to someone else, then the someone else will end up changing. There is no other way for him to exist in a changed system.

Distancing

In some families, the homeostasis is maintained and anxiety is managed through distance. Distance is emotional, not necessarily physical. It's not that distancers go to the movies or golfing alone (although some certainly do), it's more that they distance themselves emotionally by refusing to enter into any sort of meaningful conversation about anything, especially family relationships.

Figure 33 shows two types of distancing:

Sometimes only one partner distances, while the other constantly pursues him. Since it is impossible to ever catch a distancer, this pattern continues into perpetuity. At times, either the distancer or the pursuer becomes so frustrated and angry that the pattern changes to conflict and a fight ensues. Following the fight, there may be a time of closeness. The fight reinforces to the distancer that distance is best and the closeness reinforces to the pursuer that pursuing is best, and so the homeostasis is maintained with distance.

In the other pattern, both partners are more comfortable with distance, and so neither is interested much in any sort of emotional exchange with the other. There may be no meaningful conversation at all. Eventually, these couples lead virtually separate lives, more like roommates than partners. In the end, one either suddenly announces a divorce (often after 25 or 30 years), claiming they have "drifted apart" or that she just isn't getting anything she needs from the marriage. It is also possible that a distancing couple will celebrate their 50th wedding anniversary together and everyone will ask what their secret is. While they may be still married, their magic formula for staying together will not last through to the next generation. This couple's children will have no idea how to relate emotionally to another person, and conflict may easily emerge in their relationships or in those of the grandchildren.

Emotional Cutoff

Emotional cutoff is an extreme form of distancing, along with an extreme form of projection or blame. Cutoff is most evident in families where one member becomes the "black sheep" and is completely separated from the rest of the family, emotionally—whether or not it is geographically. Perhaps you are the "black sheep" in your family, and they are cutoff from you *or* perhaps you are the "white sheep" in a family apart from whom you think you'll do better in this life. Cutoff is an emotional process, which is used in families, either way, to manage anxiety. As long as the problem lies "out there," and everyone else can talk about the cutoff member or members behind their backs, then the homeostasis is maintained in the family. Whenever the cutoff member rises up and makes an appearance, even by a Christmas card, all hell breaks loose.

Cutoff *can be* a helpful way of managing stress *for a short time only,* especially in families that are very "hot," meaning there is extreme immaturity, perhaps even addiction, criminal behaviour or physical or sexual abuse. The conflict may be so great that you cannot think clearly if you're with the other, so it can be helpful to cutoff for a bit (known as "creating some space") while you sort out your thinking. But beware. Permanent cutoff is extremely unhealthy. Edwin Friedman believed emphatically that if there were cutoff *anywhere* in a family, then that family could not possibly heal.[93] This has certainly been my experience in observing and working with families where there is cutoff.

When I was doing my clinical residency in marriage and family therapy, I embarked upon a 10-year study of "healthy families." My goal was to carefully study 10 families, who did not seem to display any symptoms at all, for at least three generations. Although I found 10 families in my own congregation who qualified for the study, I very quickly observed that while these families differed in ages, cultural backgrounds, race, affluence and subjection to outside stressors, they all very clearly held one thing in common: there was no cutoff in any of their families—anywhere. And for several generations. The whole family was in fairly good contact with each other, even though four of the families were immigrants and their extended families were overseas, some in developing countries. Try as I might, I could not find one single family with cutoff that didn't have symptoms. By "symptoms" I mean chronic physical illness, mental illness, addiction, criminal behaviour or any other reason one would seek help from someone in a "helping profession." The study is still ongoing, but I was amazed at this preliminary finding.

While cutoff seems to be a good idea if you are a member of a toxic family, the adage is still true that if you go away on a trip, you take your baggage with you. What has not been worked out in your own family will get infused into every other relationship—with your own partner, children, even friends and co-workers. Show me a person cutoff from his family of origin, and I'll show you trouble in the boardroom every time. If you *are* experiencing trouble in your marriage, with your children or in work relationships, I would suggest the first place you look is to your family of origin to see if there is any cutoff. Cutoff comes in degrees, all the way from the extreme "move-to-another-country" kind to the families who get together every Sunday with the folks but never talk about anything more meaningful than the cats. Remarkably, the former type of family always has far worse problems than the latter.

I'm not sure what it is about cutoff that is so toxic to us as organisms, but I suspect that we are more fused with our families than we imagine. Like monkeys who are kicked out of the troop, we just don't fare well, no matter how many

---

[93] Edwin Friedman video, *Reinventing Leadership*.

friends we make. We need our families, as awful as that might seem to some of you reading this. One can look at organisms with a very few cells and see under a microscope that they "vibrate." Surely human beings, in every cell "vibrate" also, and these vibrations somehow intermingle with the vibrations of others in our families in a different way than they intermingle with our friends[94]. Again, "blood is thicker than water."

If there is cutoff in your family, it is up to you to begin to heal that in any way you can. This does not mean that you have to start liking your family or forgiving them for what they've done to you. But if you can't "go home" and take leadership by defining yourself, becoming more emotionally intelligent, and staying in meaningful contact with the people who get you "vibrating" in the worst way, then you won't be able to take leadership in any other area of your life. Evoking change will be impossible. My last piece of advice about the leadership trinity is this:

TRY THIS AT HOME!

If the cutoff in your family is extreme, you will need to take "baby steps." Going home at Christmas and announcing to everyone at dinner, "So, Uncle Fred, did you molest anyone else in the family besides me?" will result in *them* cutting *you* off. If you define yourself in such a way that you cannot stay meaningfully connected with that person or persons, then your leadership effort has failed. Baby steps. Perhaps go fishing with cousin Dave and talk to him about your family in general, to start.

We are all emotionally cutoff to one degree or another, in order to manage our anxiety. Murray Bowen would say that the only way to heal (Leviathan) is to do intentional family work, making a clear effort to be in contact with as many members of your family of origin as possible. Bowen therapists are very good at facilitating and coaching this "family of origin work." There is also an excellent little self-help book by Ron Richardson, *Family Ties that Bind*, which nicely outlines the process of reconnecting with family in a meaningful way.

In order to be a good leader, you will have to find some way to stay connected with your own family. If you cannot connect with them, you will ultimately not be able to connect meaningfully with anyone else in the group you're leading. Murray Bowen said, "The family is the best laboratory" (to

---

[94] Bruce Lipton, *The Biology of Belief: Unleashing the Power of Consciousness, Matter and Miracles*.

test out your emotional reactivity and maturity). It may be a good idea to work on emotional intelligence as an individual with a good therapist or spiritual director first, so that you are better able to return to your family and be less reactive to them. I suggest that the person you seek to help you in this journey:

1. Isn't afraid to delve into the area of emotion, in other words, she isn't just applying cognitive techniques to get you to "rationalize" your problem
2. Is willing to talk about your family of origin with you, and your emotional reactivity to it
3. Has done enough of his own emotional, family and spiritual work that he can be an effective coach for you

Togetherness

This family process is one that I have discovered after 25 years of observing families in my congregations, especially those who do not seek therapy. I have also observed it in families and couples in therapy. The family manages its anxiety and maintains homeostasis through togetherness. A togetherness family is like a package of gummy bears that's been left in the sun too long. Everyone is sticky and gooey and sweet, but they are all stuck together in one "gummy blob." My own nuclear family is very much like this. We "talk." Whenever there's a problem, we all get together and talk it through. There are *no* family secrets in my family! We blab everything to everyone and in front of everyone all the time. We also analyze it and "help" each other with whatever it is. I imagine that many families of ministers and therapists are at particularly high risk for gummy-blobby-ness.

It is impossible to define oneself in a family like this, because whatever you say, everyone else agrees with or, with a big group-hug, agrees to disagree with. It's almost impossible to get a rise out of anyone in these families. They're always so *understanding*; always validating one another's feelings. A teenager can't even take a good stab at rebellion. Everyone "respects" her choice of clothing or lifestyle or friends. These families may sound too good to be true. But alas, when the children of a gummy-blob family marry and form their own families, they are often dissatisfied with their partners and/or children and their un-worked-out emotional responses get manifested quickly in one of the other processes. Children of gummy-blob families may be quick to blame their partners for the problems they are experiencing because, after all, there couldn't possibly be anything wrong with them—look at the lovely family they came out of!

I had one couple in therapy for a long time where the husband came from a gummy-blob family. Both his parents were therapists, and all they did when he was growing up was attend to his feelings and those of his two siblings. Obviously, when he got into conflict with his wife, it had to be his wife's fault. He came to therapy to have me fix her. Interestingly enough, when the wife received a little coaching on defining herself and maturing emotionally, she pulled up, and her gummy-blob husband started to disintegrate. The next time the couple met his gummy parents for the weekend, his mom and dad had a fight, and momma gummy bear drove off in a huff—something he had never observed before!

I surmise that Murray Bowen himself came from a gummy-blob family. He once conducted an exercise in self-definition where he purposely wrote letters to his parents and siblings to stir them up.[95] He was trying to see if he could remain "outside" the gummy-blob while still maintaining good contact with them. The letters did indeed stir them up, and they all came together to see what on earth had happened to Murray, with one sibling concluding he must now have a drinking problem. In the end, Bowen concluded that his effort virtually forced the whole family to make a significant shift in acquiring "self," (moving up the Scale) and that this effort of his contributed to the overall health of the family.

I don't know about writing purposely misleading letters to stir up trouble in a family. But it is probably good to do whatever you can to find some "self" in a family like this, even if it means really ticking somebody off. Gummy-blob families are held up as perfect and ideal. They are not. While they may experience fewer divorces, they can be just as subject to illnesses—physical or emotional. If no one can take leadership in these families and find a way to "stand alone"—out of the lump—these families will do poorly in subsequent generations.

---

[95] Murray Bowen, *Family Therapy in Clinical Practice*, 467–528.

Chapter 26:
Emotional Process II

Happiness is having a large, loving, caring, close-knit family in another city.
—George Burns

Over- and Underfunctioning

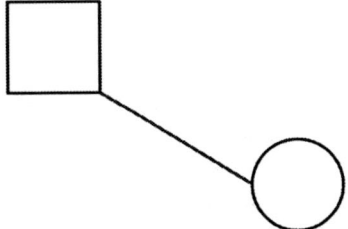

The over/underfunctioning process may be as mild as one partner doing all the banking to as extreme as one partner "looking after" the other one who is completely impaired (physically, mentally or emotionally). It is not possible for the emotional process within a system to be defined in terms of over/underfunctioning if both partners function at a high level. If they do, then they will exhibit another emotional process, such as conflict or distancing, especially when the anxiety goes high. High functioning is good! *Over*functioning is a sign of emotional immaturity.

In partnerships where one partner is chronically ill, the other is usually an overfunctioner, and was that way even before the couple met. It is not the overfunctioner's *fault* that the other one is impaired. In order to maintain homeostasis in the family, if one partner functions too high, the other one *must*, by the definition of homeostasis (balance) function low to compensate. Since our society values overfunctioning, workaholism and every effort to "get ahead," the underfunctioner is often blamed for being weak or helpless. If truth be told, both partners are functioning at equally poor levels.

Sometimes the overfunctioner is completely frustrated with his workload, and wishes or demands that the underfunctioner pull up. Unfortunately, it is not possible for the underfunctioner to pull up so long as the overfunctioner is overfunctioning! In other situations, the overfunctioner is quite "happy" to be "helping" the poor helpless (sometimes sick) partner. What he doesn't realize is that his overfunctioning is not helping and may in effect be contributing to the helpless or sick partner remaining helpless or sick.

Because it seems cruel not to help someone who is impaired, "love" prevails and the person is "helped." Far from being cruel, true love would allow the other to experience the consequences of her own behaviour or condition, for when she does, she will inevitably grow spiritually, find more fortitude than she previously thought she had, and pull up in her own health or functioning.

Janet and Paul: A Case Study[96]

Let's take a look at this fictional but typical example of an over/underfunctioning couple: Janet is chronically ill with various problems, including fatigue. Despite repeated promises to try harder or do better, she fails to follow through on her commitments. She feels badly but is still relieved that her husband, Paul, will always bail her out. Paul feels chronically resentful of Janet but continues to rescue her every time.

When friends suggest that he let her deal with the consequences herself, it sounds good to Paul, but he can never bring himself to do it. What really comes up for Paul is his image of himself as a "nice guy" that he'd have to let go of if he let his wife struggle with her underfunctioning. He fears her becoming angry toward him (rather than the "I'm such a lucky woman—what would I do without you" that he has been used to). He also fears her leaving him because, aside from his "taking care of her," he doubts that he really offers her much more. His chronic overfunctioning keeps his anxiety in check.

On Janet's side, she feels badly about herself, that she keeps letting Paul, and others, down. She tells herself that she'll do better, but whenever she begins to rise to a challenge, she feels anxiety. Dealing with things in the big outside world seems daunting. She could push through this anxiety and accomplish something she'd feel good about, but she has learned that it is easier to back down. Her "wonderful husband" will take care of it later. So Janet's underfunctioning

---

[96] I am indebted to clinical psychologist Dr. Geoffrey Carr for writing this perfectly fitting (fictional) case study for me.

maintains Paul's sense of being a fabulous, nice guy, and Paul's overfunctioning relieves Janet of having to cope with her anxiety, leading them to continue this dance despite its costs.

Just Stop That!
Underfunctioners will not pull up by themselves, or through any sort of advice, convincing or argument, no matter how "logical" it is. The only way for an underfunctioner to pull up is to have everyone stop overfunctioning for him. Now some underfunctioners I know of are so invested in their own underfunctioning that if their partner stops overfunctioning for them, they simply seek out someone else in the family (or outside of it) to "help them" from then on. So the point is not for the overfunctioner to stop overfunctioning in order to make a change in the other. The overfunctioner must think only of himself, his own emotional healing and defining himself clearly. This will have a far greater effect on the other in the long run.

It is easier said than done that an overfunctioner must just stop overfunctioning. As a card-carrying overfunctioner, I know first-hand how difficult if not impossible it is to do that. But I do have a success story in my own life that I will share, at least in part, in the next section. The thing is, it is not possible to say to someone, "You *must* start to function better." The "must" in that sentence, especially in conjunction with the you statement, implies an imposing of the will upon the other, and this is not only unhealthy, it will be fruitless in bringing about change. It merely continues the overfunctioning: "*I* have decided how *we* will get through this." But even to announce something like, "I am no longer willing to do the laundry in this house" may be fruitless as well. Whenever you make a self-defining statement, you have to be willing to endure the consequences of what you will or will not do.

It's fine to declare you'll never do laundry again, but you must either be willing to live in a house where the laundry is never done (perhaps even wear dirty clothes to work for the rest of your life) or else you must clearly outline the consequences of your decision to stop overfunctioning to others. For instance, "If someone else does not pull up and do the laundry, then I will:

- Hire a maid
- Take all the clothes to the dry cleaner
- Buy myself new clothes whenever I run out
- Put your clothes in garbage bags when dirty and deny you access to them until you're ready to launder them

> Do my own laundry only, and pile yours in hampers whenever I see them lying around

The consequence does not matter; what matters is that you must be willing to follow through with it. Now here comes the most important part: you are not waiting around for other people to change (i.e., start doing laundry). You, yourself, are changing. Only you. You are no longer going to do laundry, *and* you are going to work on emotional intelligence. This may mean figuring out how having dirty laundry or hiring a maid will affect you emotionally, sitting in those emotions, processing through them and coming out the other side.

You must still fully expect that you will have to continue this behaviour into perpetuity and that no one else in the house will ever, in fact, do laundry. You will have no cares or concerns about your children putting on dirty underwear to go to school, or your husband putting his dry cleaning (which now extends to his socks and boxers) onto his credit card. The minute your mind wanders to *them*, wondering when they'll learn (to be more like you) and help around the house, you have lost the leadership game.

Whatever consequence you decide upon, it cannot, under any circumstances be an idle threat. Threats are acceptable as long as they're not emotionally charged. Well, okay, just the word "threat" is emotionally charged, isn't it? In another's emotional reactivity, you'll certainly be accused of "threatening" or "giving an ultimatum." I personally think there's nothing wrong with ultimatums. Ultimatums have been given a bad rap. I would appreciate hearing one from someone because then I'd be crystal clear on where I stood. If someone said to me, "If you do such-and-such, I will quit this group and never come back," I would even appreciate that. I might respond with, "Thank you for being so clear." If they said it in an emotionally charged way, then it would be the emotion I would want to address not the "ultimatum" anyway. And if they said it calmly, I would take it as a purely self-defining statement, which I appreciate coming from anyone. Never take to heart anyone's accusation that you are "threatening" or "giving an ultimatum" if you are not emotionally reacting but are just plain defining yourself.

The trouble with this theory is that most overfunctioners are *not* willing to live with the consequences despite their protests to the contrary and would rather overfunction forever. Mothers are not willing to let the house look the way it would if they didn't overfunction. Husbands are not willing to let the bank account and charge cards get into the state they would get into if they didn't overfunction. As this emotional process (like the others) extends to the workplace, most bosses/owners/managers are not willing to lose money if they cease to overfunction. The list goes on.

An Overfunctioner's Story

A few years ago, I came to the point in my own life where I was faced with few choices. It was driving me nuts that my husband, although a successful law partner, sat on the couch every night and watched TV. He seldom interacted with me or took part in the homemaking. The only way I could define myself was to say calmly that if he were to continue to underfunction in this manner, then I did not want to live that way the rest of my life, and I would walk away from the marriage. It was a fascinating time in my life when I did that. It took me months to sort it out—both with a supervisor and some other family members. I did not really want to leave my husband. I had not ceased loving him at all. We weren't fighting, and I wasn't hopelessly unhappy. But I was exhausted from more than 20 years of overfunctioning, and I was not willing to live with the consequences of ceasing to overfunction. I had tried it about five years earlier with consequences I didn't like—the house ended up filthy and unorganized, meals were never prepared, and all the little "fix-it" tasks around the place were never done. I had assumed that if I stopped doing and nagging, that eventually he would pick up where I left off. But remarkably, not one thing changed, and I'm talking about *years and years*. In response, I gave up this stupid theory and went back to overfunctioning and nagging, which meant that although I was miserable, I could at least live in the place, invite people over and eat.

But as more years passed, I became increasingly exhausted, and, of course, there was always underlying resentment, which I was trying to manage as best I could and not project back onto him (resenting someone else is quite a useless expenditure of life energy). Finally, the real choices in my life became clear: I could either grow old and die exhausted from overfunctioning, or I could move out on my own and try to deal with the loneliness or the task of finding someone else in my life who didn't underfunction *and* was at least as emotionally mature as the partner I just left. I was leaning toward the second option. But I had to be comfortable enough with choosing it so that I could define myself clearly with him and *not* expect him to change.

Finally, the day came when I calmly and clearly confronted him with what I was thinking about. That initial conversation went badly, as I had expected. He reacted with anger and accusatory statements, in the predictable "three-fold formula": you are wrong, change back, if you don't, there will be consequences. I held my ground, and refused to get emotionally reactive. After all, I had already done that on my own; I had sorted through and processed a whole truckload of emotions. I was able to have *this* conversation with my neocortex fully engaged.

Since my husband is actually not an immature idiot and pretty much an all-around great guy (except for the bit about lying around on the couch), he quite quickly saw the immaturity of his own reaction and returned to the conversation. (He had originally walked away in a huff.) The next time we talked, it was more thoughtful and mature. It's almost as if family members can "smell" self-definition and emotional intelligence. There's certainly something in the air, something perhaps in our subtle body language or facial coding that tells the tale: I was serious. I was not angry, not reactive, not demanding he change or do anything. I was calmly, maturely, dead-serious, and he knew it.

Things changed—in both of us. Finally, after over 20 years, he pulled up. *And*, equally importantly, I learned wherein *I* was underfunctioning in this relationship. I learned wherein I needed him and relied on him. So he doesn't do much at home. Okay, but he's a very successful lawyer and makes a lot of money. He worked his way up the corporate ladder, went to night school for 13 years to get a BA while raising a family and quit a corporate executive job at 38 to go to law school. Hardly a lazy bum. He manages the household money fairly well, negotiates mortgages, pays the taxes and runs errands. He does all the dishes and his own laundry—even though he complains bitterly about that on a daily basis. Moreover, he's my best friend. He's the first person I call if I have good news or bad news. He has learned to listen. He loves me and loves the children. He thinks he's funny, and there's something funny about that that I just love. He cries at sad movies and sad telephone company commercials. He loves kids so much, he cried all the way through the movie *Mrs. Doubtfire* because the poor bloke had to dress up like a woman just so he could be with his kids. (To everyone else, this movie was a hilarious comedy.) He still believes in Santa Claus, and at Christmastime he thinks he is Santa Claus. His extravagant giving of gifts to everyone else in the family is a type of overfunctioning to which I respond with underfunctioning (*I'm* the one who forgets birthdays and anniversaries.)

When I thought about leaving him and finding someone else, I took a look on one of those match-up websites and read the bios of the 50-year-old men out there looking. Yeesh! Who was I kidding? Not only did I come to realize that they were all infinitely less mature than my own husband, but my eyes were opened to how little I, too, had to offer someone else. For instance, although I don't lie around on the couch watching *Matlock* reruns, I do spend most of my spare time reading about brain function and writing a book. Whoop-de-doo! How appealing is that? I had read page after page about how much "fun" these single people were and how they loved adventure, hiking, sailing, etc. Give me a break. My idea of adventure is to find some book in the library on a philosophical premise I'd never considered before or sit in a coffee shop with some other geek talking about quantum theory or the problems with substitutionary atonement. So perhaps the very best mate I could find would be someone who isn't into doing too much more than watching TV. I learned a lot about myself.

Charlie and I still struggle with over and underfunctioning in our relationship. But I see now more clearly how it moves back and forth; overfunctioning doesn't only belong to me. We are now both more committed to telling each other what we need and truly listening to one other. Our relationship is not only enriched, it's more genuine. And I've solved a lot of my exhaustion problems by hiring a gardener and a maid and charging it to him!

Projection onto a Child

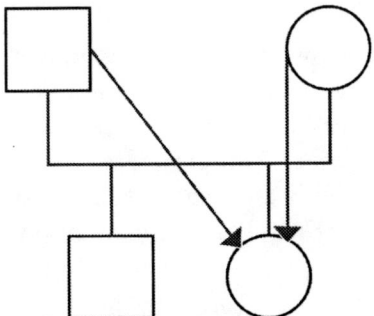

The final emotional process that a family may use to manage its anxiety and maintain homeostasis is by projecting all, or a large part, of its anxiety onto a child. This is the reason, more than anything, that children in the same family turn out differently. One may appear to be "normal" and function quite highly, while another one is riddled with problems. Because they were raised by the same parents, often it is concluded that the child's problems must be genetic or she was just born to be a pain in the ass. Parents refuse to look at themselves, or their own families, and conclude that the problem lies solely in the child. It is amazing to me that on the one hand in our current societal culture we do not want to "blame the victim" (as in cases of rape, domestic violence, etc.) yet we seem to have no trouble blaming children for their own problems because God forbid that we should "blame the parents." The trend that I have observed, of which I gave a full treatment in chapter 9, is to blame neither the parents nor the child, but to blame genetics.

As I have said, blame and responsibility are two different things. Because every family manages its anxiety *somehow*, there is really no point in blaming anyone for anything. But taking responsibility is something different. If you can take responsibility for your child's impairment by at least admitting that family emotional process might be contributing to it, then would this not give you tremendous hope and an unbelievable sense of power over your child's problems?

If you are incapable of taking any responsibility whatsoever in regard to your children, it is probably because you cannot deal with your own shame in doing so. The fear of shame is nothing less than Leviathan. Better to attribute the problem to a gene, a disorder, a virus or the child himself than to deal with Leviathan. Most cannot sit in their shame for one minute, let alone long enough to admit that perhaps they made a mistake as a parent or neglected to take enough care and attention to their parenting or anything else that would hold them responsible. Emotional intelligence is the best resolution to this problem.

You might well ask how projecting anxiety onto a child, or an impairment in the child, "manages" the anxiety in the family or maintains some sort of homeostasis. Aren't families with impaired children in perpetual chaos? It's a good question with a rather complicated answer. Murray Bowen, through his research on families with an impaired child (originally schizophrenic), discovered the following principles in this emotional process, which I have simplified below:

> ➢ Mom and Dad have not worked out their own lack of maturity (healing what's under their trap doors)—something that has its roots in their

own families of origin. (For instance, if they fall at 70 on the Scale, they still have 30 "units" of emotional immaturity and lack of integration to make up for.)

- When one parent notices that something may not be quite right with a child, the parent's amygdala flares up a **DANGER!** signal. The danger is obvious; as parents we instinctively want to protect our children from all harm, so if anything looks like it's threatening them (even a virus), our amygdala kicks in. Our bodies prepare themselves to take the child and flee, or fight off the predator.

- When a parent's amygdala is firing madly, he appears anxious to the child even if he can fool others with his apparent calm. You may think you are able to "fake" being calm with a child, but this is not possible. Your body language and facial coding will betray your words and calm tone of voice. It will be subtle, but it will be there.

- If the parent is saying he's calm, but his body is sending another message, the child becomes confused and therefore anxious.

- If the parent is visibly anxious, and acting so or saying so, then the child becomes anxious. The only way for children to be anxious children is if one of their parents is anxious. Show me a kid with an anxiety disorder, and I'll show you an anxious (or an absent) parent every single time.

- Throughout this entire process, the parent's cognitive functioning has slowed down or shut down, adding to the anxiety of the child.

- The other parent "smells" the anxiety in this situation and becomes anxious, compounding the anxiety of the child.

- In their anxiety, the parents hurriedly (and without much clear thinking) look for a diagnosis of the child and usually consult someone outside the family such as a doctor, psychologist, teacher, police officer or clergyperson—sometimes all of the above. If the child's "problem" is behavioural, even the most well-meaning parents in the most educated families will start to consult books, take parenting courses and seek out other advice.

- Throughout this process, the two parents have now "forgotten" about the amount of immaturity they have from their families of origin and perhaps even the conflict they had between one another. They do not spend time working on themselves as individuals: all their time and energy is spent on the "problem" child.

- At some point in this process, the child is "diagnosed" by a well-meaning expert: the child has chronic tonsillitis, dyslexia, anaemia, constitutional growth delay, allergies, asthma, stress, obesity, anorexia, ADHD, a chemical imbalance, depression, social anxiety, phobia, epilepsy, IBS, diarrhoea, indigestion, arthritis, constipation, dysmenoria, is a daydreamer, artistic, autistic, energetic, lethargic, rude, dirty, overly sexual, asexual, fantasizer, uncreative, underachieving, overachieving, superachieving, is "special needs," is "special gifts."

- Once the parents receive a diagnosis for the child that they are satisfied with, their anxiety goes down significantly. This may seem odd. But I experienced it myself one time when I waited in a hospital emergency room for two hours with my seven-year-old daughter. Once the doctor finally came along and looked at the gash in her arm and declared she needed stitches, I felt tremendous relief. The relief was so tremendous that I took note of it at the time and wondered about it for years until I learned more about Family Systems theory. I thought to myself, "Now why was I happier knowing the cut was bad enough to need stitches? Shouldn't I have been more relieved if he'd come along and said, 'It's nothing. It'll heal. Take her home.'?" The thing is, I imagine I would have been embarrassed then for bringing her to the emergency room, and so the diagnosis of stitches being needed was more welcome than my own shame. Aha!

- When parents get their child diagnosed with something there is inevitably an internal process in their minds that says, "Thank God it wasn't just me or my parenting; there really is something wrong with this kid." Since we are unaware of this internal process, because we'd much rather keep *that* under the trap door, we cannot process it and deal with it within ourselves. Like it or not, once we get our child diagnosed, we feel better and calm down. If you don't like how all this is sounding right about now, there is another reason you feel relieved, which you may like better: once you receive a diagnosis for your child, you feel better because there will inevitably be some form of treatment that goes along with it. Also, there are more people working with you to "help" the child. You are no longer alone in it. The school will start remedial work or counselling, the rabbi will take him under her wing, there will be a drug prescribed or physiotherapy or a support group you can attend with parents of other children with the same problems.

> Now that the parents have calmed down with this diagnosis, the child learns that so long as he is "sick" or has a "problem," his parents are calmer. It makes no difference if the parents feel calm because help is on the way or if they feel calm because they now have evidence that they are not ineffective parents after all. Again, this is such a subtle process that neither the child nor his parents will be aware of it. It is the living system's natural response to do what works for it with as little stress/anxiety as possible.

> As time goes on, if the child improves, the other stressors in the family system start to rear their ugly heads. Far from it being true that if the child does better, everyone is happier, in families with an impaired child, no one does better for very long. So if the child starts to function better, the homeostasis in the family once again becomes upset. Mom and Dad might have to deal with their own issues, both as individuals and as a couple.

> The tension rises in the family. Meanwhile Junior "knows" (meaning some part of his brain and his body knows; it will not be a conscious thought of his) that if he were just in trouble again, everyone's anxiety would calm down. So he gets into trouble again. The family focus goes back onto him and round and round she goes.

The most obvious reaction to this theory of family process is: So what am I supposed to do if my child has a problem? Ignore it? Of course that is not only impossible, but it would be unethical. It behoves you as a parent, however to:

1. Do what you can to remain calm and make up your mind to be *more relieved if the child is not diagnosed with something serious than if he is,*
2. Focus more on your own anxiety/shame related to the child's problem than the problem itself,
3. Seek whatever help is necessary for the child, as a faithful and caring parent, but not make a big deal out of the child's problem—to him or anyone else—no matter how serious it is,
4. Only devote as much life energy into the child's problem as is needed to address the problem and
5. Refuse to fret, fuss and worry excessively about the problem.

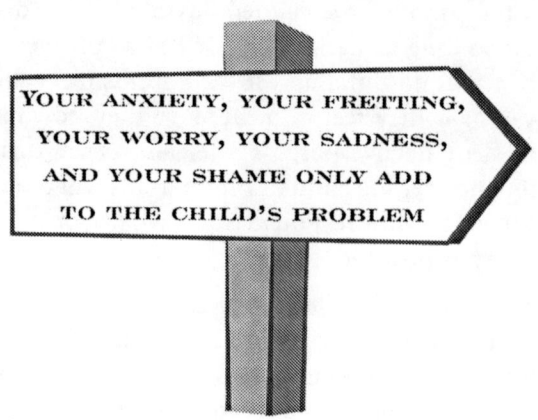

> YOUR ANXIETY, YOUR FRETTING, YOUR WORRY, YOUR SADNESS, AND YOUR SHAME ONLY ADD TO THE CHILD'S PROBLEM

I've Been There[97]

I have been through the terrifying and heart-breaking experience of having a "problem child." Our oldest son and our next-oldest, a daughter, sailed through childhood and the teen years pretty much unscathed. Alex was the "problem." We thought she was born that way. Born on a Wednesday, and as the old Mother Goose poem goes, "Wednesday's child is full of woe," Alex was beautiful, smart and delightfully unique but frankly, just a little bit weird. Even her kindergarten teacher said to us, "You can't put a label on Alex. She's really…*different*." We didn't mind "different" one bit—we enjoyed her distinctive character.

Alex went through some tough times being the youngest, always bossed around by the other two, as well as a couple of neighbour kids who were older. We found out later that she really got picked on and virtually oppressed: bullied, treated like a slave. We had no idea as parents that this was going on. We were both wrapped up in our careers and assumed that as long as kids were loved, fed, clothed, safe and taken to ballet and soccer, there was no problem. Besides, we had a great nanny.

Eventually Alex's "woe" imploded upon her when I got diagnosed with cancer when she was only 11. That's pretty tough. She seemed to be handling it fine, but what did I know? I was even more wrapped up in myself at that time. She was angry, but Alex was always angry. Little did I realize, that for the next three years or so, she would find a secret coping mechanism for "controlling"

---

[97] I am indebted to my daughter, Alexandria Bois, for her permission to use this story. As of this writing, Alex is a candidate for Ordained Ministry in the United Church of Canada.

a life that she perceived was out of her control. During those same two years, I happened to be on a steep learning curve, ascertaining as much knowledge as I could about Family Systems theory. This was something I later came to be very thankful for.

I'll never forget the day Alex came to me in tears when she was 14 years old. I even remember where I was standing—right in the kitchen at the top of the stairs, across from the fridge. It's a flashbulb memory, burned in my brain. "Mom," she cried. "Today in health class we learned about anorexia nervosa, and I think I have that! They said it can get worse and worse until you die. *I don't want to die!*" She buried her face in my chest and sobbed, and right there, my heart broke. Shattered. Disintegrated. I held her so tightly, I dared not risk the inhaling of a breath. Time, and my spirit, languished in her arms.

When the fog in my brain cleared, one thought was apparent: *this is not about her*. If my knowledge and training in Family Systems was of no other value in my life, in these circumstances, it was crucial. I knew at that very moment that in order for my daughter to get better, I must focus on myself, as well as my relationship with my husband, and not on her and her problem.

I said something like this, "Alex, I am so sorry. This isn't your fault. I promise you that I'm going to work on being more calm and helping the rest of the family be more calm, so it's easier for you to work this out." Her reply was, "Well…okay…but can I go to a doctor or something too?" I will never know what her response would have been if I had responded the way I normally would have, insisting she see a doctor right away. I can imagine, though, that she would have been less motivated to get help or stick with it. When I shifted the focus from her to myself and the whole family, she immediately took responsibility for her own healing—at only 14 years of age. I am still astounded when I think of it.

Of her own choosing, Alex saw an adolescent psychiatrist and took antidepressant medication for one year. She spent several years with a therapist, also of her own choosing, working on processing her childhood issues, her subsequent anxiety, and her own personal and spiritual growth. Alex is a tall girl with a large, athletic frame. She was a star softball player for many years. At her lowest weight she was about 110 lbs—luckily she caught the disorder early enough that her health was not significantly affected. Today, eight years later, she's a healthy, and gorgeous, 150 pounds. Right now, she's downstairs eating a clubhouse sandwich and writing an essay. She still struggles with food issues when her anxiety rises. But Alex is one of the wisest, most integrated, emotionally intelligent and mature people I know. She is and will be an extraordinary leader.

I share this story because I have been there. I know that the most difficult, near-impossible, counterintuitive thing to do when your child is sick or troubled is to focus on yourself and your own growth, rather than hers. Somehow, I found within myself, and through the grace of God, the will to do so. If I did not believe that this theory would work for you and your family, I would not have embarked upon the journey of writing this book. When your closest relationship systems are screaming out for you to "do something" other than focus on your own spiritual growth, it takes incredible courage to stay the course. But *you* have the power to do that. If you didn't, you would not have bought this book, or read this far.

Chapter 27:
Curious Change

The important thing is not to stop questioning.
Curiosity has its own reason for existing.
—Albert Einstein.

All of the emotional processes in the previous two chapters are visible and present to some degree in any living system. This includes any place where more than two human beings gather: an office, a temple, a Rotary club, a sports team or the United Nations. Although it will not be as pronounced and will be more fluid than in a family, emotional process will be present and visible to the leader with a keen eye and a commitment to curiosity rather than involvement in the content of issues. "Content" means whatever the issue is about: incompetent staff, falling sales, same-sex marriage, tax regulations, personality differences, the budget, restructuring.

When there is conflict, staying neutral and being curious is particularly difficult. You will assume you can evoke some change in the system, or in the people involved in the conflict, by imposing your will in the form of "teaching," "telling them things" or providing some "expertise" on the matter.

THE ISSUE IS NOT THE ISSUE

Playing Detective

When any system is in crisis, anxiety will rise such that everyone's clarity of thought is impaired. There will be less expression of facts and more assumption and innuendo. The anxiety will become apparent in one or more of the following ways, as outlined in chapter 23:

- We-thinking
- Resistance and sabotage
- Overfunctioning
- Diagnoses and blame
- Herding
- Cutoff
- Secrecy

The leader may be the target for any or all of these factors. If the leader can manage her own anxiety and define herself in the matter, she will be told, one way or another:

- You are wrong.
- Change back.
- If you don't, there will be consequences.

In order to stay meaningfully connected, the leader must first take on the role of detective in order to bring anxiety down.

When Anytown Baptist Church experienced a complete culture shift in terms of their mission, vision and purpose, the anxiety began to rise among the dissenters. Being contagious as in a herd of wildebeests, this anxiety spread to nearly everyone. Rev. George and the board of deacons became the target. George's response, after examining himself in terms of the leadership trinity—what he thought and what was going on with him emotionally—was curiosity. He decided his role would be detective. He would meaningfully connect with everyone who was upset and ask questions. This involved a multitude of visits, meetings and cups of coffee with members of the congregation. At each of these meetings, George asked direct questions such as these:

- What happened?
- What exactly was said?

- ➢ Who said it?
- ➢ Who are the other people whom you say feel the same way? What are their names? (George wrote all their names down, met with each of them and asked the same questions *until no new names turned up on the list.*)
- ➢ What do you think about it?
- ➢ What's your greatest fear?
- ➢ What else do you think I should know?

George did not only get at the facts of who said what and who felt what, he also gained invaluable understanding of his people and what they were thinking. It paid off. After about five months of engaging in this detective work, no one was able to pull the old "a lot of people are upset about this" with George. He could calmly respond with something like, "Actually, four people are upset about it besides yourself—Mabel, Tom, Elsie and Hugh. Have you heard from anyone else that I should also speak to?" It turned out that only about 10 people out of the 400 members of Anytown Baptist were "upset." These 10 had managed to make another 50 quite anxious that "everyone was upset," and had nearly convinced the majority to go along with the wishes of the 10!

George stayed the course. The 10 left and took their financial support with them. Anytown church got a temporary grant from the judicatory's mission fund, re-mortgaged, flourished and grew. The change in George (to curiosity and calm rather than reactivity and problem solving), evoked the eventual change in his closest relationship system: the congregation.

Turning Up and Down the Heat

Ron Heifetz in his brilliant work *Leadership without Easy Answers*, teaches leaders that it is their job to force the organization to do the difficult work of adaptive change, rather than seek a quick fix or "technical solution" to their immediate problems.[98]

As soon as you arrive in a new position, the heat (anxiety) will already be up because of your very arrival. A new leader is wise to work at turning down the heat, or as Heifetz says, "manage the distress" by meaningfully connecting with others. Watch process, listen. Don't do much. I would suggest you keep this up for at least six months to a year, if you can.

---

[98] Ron Heifetz, *Leadership Without Easy Answers*, Chapter 6.

If the system seems relatively calm and complacent, define yourself in such a way as will stir up a little trouble. Not too much! Clergy could try something like, "I think the baptismal font would look better on the other side of the chancel." Then sit back and watch the fun. (Don't forget your detective work.) A new CEO, who's been sitting at meetings quietly for months, may try saying, "I don't think that idea will work." She has to mean it, of course. I'm not suggesting you make something up just to turn up the heat. Merely announcing one of your clearly thought-through values, goals or visions will be enough.

If your family appears to be calm and everyone's happy, it may be time for you to say, "Gee, Dad, I've noticed that every time we all get together, you drink too much." Watch what happens, to whom and how people respond to it. See if you can determine the emotional process at work. Try to identify the triangles. Ask *yourself*, "What's happening with me?" Turn up the heat and watch. Heifetz compares this process with getting up on the balcony and watching the dance below rather than being caught up in it.[99]

If the heat is already high and anxiety is running rampant, then according to Heifetz, the leader's job is to manage the distress. Worry less about defining yourself; don't stroll into meetings and declare your profound and scholarly opinion. Spend your time being meaningfully connected. Visit people. Arrange coffees, lunches and "fireside chat" meetings. Observe; be curious. Reassure the anxious. Do not involve yourself in the content of issues and try not to ally yourself with any groups or "camps," no matter how you personally feel about the issue itself.

Empowerment

It is difficult to talk about empowering others in leadership without falling down the slippery slope of imposing one's will or overfunctioning. However, it can be an important part of a good leader's self-defining effort to seek out gifted people in his organization who have good ideas but no authority or *position* of leadership to carry them out.[100] If you hear someone's idea and think it is valid, then it is a matter of defining yourself to say so. As a leader of an organization or institution, you also have a duty to speak up. It is perfectly acceptable for you to say, "I think Joe's idea is a good one." If *you* have the authority, then people may listen. Of course, once you define yourself, the response will be predictable; there will be allies and saboteurs. If you support an idea from a voice without

---

[99] Ron Heifetz, *Leadership Without Easy Answers*, Chapter 11.
[100] Ron Heifetz, *Leadership Without Easy Answers*, 128.

authority, you will be blamed for the idea if it doesn't fly. On the up side, you will also be credited if it's a success.

Assuming Authority

Leaders must embrace the leadership trinity in all that they do. Even so, at times, the anxiety in a system will shoot up and continue to escalate despite the leader's clearly expressed thinking, and calm, mature effort to stay connected. If this happens, then the leader has not defined herself strongly enough or emphatically enough. Sometimes it is necessary to put one's foot down. Perhaps even reach down deep and drag out some of that adaptive, self-righteous anger. Be firm and fair. Beware, however, of the plethora of material written about "strong leadership." Desperate times call for thought-filled measures, not emotional reactivity.

Back at Anytown Baptist, the congregation was enjoying getting on with their articulated mission and vision after going through almost a year of conflict. Rev. George had provided excellent leadership, but anxiety continued to spiral upward. It seemed like it was one thing after another. It was time for George to put his foot down. He knew what his own, and the congregation's, values, goals and visions were, and he was not willing to put up with any further pettiness, foolishness or sabotage. It was expressed in a simple, non-anxious, "That's enough now" followed by the best I-statement George could muster: "I am no longer willing to tolerate this nonsense." No more home visits or cups of coffee to meaningfully connect. No more information-sharing meetings where grievances would be aired. No more time taken up on the board of deacons' agenda. Because *that was enough.*

One risk of suggesting something like this is that immature leaders may assume authority too soon or do it anxiously. It is very tempting to make an end run around the quest for emotional intelligence or meaningful connection. If you do not know what you think or value because you have not thought through it carefully enough, you will "put your foot down" while you are still anxious in order to impose your will or avoid the emotional reactivity in yourself or others. This usually results in cutoff or dismissal.

If the leader is anxious when he defines himself, then the anxiety will zap around the system like a fart in a mitten. It may go below the radar for a bit, but it will surface with the fury of a school of sharks. When you assume authority, you have to really examine yourself to make sure you're just not unable to cope with your fear. That you haven't skipped over the bourn of *self*. If you're positive you haven't, then it is time to assume the authority of your leadership position with the self-defining words, "*I will not.*" Rev. George had done nearly a year of self-examination, spiritual growth, and detective work in the system before he uttered his firm "I am no longer willing to" words.

When the leader is leading, the people feel safe. Even if they do not agree with what the leader is saying, and even if they don't like the leader very much. A self-defined leader is like a solid concrete structure in a hurricane. You may not like it, you may never want to live there, but you know it will stand in a storm.

Chapter 28:

Extraordinary Leadership

A leader must have the courage to act against an expert's advice.
—James Callaghan

Extraordinary leaders are, first of all, good leaders: they understand that they can only bring change to themselves, and, by embracing the leadership trinity, to those within their closest relationship systems. As such, they are wise, integrated human beings. They do not need any other gifts in order for their organization to flourish. Whatever gifts they lack, they will see in other people and surround themselves with those people. They will not act as if threatened by the gifts of others, as they will be emotionally aware of their feelings and will process them in healthy ways without projecting them negatively upon others. They will be aware that their primary job is to lead, not to be an expert on everything. Good leaders who are blessed enough to possess other gifts such as creativity, vision and a sense of adventure, may become extraordinary.

Creativity and Vision

"Creativity" literally means starting with nothing and making something. It means coming up with great ideas to either solve problems or move your organization forward: events, fundraisers, programs, merchandise, services, training methods, marketing plans or forms of governance. To be visionary means that you can virtually "see" a picture of the future of your organization. This doesn't mean that it will turn out that way, but you can see its potential. People who have a great deal of expertise and creativity as well as vision can put into place what is necessary to head toward that vision. When circumstances change, and when others come up with new ideas along the way, extraordinary leaders quickly adapt, change gears and implement new ideas to move the organization forward.

Adventure

Edwin Friedman in his video *Reinventing Leadership*, says that great leaders always have a sense of adventure. They are willing to risk for the sake of the group. A leader completely unwilling to risk is usually too anxious to lead well. If your anxiety is so high that you feel an adventure is a threat, then you'll probably never really do anything, including define yourself.

It is easy to be loved as a leader but not if you want to accomplish something. As soon as you embark upon an adventure, the system will respond predictably to restore the homeostasis. Prepare to be hated. Prepare to fail. Or prepare to risk nothing and do nothing. I have seen businesses go bankrupt and churches close down where the "leader" was embraced and loved. He was described as perfect and wonderful: a brilliant chef, a nice guy, a God-like clergyman. The failure was "not his fault" they said when the bailiff changed the locks. It was the neighbourhood, the silly consumers, the kids these days, the world-going-to-hell. The truth was that he was not willing to risk one thing because he was afraid of not being liked or afraid of "people getting upset."

Adventure and recklessness is not the same thing. If a leader is going to risk, she must be willing to experience the consequences of the risk somehow herself. It isn't fair to risk what only affects your constituents' or employees' livelihoods and not your own.

But leaders who are very successful do risk failure. Babe Ruth held the record not only for home runs but also strikeouts. Why? Because he *swung the bat*. He went for it. If he had not, he would not have successfully hit the ball over the fence so many times.

Life-Long Learning and Spiritual Growth

Extraordinary leaders are committed to learning and growing for life. This includes their particular field of expertise, but also things like leadership and human behaviour, current events, trends and realities. You've already shown that you're interested in life-long learning by reading this book. But don't go around quoting me 10 years from now. Use this book to inspire you to think for yourself and keep learning.

Work on learning more about your own family—both factual (historical) information as well as how your family members think. According to Murray Bowen, it will take *90* trips home to your family of origin where you are making every effort to define yourself and stay connected, watch process and look for triangles, in order to heal. Ninety. Not one or two, or even 10. It's a life-long process.

If possible, work diligently with a therapist, counsellor, emotion coach or spiritual director. Extraordinary leaders have done far more personal work than have the people they lead. You being your only teacher of emotional intelligence is akin to performing your own surgery.

You will learn a great deal more about yourself, others and the supernal by becoming part of a spiritual community with other people. If you do not belong to a faith community, return to that of your parents or grandparents. You may believe that organized religion has betrayed you, but it has not betrayed everyone. I am not saying that religion by itself is a solution to your pain or the only vehicle for your spiritual growth. Many people are religious; very few are truly close to the supernal. Those who take a spiritual path, however, are often led naturally back to the religion of their parents or ancestors.

Teaching

Lloyd Ogilvie, minister of the largest Presbyterian church in the United States, said, "Nothing can happen *through you* which is not happening *to you*." Teach what you know, what you have learned and what you are learning.

In my congregation, almost half of the active adults have taken part in my two-year-long course on leadership. My last class learned significantly more than my first, but even that first class produced several graduates who have gone on to become good leaders not only within the church but in the community, as well. The most significant change is that they understand the importance of their own spiritual growth.

Extraordinary leaders teach others how to lead. Not only will they teach skills, knowledge and expertise particular to their trade, but they will invest time in the spiritual growth of others by teaching them ways to grow. Once you have worked at the concepts in this book and believe that you have grown, set up training events or informal discussion times at work or with your family. Create a "learning environment" of listening and curiosity toward emotional process. Teach the concepts of the leadership trinity to others so that one day they, too, may evoke change in their closest relationship systems. This ripple-out effect is the vehicle for significant change in every bourn.

Caring for Others

Extraordinary leaders are people who care about the whole earth, its people and their own communities. They give back—not just for a tax receipt or for the sake of their reputations. They strive for justice, peace and a better existence for all of humanity. They long for *shalom*. Although they deeply understand that they cannot change the world except by working on themselves and within their closest relationships, they will nevertheless reach out to others and to a hurting world because their compassion cannot possibly be contained.

Part Four

Distant Bourns: Societal context, nature and the supernal

Chapter 29:

Changing the World

Sole bourn, sole wish, sole object of my way.
—William Wordsworth

I don't know about you, but I would like to change the world. I long for my life to make a difference. I want to reach out to others in such a way that they will come to know that there is another path to be taken than the one most choose to travel. I want to leave a legacy with those who remain after I am gone. The absolute truth that I will not see significant change in the world in my own lifetime brings me sadness. It is a loss of hope, a loss of innocence, a loss that I must grieve.

Take a moment to refer back to the list you made in chapter 2 of the things you'd like to see changed in the world. Probably "the world" that you would like to change is either the bourn of societal context, or the bourn of nature. Sadly, you as a single individual have no *direct* power to evoke such change. Moreover, you cannot bring change yourself, as one person, to the supernal. You cannot change "the course of history" or bring about anything on your list, single-handedly—not even with one big barn-burning, gut-wrenching prayer.

A Postmodern View of Change

We live in postmodern times where even the nature of change is changing. Modernity brought with it some idea that we could know virtually everything—that the Enlightenment period was the be-all and end-all of history. Since the turn of the 20th century, human beings pretty much all bought into the idea that we would just get smarter and smarter and one day be able to prove everything (scientifically). Today there is skepticism of scientific knowledge altogether. Postmodernity, according to the French philosopher Jean-Francois Lyotard, is rejecting the grand "metanarratives" of modernity. A metanarrative is a big-picture explanation of everything: the idea that "truth" can be fully known. This includes, of course, almost everything in the bourn of nature.

Science is based on the assumption that *matter* and *energy* (that which we can perceive in the material world) is all that there is. The microscopic atom has been split into three incomprehensibly small parts, and it was once thought that each of these might be made up of some particle even smaller. Whatever that may be, it is *something*. The problem is that quantum physics, grossly oversimplified, reveals that when we break these small parts down even further *there is nothing left*. So if we're not looking, material things may not even be there. Quantum theory also allows for the fact that there might be another universe somewhere, and it may look remarkably like ours or exactly like ours. We might even borrow stuff back and forth from it like energy, life forms, ideas, archetypes, cabbages or people. Don't worry, trying to make sense out of this kind of stuff makes my brain hurt, too.

Many scientists believe that everything is governed by the laws of science. They think we just need to discover more about these laws, and then we will know everything. Today, at the dawn of the 21st century, this very assumption is being questioned. We are coming to believe that the bourn of societal context *decides* what is possible, what is true, what is even miraculous. We already understand that societies, religions and lawmakers decide whether homosexuality is normal or a mental illness; whether there is a "natural order" wherein men are superior to women; whether humans have inherent rights or not. But what about questions like: What is nature? What is the universe? What is reality? These are the questions of a new age that is only beginning to emerge.

The more we discover about nature/the universe, the more it changes. At one time, the world was flat. A postmodern view could argue that there is no difference between this statement and "at one time *we thought* the world was flat." If someone in 1700 saw a man coming back to life after death because that man was administered an electric shock, it would be perceived as a miracle—a change in the very reality of nature. Today it is accepted not as a supernatural event at all, but a routine medical procedure with a "scientific" explanation. Do the perception and knowledge of humanity and the ideas put forth by the social context *shape* the universe? Who knows? Perhaps there is no ultimate reality of the universe beyond what we perceive it to be or beyond what our societal context tells us it is.

The Bourn of Societal Context

We are creatures who evolved into, or were created for, life in community with one another. We exist together in *living systems* or *the bourn of relationship systems*. There is something that joins us together as one with those we love as well as those we interact with on a daily basis. When systems as small as families or organizations begin to grow spiritually because the individuals within them have embraced the leadership trinity in their own lives, slowly, painstakingly, the social context begins to change. Groups of people change laws and cultural norms. Knowledge grows; new ways of thinking and being emerge that shape us and shape the life that is to come—that which we may never know.

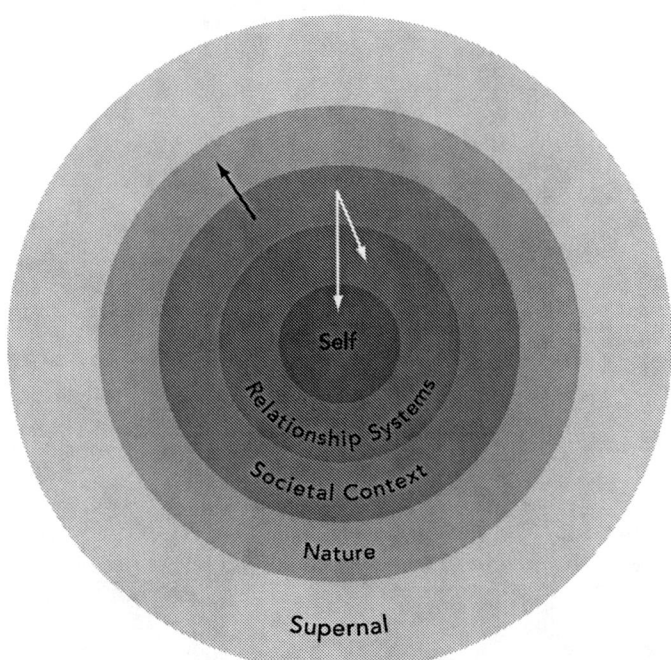

The bourn of societal context in which we live and move (societies, cultures, governments, religions) is ever changing. This is partly due to the influence that groups of people—relationship systems—have over it, and partly because of the influence that nature and the supernal have over it. The societal context makes rules, sets standards and comes up with morals, values and belief systems that influence communities of people: families, churches, businesses and friends. Societal context is in symbiotic relationship with these communities, however.

For communities of people together make up a large part of the context in which they exist. Expressed another way, a relationship system, once it grows large enough, *becomes* the societal context.

If the community is large enough, has one leader (such as a pope or president) and if it becomes dedicated to its own spiritual growth, it will have a tremendous effect for change on the societal context. The Berlin Wall came down. World War II ended with a single bombing. Groups of blacks protesting in the southern United States changed the country's view of human rights. Families may nurture children or abuse them—both will have a life-long effect on the whole family, as well as other families and communities of people with whom they have a connection. Cultures, governments, religions, belief systems or worldviews can change how we understand the universe or even change the universe itself.

The Bourn of Nature

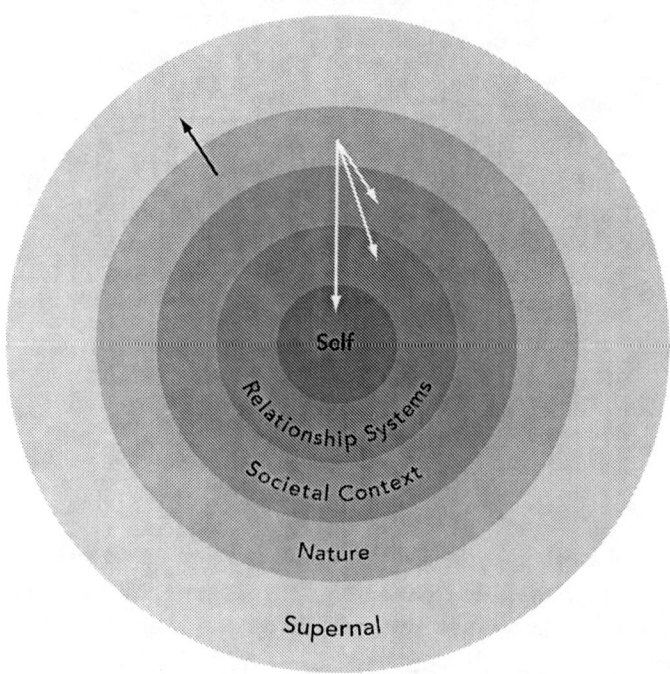

Nature may influence every other bourn, including the supernal, its next closest neighbour. It is well within the realm of our common understanding that nature, in the form of the wonder of the brain or the wonder of disease or disaster, brings change in many forms to both individuals and groups of people. Nature influences societal context, relationships and individuals. Nature can change the world.

Let's face it: we believe what we believe because the universe is a certain way. We make laws, think up ideas, create art and poetry and even write religious doctrine that is in sync with the universe as we know it. But if the universe were static in time and space, our ideas and beliefs would be static as well. Change happens in our beliefs, ideas and cultures not only because we *discover* more truth as time goes on, but because the universe also changes.

Probably all of the items about changing the world that you put on your list in chapter 2 can easily be accomplished by the power of nature or the power of the supernal. Neither one are talking. Frustrating, eh?

Nature and the supernal are in an intimate, and reciprocal, relationship. It is most arrogant for us as humans to believe that the supernal may only relate to humans or human communities. How do we know this? If we can pray and summon up cosmic power through our act of prayer that brings change to ourselves or others close to us, then why is it impossible to believe that the universe cannot also "pray" (somehow communicate with the supernal) and bring change to itself? We have no idea of the power of the universe outside of our human understanding, which, although vast, is severely limited.

Perhaps the supernal and nature depend upon one another. They may be like a pregnant mother carrying a child that is growing and waiting to be born. Whatever this relationship is like, the supernal and nature have some kind of a "deal" going that is unknown to humankind. Nature and the supernal *agree* on how things will normally work and on what is "real" and what is "miraculous." The supernal cannot act alone and "break the deal." Nature must give its consent. And vice versa. We do not know, and never will, what this consent might look like. If this concept is confusing, let it be. It is enshrouded in some amount of mystery anyway. You and I cannot know everything. We are not supernal.

I conducted a discussion session at my church after the horrific tsunami of 2004 in Southeast Asia. The question on everyone's mind was, "Why would God do this (to humans)?" Nobody thought of the idea that the earth itself might have a relationship with God, apart from the humans who live on it. Perhaps the earth was wounded or "sick" that day, just as we get wounded or sick. Maybe it groaned in agony and then simply cracked. The human death toll may have had nothing to do with God's relationship to the human beings on the planet. It may have had everything to do with God's relationship to the planet itself.

Nature may have power beyond our wildest dreams. There is no evidence apart from human construction (our experience, theological doctrine, sacred writings) that we humans have the "top" relationship with the supernal, and the universe, apart from us, does not. Nature may be as capable of love as we are. This love would influence the supernal—change it, even—in ways that we humans cannot even perceive.

The Problem of Evil[101]

Evil is a part of the bourn of nature. It is some kind of mysterious cosmic force. Do not misunderstand me: I am not saying that nature *is* evil, but rather that evil exists in its bourn. So do plants, animals, the human race *as a whole*, the planets and the weather. None of these *are* evil. Evil is something separate—an entity in and of itself.

Unlike the supernal, evil does not move humans or the universe toward the good. Evil knows nothing of love. Evil is a compelling energy that pulls us downward and almost "beckons" us *not* to grow. Evil thwarts our efforts at growth, increasing our pain. Evil tempts us away from growth with temporary, hedonistic satisfactions. Evil is the force that has us saying, "Oh, what's the point? I'm just going to party!" Not that I'm pooping on parties. Fun is fun, and fun is good for the soul. It is only when it consumes a person and keeps him from the (hard) work of spiritual growth that evil is hovering in the shadows.

Evil is the opposite of the supernal, which is wholly good. The supernal is infinite in its capacity to grow, even in size. Evil is limited and finite. It will also be slowly reduced in size over time. When this happens, the universe will evolve into *shalom*. Whenever even one human being grows spiritually, becoming more loving, evil is diminished. If everyone were committed to growth, over a long period of time (even billions of years), evil would eventually disappear. Whenever someone (or perhaps even the universe itself) grows spiritually, there is a little less evil in the world.

People are not evil. People are damaged, wounded, sick or in pain—to varying degrees. Every person's pain is one manifestation of the presence of evil in the world. Depending on the character of it, people's pain will often be projected onto others, sometimes in heinous ways. The pain of the severely depressed kindly pastor who commits suicide and the pain of the sociopath are

---

[101] I am indebted to M. Scott Peck's theory in his book, *People of the Lie*, for many of the ideas in this section.

two extremes of the same kind of pain. It is too overwhelming to be addressed in one lifetime. The sociopath is to be pitied, not despised and executed. At the time of this writing, it is not possible to "cure" a sociopath. Depression at least has some medical treatment. Unfortunately, until sociopaths commit a crime and are caught and incarcerated, they have the potential to become yet another contributing factor to the pain of many others.

As part of the bourn of nature, evil has an influence on the supernal. Evil is basically a pain in the supernal's neck. Evil messes with every bourn below it, thwarting the supernal's bidding that each of them grow. As a result, the supernal must change its very nature over time, in order that its mission of the restoration of the universe to wholeness and healing may be accomplished.

Evil is the opposite of love, and incapable of love, or even of understanding it. Love is consistent and predictable. Love can be counted on. Evil, therefore, cannot be counted on for anything—even to show up when we expect it. It is random by its very nature. Disease, mental illness, disaster, injustice, oppression, poverty and war often fall upon the undeserving in some random way. Evil has us screaming, "Why did this happen?"

Because evil is part of the bourn of nature, as is all the rest of the universe, we do not know if some such thing as a virus or a tsunami is evil or not. Perhaps it is merely the work of the universe itself, which has a relationship with the supernal just as we do. And humans are occasionally the "innocent bystanders." Since it is something we will never know, we will waste a lot of our time and effort asking the "why did this happen" questions.

Whatever the makeup of evil, it is a problem for us, both personally and as a human race. Reacting out of our own fear of the effect of evil upon us and upon those we love, we anxiously skip over bourns and attempt to eradicate various forms of evil from the earth. We find cures for diseases and claim victory over nature, only to discover that some new disease has sprung forth from the universe to kill us. We create seat-belt laws, but people drive faster and accident rates stay the same.[102] We get rich in the "first world" to abate our fears of the effects of evil (random pain), while the rest of the world gets even

---

[102] N. Gregory Mankiw, *Principles of Economics*, Orlando: Harcourt, 1997.
"Now consider how a seat belt law alters the cost-benefit calculation of a rational driver. Seat belts make accidents less costly for a driver because they reduce the probability of injury or death. Thus, a seat belt law reduces the benefits to slow and careful driving. People respond to seat belts as they would to an improvement in the road conditions—by faster and less careful driving. The end result of a seat belt law, therefore, is a large number of accidents…the net result is little change in the number of driver deaths and an increase in the number of pedestrian deaths." (p. 7)

more poor and desperate. We have had wars to end all wars, and, well, you know how that worked out. The solution to changing evil is the same as the solution to everything else. We must begin within our own bourn, the bourn of self, embrace the leadership trinity and grow. Our growth increases our ability to love, and thus the amount of love we express. The increase of love in the universe increases the size of the supernal.

The Bourn of the Supernal

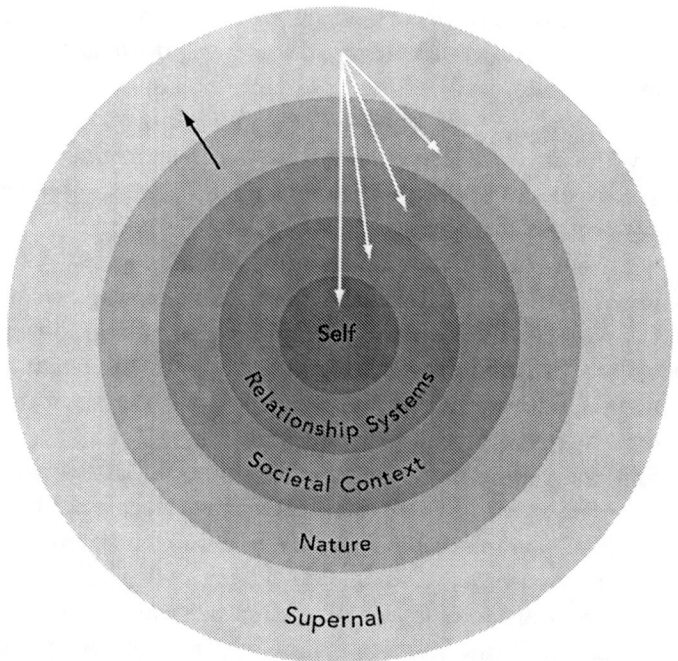

I do not know exactly what the supernal is. I can't explain God to you or the experience of Enlightenment. I cannot *prove* that such things exist. Any philosophical argument I would give would be *a posteriori*, meaning based on my experience. I have had a powerful experience of God in my own life, and I would be glad to tell you about it anytime you come to my church, or if we ever meet for coffee. I have no power to make you see it, however, and particularly I have no power to make you see it *my way*. But I know for *myself* that God exists.

It makes no sense to me that the supernal existed at one time in a vacuum, apart from the universe. Perhaps the supernal and the universe were just "always here." For what is time anyway but a creation of human thinking? This would mean that the supernal exists in relationship with a universe that may not be its own creation. This is radical thinking and perhaps offensive to some religious people. Many like to think of the supernal as big and dominant and in control over everything. But what if the supernal is ultimately *in relationship* with all forms of life, from the largest configuration of galaxies to the smallest, most insignificant human, and the smallest most insignificant one-celled organism? If this is true, then the supernal needs "us" (i.e., the entire universe, including humans) as much as we need it. It changes as "we" change. It grows when "we" grow. The supernal may be nothing more than a simple but powerful call to growth.

There is a very simplistic atheist argument that God cannot possibly exist because such existence cannot be proven scientifically. To which my scholarly response is: "*Duh!*" I once heard an interesting analogy on a television show about the paranormal. I cannot cite the reference, as I only watched it for a few minutes during the commercials in the infinitely more intellectual show, *America's Next Top Model*. That was a joke. Anyway, this analogy compared the universe with an apartment building; I mentioned it briefly in chapter 3. If you think of every bourn on a different floor, remember that the elevators only go up one floor, but they'll go all the way down.

The supernal exists on the top floor. It can come down to our floors if it likes, but we can't go up there. Downstairs (in the societal context), atheist-type scientists are running all sorts of tests, according to the "laws" of life on our very human floor. They cannot find evidence of the supernal. The supernal cannot be seen or *discovered* anywhere on our floor, so the atheist-scientists all agree that there is no such thing. The only problem is, lots of people (including many scientists) keep running into the supernal in the elevator, the lobby and sometimes wandering down the hallways on our floor. Occasionally, there's even a knock at someone's door, and the supernal comes right in for tea. Christians believe that one Bethlehem night, God decided to come and hang out here for about 30 years.

The Celtics refer to the experiences of God's realm breaking into ours as "the thin places." A thin place is a time when the supernal breaks into our "world," even if just for a moment. Sometimes you will encounter a thin place when you are communing with nature, singing a hymn, admiring a sunset, laying by the fire with a dog's head in your lap, listening to a sermon, looking into the eyes of a loved one, learning something insightful or new, praying, meditating or holding a newborn child.

One thing that I believe about the supernal, which I think is pretty much universal among spiritual people of all varieties: the supernal is a good thing, a powerful thing, a force that draws everything toward *shalom*. There is within the universe some cosmic power that moves in the direction of love. It calls forth love in every one of us, at every level of our human existence. It also calls forth love from the universe itself, beckoning it to grow.

The self is in relationship with the supernal. It can go "up the elevator" to the supernal's floor whenever it wants, but is not able to change the supernal. This concept may also be objectionable to some religious people, or it may be blatantly obvious, depending on your theology. "Does the supernal not answer prayer?" you may ask. Of course it does, because it is able to influence the self if it desires to do so. The supernal seems to be particularly amenable to prayers that ask for help in changing *you*, though, rather than outside factors, others or nature.

The supernal is in relationship with everything, including the self. But one person cannot pray for the supernal to change itself. Prayer is a powerful force in the universe, don't get me wrong. I'm a huge advocate for prayer. But it will take more than one person's or one family's prayers to change the supernal. The whole of our societal context—our belief system, our culture, our very thoughts—would have to change first, and then the universe (nature) would have to agree. This just might bring change to the supernal. But you cannot do it alone. Trying is a waste of time that could be spent on a much more fruitful exercise: changing *yourself*.

When *you* grow, you influence those closest to you, which eventually influences the societal context, nature and then the supernal. Wise, integrated individuals are committed constantly to their own growth. They are always aware of their pain and pursue their own healing. They have, as a result, seen healing in their families and among others they associate with; they are true leaders among everyone with whom they live and work. Their wisdom is infectious, and their influence gets larger and larger. Their effect on the world is like the ripples spreading out to the far shores of the pond, begun by a single stone tossed in the centre.

There is something even more miraculous than the ripple-out effect of your own spiritual growth. When you grow, the supernal grows also because *it* is in relationship with *you*. It influences (calls, beckons) you to grow because your own growth adds to the size of the supernal itself. *As long as the supernal is growing, the world will change. It is therefore your own growth that changes the world.* It is not your effort to bring change to the world that has an effect. It is your effort in your own life.

Afterword

Those who aspire to greatness aspire to crucifixion.
—Anna Christie

I am deeply honoured that you have taken the time to complete this book, and I genuinely hope that it will provide you with a way of thinking that may help you in your spiritual journey.

Regardless of what your beliefs are, I encourage you to grow until the day you die. Do not fear Leviathan, for Leviathan does not exist. Open the trap door, and let the painful feelings come. You will assume that you could never tolerate them, but you can. There are no monsters dwelling below; there are only your memories, and they cannot hurt you. You may weep with sadness or experience great anxiety, but you are not in danger. Your amygdala is lying to you. These are only body memories you have. The world is not a dangerous place.

What is the worst thing that can happen to you? No matter what you do in this life, you will die and so will everyone you love. You may die young, but you should not live in fear of this, saying "what if?" at every turn. What if you spend your whole life afraid and never change anything? If you take even a small chance on life, on spiritual growth, on allowing yourself to experience your pain, your life will not have been in vain. For as much as you have grown spiritually, you have added to the size of the supernal.

In my own experience, I still struggle with many of the concepts outlined in this book. My Christian faith is helpful in this regard, as my own belief is that the supernal—God, as revealed in Jesus Christ—is the power of love in the universe. It gives me comfort to know that as others and I grow and love, God is growing, too. One day, when God is large enough, evil will be eradicated and God will provide for the world the kingdom of *shalom*.

It also helps me to remember, from time to time, that I am not God—or any sort of Messiah either, capable of riding in on a white horse and saving the world. I do believe that God will save the world, and it doesn't matter that I never live to see it.

Suggested Readings: Leadership and Personal Growth

There are a plethora of books written and being written on these topics. Below is a list of my top five "must read" classics. Publisher information is provided in the bibliography section.

Peck, M. Scott	*The Road Less Traveled*
Heifetz, Ronald	*Leadership Without Easy Answers*
Gilbert, Roberta	*Extraordinary Relationships*
Friedman, Edwin	*Generation to Generation*
Covey, Stephen	*The 7 Habits of Highly Effective People*

Bibliography

Ainsworth, M. D. S. *Infancy in Uganda: Infant Care and the Growth of Attachment.* Baltimore: Johns Hopkins, 1967.

Ainsworth, M. D. S. et al. *Patterns of Attachment: A Psychological Study of the Strange Situation.* Hillsdale, NJ: Erlbaum, 1978.

American Psychiatric Association. *Diagnostic and Statistical Manual of Mental Disorders,* Fourth Edition, Washington DC: American Psychiatric Association, 1994.

Arnold, M. B. *Emotion and Personality.* New York: Columbus University Press, 1960.

Augsburger, David W. *Conflict Mediation across Cultures.* Louisville, KY: Westminster John Knox, 1992.

Augsburger, David W. *Caring Enough to Confront: How to Understand and Express Your Deepest Feelings toward Others.* Ventura, CA: Regal Books, 1981.

Bardill, Donald R. *The Relational Systems Model for Family Therapy: Living in the Four Realities.* New York: The Haworth Press, 1997.

Beck, A. T., and G. Emery. *Anxiety Disorders and Phobias: A Cognitive Perspective.* New York: Basic Books, 1985.

Bekkedal, M. et al. 1997. Brain Systems for the Mediation of Social Separation-Distress and Social Reward; Evolutionary Antecedents and Neuropeptide Intermediaries. *Ann. N.Y. Acad. Sci.* 807: 78–100.

Bibby, Reginald. 2004. "Religious Services Attendance Trends" (Press Release), University of Lethbridge, November 25.

Bouchard, T. J. 1994. Genes, environment, and personality. *Science* 264: 1700–1701.

Bouchard, T. J. 1997. Whenever the Twain Shall Meet. *The Sciences*, 37(5): 52–57.

Bowen, Murray. *Family Therapy in Clinical Practice.* Lanham, MD: Jason Aronson Inc., 1985.

Bowlby, John. *Attachment and Loss: Volume I. Attachment.* New York: Basic Books, 1969.

Bowlby, John. *Attachment and Loss: Volume II. Separation: Anxiety and Anger.* London: Penguin, 1973.

Bowlby, John. *Attachment and Loss: Volume III. Loss: Sadness and Depression.* New York: Basic Books, 1980.
Bowlby, John. *The Making and Breaking of Affectional Bonds.* London: Tavistock, 1979.
Bowlby, John. *A Secure Base: Parent-Child Attachment and Healthy Human Development.* New York: Basic Books, 1988.
Bowlby, John. *Maternal Care and Mental Health.* Geneva: World Health Organization, 1951.
Bradshaw, John. *Homecoming: Reclaiming and Championing Your Inner Child.* Toronto: Bantam, 1990.
Braitenberg, V., and A. Schulz. *Anatomy of the Cortex.* New York: Springer-Verlag, 1991.
Brown, Juanita, *The World Café: Shaping Our Futures Through Conversations That Matter.*, San Francisco: Berrett-Koehler, 2005.
Chambers, Julie A. et al. 2004. Parental Styles and Long-Term Outcome Following Treatment for Anxiety Disorders. *Clinical Psychology & Psychotherapy* 11(3):187–198.
Cherer, Klaus, and Paul Eckman. *Handbook of Methods in Nonverbal Behavior Research.* Cambridge: Cambridge University Press, 1982.
Cornelius, Randolph R. *The Science of Emotion: Research and Tradition in the Psychology of Emotions.* New Jersey: Prentice Hall, 1996.
Covey, Stephen R. *The 7 Habits of Highly Effective People.* New York: Fireside, 1989.
Damasio, A. *Descartes' Error: Emotion, Reason and the Human Brain.* New York: Grosset/Putnam, 1994.
Darwin, C. *The Origin of Species by Means of Natural Selection; or, the Preservation of Favored Races in the Struggle for Life.* New York: Collier, 1959.
Davis, M. 1992. The Role of the Amygdala in Fear and Anxiety. *Annual Review of Neuroscience* 15: 353–75.
DePree, Max. *Leadership Jazz.* New York: Dell Publishing, 1992.
Eckman, P. 1992. An Argument for Basic Emotions. *Cognition and Emotion* 6: 169–200.
Eckman, P. 1992. Facial Expressions of Emotion: New Findings, New Questions. *Psychological Science* 3: 34–38.
Eckman, P. 1993. Facial Expression and Emotion. *American Psychologist* 48: .
Field, Tiffany. *Touch.* Cambridge: MIT Press, 2001.
Firestone, Robert. *Conquer Your Critical Inner Voice.* Oakland, CA: New Harbinger, 2002.
Frankl, V. E. *The Unconscious God.* New York: Simon & Schuster, 1975.

Friedman, Edwin. "Bowen Theory and Therapy," in A. Gurman and D. K. Kniskern, eds., *Handbook of Family Therapy* Vol. II, New York: Brunner/Mazel, 1991.

Friedman, Edwin. *Generation to Generation: Family Process in Church and Synagogue.* New York: The Guilford Press, 1985.

Freidman, Edwin. *Emotional Process and Process Theology* (video). Alban Institute, 1991.

Friedman, Edwin. *Reinventing Leadership.* (video and discussion guide), New York: The Guilford Press, 1996.

Gilbert, Roberta M. *Extraordinary Relationships: A New Way of Thinking about Human Interactions.* Toronto: John Wiley & Sons, Inc., 1992.

Ginott, H.G. *Between Parent and Child.* New York: Avon Books, 1994. (Originally published 1965)

Goldstein, A. "Neurobiology of Heroin Addiction and of Methadone Treatment." Delivered to the U.S. National Methadone Conference, April, 1997.

Goleman, Daniel. *Emotional Intelligence.* New York: Bantam, 1995.

Gottman, John et al. *Meta-Emotion: How Families Communicate Emotionally.* New Jersey: Lawrence Erlbaum, 1997.

Gottman, John. *Why Marriages Succeed or Fail.* New York: Simon & Schuster, 1994.

Gottman, John. *Marital Interaction: Experimental Investigations.* New York: Academic Press, 1979.

Gottman, John. 1994. The Family as a Meta-emotion Culture. *Cognition & Emotion* Spring:.

Gottman, John. *Raising an Emotionally Intelligent Child.* New York: Simon & Schuster, 1997.

Greenberg, L. S. 2004. Introduction to Emotion. Special Issue, *Clinical Psychology and Psychotherapy*, 11: .

Greenberg, L. S. 2004. Emotion-Focused Therapy. *Clinical Psychology & Psychotherapy* 11(1): 3–16.

Greenberg, L. S. *Emotion-Focused Therapy: Coaching Clients to Work Through Their Feelings.* Washington, DC: American Psychological Association Press, 2001.

Greenberg, L. S., and S. Paivio. *Working with Emotion in Psychotherapy.* New York: The Guilford Press, 1997.

Greenberg, Leslie S., and Jeremy D. Safran. *Emotion in Psychotherapy.* New York: The Guilford Press, 1987.

Greenspan, Stanley. *The Growth of the Mind.* New York: Basic Books, 1998.

Harlow, H. F., and R. R. Zimmerman. 1959. Affectional Responses in the Infant Monkey. *Science* 130: 421.

Heifetz, Ronald A. *Leadership Without Easy Answers.* Cambridge: The Belknap Press of Harvard University Press, 1994.

Izard, C. E. *The Face of Emotion.* New York: Appleton-Century-Crofts, 1971.

Izard, C. E. *The Psychology of Emotions.* New York: Plenum Press, 1991.

James, W. *The Principles of Psychology.* New York: Henry Holt, 1890.

Kagan, J. *Galen's Prophecy: Temperament in Human Nature.* New York: Basic Books, 1994.

Kerr, Michael, and Murray Bowen. *Family Evaluation.* New York: WW Norton and Company, 1988.

Kubler-Ross, Elizabeth. *On Death and Dying.* New York: Touchstone, 1969.

Larson C. L., et al. 2006. Fear Is Fast in Phobic Individuals: Amygdala Activation in Response to Fear-Relevant Stimuli. *Biological Psychiatry* 60(4): 410–417.

Lazarus, R. S. *Psychological Stress and the Coping Process.* New York: McGraw Hill, 1966.

Lazarus, R. S. 1984. On the Primacy of Cognition. *American Psychologist* 39: 124–129.

Lazarus, R. S. Cognition and Motivation in Emotion. *American Psychologist* 46 (4): 352–67.

Lazarus, Richard S. *Stress and Emotion: A New Synthesis.* New York: Springer, 1999.

Leacock, Stephen. *Nonsense Novels IV.* New York Review Books Classics, 2004. (Originally published 1911.)

LeDoux, Joseph. *The Emotional Brain: The Mysterious Beginnings of Emotional Life.* New York: Touchstone, 1996.

LeDoux, Joseph. *Synaptic Self: How Our Brains Become Who We Are.* New York: Penguin, 2002.

LeDoux, Joseph. "The Neurobiology of Emotion" in *Mind & Brain: Dialogues in Cognitive Neuroscience.* Cambridge University Press: 1986, 301–354.

Lerner, Harriet. *The Dance of Anger.* New York: Harper & Row, 1995.

Lipton, Bruce. *The Biology of Belief: Unleashing the Power of Consciousness, Matter and Miracles.* Santa Rosa CA: Mountain of Love/Elite Books, 2005.

Lyotard, Jean-Francois. *The Postmodern Condition.* Manchester University Press, 1984.

MacLean, P. D. The Triune Brain: Emotion and Scientific Bias," in *The Neurosciences: Second Study Program,* F.O. Schmitt, ed., New York: Rockefeller University Press, 1970, 336–49.

MacLean, P. D. *The Triune Brain in Evolution: Role in Paleocerebral Functions.* New York: Plenum, 1990.
Mankiw, Gregory N. *Principles of Economics.* Orlando: Harcourt, 1997.
Maté, Gabor. *Scattered Minds.* Toronto: Vintage, 2000.
Miller, J. G. *Living Systems.* New York: McGraw-Hill, 1978.
Miller, J. G. *The Earth as a System.* Center for the Study of Democratic Institutions, University of California at Santa Barbara, c. 1985.
Montagu, Ashley. *Touching: The Human Significance of the Skin.* New York: Harper and Row, 1978.
Morowitz, H. J. *Energy Flow in Biology.* New York: Academic Press, 1968.
Oatley, K., and E.Duncan. 1994. The Experience of Emotion in Everyday Life. *Cognition and Emotion* 8: 369–381.
Panksepp, Jaak. "Toward a General Psychobiological Theory of Emotions." in *Behavioral and Brain Sciences* 5, 1982: 407–67.
Panksepp, Jaak. *Affective Neuroscience: The Foundations of Human and Animal Emotions.* New York: Oxford University Press, 1998.
Papero, Daniel. *Bowen Family Systems Theory.* Boston: Allyn & Bacon, 1990.
Peck, M. Scott. *The Road Less Traveled: A New Psychology of Love, Traditional Values and Spiritual Growth.* Toronto: Touchstone, 1978.
Peck, M. Scott. *People of the Lie: The Hope for Healing Human Evil.* New York: Simon & Schuster, 1983.
Richardson, Ron. *Family Ties That Bind.* Vancouver: Self-Counsel Press, 1987.
Salovey, P., and J. D. Mayer. 1990. "Emotional Intelligence." *Imagination, Cognition, and Personality* 9: 185–211.
Sapolsky, R. 1997. A Gene for Nothing. *Discover* 18(10): 40–46.
Schore, Allan N. *Affect Regulation and the Origin of the Self.* Hillsdale, NJ: Lawrence Erlbaum, 1994.
Senge, Peter. *The Fifth Discipline.* New York: Doubleday Currency, 1990.
Siegel, Daniel J. *The Developing Mind: How Relationships and the Brain Interact to Shape Who We Are.* New York: Guilford, 1999.
Steinke, Peter M. *Healthy Congregations: A Systems Approach.* Bethesda MD: Alban, 1996.
Stern, Daniel N. *The Interpersonal World of the Infant.* New York: Basic Books, 1985.
Stossel, J. The Mystery of Happiness. *ABC News*, September, 1997.
Valenstein, Elliot S., et al. 1970. Reexamination of the Role of the Hypothalamus in Motivation. *Psychological Review* 77: 16–31.
Wheatley, Margaret J. *Leadership and the New Science.* New York: Berett-Koehler Publishers, 1992.

Whelton, William J. 2004. Emotional Processes in Psychotherapy: Evidence Across Therapeutic Modalities. *Clinical Psychology & Psychotherapy* 11(1): 58–71.

Winnicott, D. W. *The Child, the Family and the Outside World.* Addison Wesley, 2nd ed., 1992.

Yalom, I. *Existential Psychotherapy.* New York: Basic Books, 1980.

Zajonc, R. 1980. Feeling and Thinking: Preferences Need No Inferences. *American Psychologist* 35: 151–75.

Index

Aboriginal, 222
Adaptive Anger, 136–140
Adventure, 3, 265, 279–280
Ainsworth, 116, 299
Alex, xiii, 155, 270–271
Amygdala, 105–113, 115, 120, 124, 129, 136, 139, 141, 151, 153, 164, 166, 174–175, 177, 180, 186–187, 204–205, 208–209, 227, 267, 295, 300, 302
Anorexia nervosa, 271
Anxiety, xv, 8, 53–54, 57, 64, 71, 75, 78–79, 85–86, 88, 92, 94, 96, 98, 109, 118–119, 131, 133, 135, 139–140, 150, 152, 156–157, 163–166, 173–175, 178–179, 186–187, 199, 201, 216, 221–222, 225, 227–229, 231–239, 241–243, 245, 247, 249, 251–253, 255–256, 259–261, 266–269, 271, 274, 275–277, 280, 295, 299–300
Apologize, 115, 143, 149, 204, 206, 207–208
Appreciation, xiii
Assumptions, 193, 195, 197, 241
Augsberger, 209, 250
Authority, 184, 276–277

Blame, xvi, 16, 41, 49, 54, 85, 94–97, 124, 144, 188, 203, 205–206, 209, 210, 223, 232, 234–235, 253, 257, 266, 274
Blaming, 92, 94–96, 124, 137–138, 209–210, 219, 235, 238, 266
Body language, 132, 144, 149, 192, 198, 200–201, 264, 267
Boundaries, 51, 218–219, 220, 222
Bourn, 13–19, 21–22, 27, 31, 35, 51–52, 54, 63, 84, 180, 183–185, 211, 213–214, 217, 277, 281, 285–287, 288, 290–293
Bourn of Relationship Systems, 16, 31, 185, 213, 287
Bourn of Self, 16, 22, 27, 31, 51, 63, 180, 183–184, 213–214, 277, 292
Bourn of Societal Context, 17, 184, 285–287
Bowen, xiv, xvii, xviii, xix, 27, 45, 68–69, 91, 185, 223–224, 230, 241, 245, 255, 257, 266, 280, 299, 301–303
Bowlby, 116, 120–122, 299–300
Brain, 6, 39–40, 45, 75, 88–89, 91–92, 94, 98–99, 101–115, 116, 124–126, 129–131, 134, 145, 151, 152, 155–156, 162–163, 166, 169–171, 173–175, 177, 180, 197, 205–206, 209, 213, 218, 265, 269, 271, 286, 289, 299–300, 302–303
Breathe, 7, 118, 134–135, 217
Buddhist, 7, 18, 29
Bugs Bunny, 84

Cancer, xv–xvi, 82, 92–93, 97, 180, 237, 270
Case study Charlie, Ellie, Grandma, Janet and Paul, Olivia. See: Alex, 260
Change back, 178, 204, 230–231, 238, 246, 264, 274
Change is loss, 228
Charlie, xiii, 88, 155, 192, 242, 265
Church, xiv–xv, xvii, xix–xx, 6, 42, 44, 60, 68, 73, 78–79, 161, 174, 180, 184, 194, 227, 229, 230–231, 233, 242, 251, 270, 274–275, 281, 289, 292, 301

Community, xv, xvi, xviii, xix, 3, 10, 16, 24, 44, 94, 112, 121, 130, 132, 180, 184, 222, 231, 281, 287–288
Conflict, xv, xvi, xix, xx, 5, 29, 82–83, 131–132, 203, 205, 209, 222–223, 249–254, 257, 259, 267, 273, 277, 299
Core Narrative, 65–66, 124
Core values, 31, 39–40, 42–43, 177, 191, 222, 238, 244
Covey, xiv, xvi, xx, 46, 197, 243, 250, 297, 300
Creativity, 108, 279
Criticism, xiv, 32, 53, 185, 190, 203–206, 208–209, 221
Crocodile, 107
Curious, 84, 122, 209, 236, 249, 273, 276
Cutoff, 232, 238, 247, 250, 253–255, 274, 277

Define yourself, 41, 44, 51, 177, 203, 213, 223, 237, 244, 255, 276, 280–281
Depression, 5, 71, 75, 78–79, 85–86, 88, 92, 94, 96, 118, 140, 150, 152, 170, 172, 268, 291, 300
Detective, 274–276, 278
Diagnosis, 98, 267–269
Distancing, 67, 131, 249, 252–253, 259
Drugs, 5, 79, 87–89, 162, 180, 218

Ellie, 81–83
E-mails, 187
Emotional Intelligence, xix, 31–32, 45, 60, 61, 63, 66, 101, 107, 112–113, 124–125, 127, 131, 138, 148, 164–165, 208–209, 219, 231, 244, 256, 262, 264, 266, 277, 281, 301, 303
Empowerment, xvii, 30, 276
Evil, 290–292, 295, 303
Evoking change, xix, 6, 21, 52, 111, 255
Evolution, 6, 7, 171, 219, 249, 303
Extraordinary leader, 28, 33, 172, 271, 279, 280–282
Extraordinary leadership, 28, 33, 279

Facial expression, 117, 119, 192, 200, 300
Facts, 31, 195, 197, 208, 227, 241–242, 244, 274–275
Family of origin, xv, 16, 78, 112, 185, 249, 254–256, 280
Family work, 255
Feelings, 9, 32, 40, 41, 49, 51, 58–59, 64–67, 72–73, 79, 83, 95–96, 118–119, 129, 134–135, 137, 142, 145, 148–149, 151–153, 157, 159, 162–165, 167, 169, 172–173, 178–179, 189–190, 195, 203, 205, 208, 241–242, 244, 251, 257, 279, 295, 299, 301
Figure, xvi, xix, 15, 21, 40, 67, 69, 80–81, 99, 105, 107, 110, 199, 215–217, 219, 220, 223, 228, 237, 241, 252
Friedman, xiv, xvii–xviii, xx, 8, 32, 235, 245, 254, 280, 297, 301
Fusion, 218–222, 224, 252

Genetics, 82, 91–93, 266
Gibran, 151
Gifted leadership, 28–29, 33
Giuliani, 42
God, xiv– xvi, 6–7, 10, 18–19, 31, 56, 71–72, 84, 87, 147, 192, 245, 266, 268, 272, 280, 289–290, 292–293, 295, 300
Good leadership, xix, 27–30, 32–33, 44–45, 52, 55, 59–60, 64, 110, 124, 126, 194, 205, 213, 221, 222, 227, 230, 232, 237, 244, 245
Gottman, xiv, xviii, 301
Grandma, 117, 151, 188–190
Greenberg, xiv, 126–127, 136, 301
Grief, xvi, 9, 59, 86, 97, 122, 138, 151, 163, 165, 208–209, 217
Ground of all being, 18
Gummy, 256–257

Happiness, 5, 13, 63, 79, 91, 117, 259, 303
Harlow, 116, 121, 122, 302
Heifetz, xix, 275–276, 297, 302

Herding, 163, 222, 232, 235, 274
Homeostasis, 111, 217, 229, 234, 245–246, 249, 252–253, 256, 259, 266, 269, 280
Husband, xiii, xv, 59, 81–82, 86, 88, 140, 148, 155, 170, 174, 192, 198–200, 246, 257, 260, 262–263, 264–265, 271

Impermanence, 7–8
Impose your will, 10, 23, 277
INAM, 53, 210
Integrated wisdom, 69, 219, 221, 227
Investment in the outcome, 55, 57
I-statements, 49, 50, 53–54, 189, 244

Janet and Paul, 260
Jesus, 7, 19, 39, 71, 73, 85, 295
Jewish, 7

Kagan, 104, 302
Kayla, 188–189, 190

Laundry, 261–262, 264
Laziness, 94, 170
Leadership, xiv, xvi–xx, 5, 8, 10, 14, 16–17, 22–25, 27–33, 40–42, 44–45, 48, 51–53, 55, 59–60, 63–64, 66, 75, 84, 110–111, 113, 124, 126–127, 129, 131–132, 140, 149–150, 153, 157, 166, 172, 174, 177, 180, 185–186, 188, 194, 203, 205, 213–214, 220–222, 224–225, 227, 230–234, 237–239, 244–245, 247, 254–255, 257, 262, 274–277, 279–281, 287, 292, 297, 300–303
Leadership trinity, 27, 30, 31, 33, 45, 124, 185–186, 220, 224, 227, 231–233, 239, 244–245, 255, 274, 277, 279, 281, 287, 292
LeDoux, 39, 99, 302
Leviathan, 77–79, 81–83, 88–91, 119, 123, 129, 132, 136, 138, 145, 149, 156, 163, 175, 177, 251, 255, 266, 295

Lipton, 255, 302
Living system, xiv, xvii–xviii, 25, 27, 111, 213–218, 224–225, 227–229, 241, 247, 249, 269, 273, 287, 303
Love, xiii, xiv, 3–5, 13, 18–19, 23, 39, 59, 68–69, 72–73, 75, 79, 85, 95, 102, 120–121, 127, 130–131, 151, 157, 161–167, 190, 194, 196, 203–224, 252, 260, 264, 287, 290–292, 294–295, 302–303

MacLean, 104–106, 109, 302–303
Maladaptive Anger, 136–138, 140
Martin Luther King, 84, 184
Maté, 118–119, 303
Meaningful connection, 31, 33, 185–187, 203, 222, 231, 247, 277
Miller, 213–214, 216–217, 303
Mind-Body-Spirit Connection, 82, 94, 179

Nature *See also* Bourn of Nature, 18, 137, 285, 286, 290, 291, 294, 302
Nurture, 84, 91, 92, 120, 127, 130, 161, 162, 163, 164, 165, 166, 167, 173, 179, 288

Offensive leadership, 29
Ogilvie, 281
Olivia, 143–144, 148–149
Operating principles, 40, 42, 44, 191
Over and underfunctioning, 265
Overfunctioning, 232, 234, 259–261, 263–265, 274, 276

Pain, xx, 3–6, 8–10, 14, 16, 19, 24, 48, 63–69, 71–73, 75, 77–79, 81–82, 84–90, 93, 95, 97–98, 109, 111–113, 119, 124, 136, 141, 145, 151–153, 156, 164–165, 177, 183, 186, 204, 266, 281, 290–291, 294–295
Pathology, 75, 91, 94
Peck, xiv, 7, 19, 72, 290, 297, 303

Phobia, 54, 108, 110, 118, 130, 268
Postmodern, 3, 18, 250, 285–286, 302
Pride, 173–174, 179, 209, 216
Projection, 5, 53, 67, 144, 210, 250, 253, 265
Psychotherapy, xiv, xviii, 85, 126–127, 300–301, 304

Rebellion, 222, 224, 257
Resistance, 230, 232–233, 274
Rev. George, 274, 277
Richardson, 255, 303
Rigidity, 41, 45, 57, 132
Rising Anxiety, 228, 232, 234

Sabotage, 222, 230, 232–233, 274, 277
Sapolsky, 91–92, 303
Scale, xviii, 68–69, 71–73, 75, 78–81, 84, 87, 89, 132–133, 148, 172, 204, 219–221, 225, 242, 249–251, 257, 267
Seat belt law, 291
Secrecy, 201, 232, 236–237, 274
Secure Base, 122, 300
Self-defined, 31–33, 49, 191, 220, 222–224, 239, 278
Shalom, 7–9, 25, 63, 75, 79, 85, 282, 290, 294–295
Smoking, 223–224
Soothing, 5, 73, 84–85, 87, 90, 131, 134, 162
Sorry, 149, 194, 196, 204, 206–207, 271
Spiritual growth, xx, 5–7, 19, 23–24, 40, 54, 60, 63, 69, 71–73, 75, 81, 86, 94–95, 103, 112–113, 141, 166, 177, 179, 185–186, 207, 225, 271–272, 278, 280–281, 288, 290, 294–295, 303

Stossel, 91, 303
Stress, xviii, 57, 78–79, 81–82, 93, 103, 108, 110–112, 115, 118, 133, 156–157, 180, 190, 201, 246, 253, 268–269, 302
SUD scale, 133
Supernal, 16–19, 22–24, 55–57, 63, 69, 71–72, 75, 84, 281, 283, 285, 287–289, 290–295
Synapse, 100
Systems theory, xvii–xviii, 27, 51, 67, 216, 225, 245, 268, 271, 303

Tasmanian Devil, 83
Togetherness, 59, 219, 221, 223–224, 232, 235, 241, 249–250, 252, 256
Toy store, 136
Trapdoor, 79
Triune Brain, 104, 106, 302–303
Tutu, 23
Twins, 91–92, 102

Universe, xvi, 7– 9, 11, 14–15, 17–19, 22–23, 56, 63, 72, 88, 99, 124, 286, 288–295

Vision, 28, 30, 40, 46, 110, 171, 180, 194, 274, 277, 279

We-thinking, 222, 232–233, 235, 274
Wildebeests, 216, 227, 274
World Café, 222, 300

You are wrong, 206, 230–231, 264, 274